EMOTIONAL
INTELLIGENCE
AT WORK

HOW TO MAKE
CHANGE STICK

Published by Spa House Publishing,
Cheltenham, Gloucestershire, UK.
Copyright © 2018 JCA Global Ltd.

EIP™ is a trademark of JCA Global Ltd.
jcaglobal.com

A CIP catalogue reference for this book is available from
the British Library.

ISBN 9780992808914

Design and artwork by Aaron Wedgbury
Cover graphic from Shutterstock.com

ACKNOWLEDGEMENTS

It was 25 years ago that John Cooper and I founded JCA Global with the purpose of helping organisations to get the best out of their people in a sustainable way. The key word here is sustainable; how to make change stick so people do not return to their old ways of behaving. This led us to the work of Will Schutz and The Human Element as a means of exploring the feelings and attitudes that underpin sustainable behaviour change and effective performance. Another key influence has been the work of Joe Griffin and Ivan Tyrell from The Human Givens Institute, who have produced some of the most profound explanations for the psychology of human behaviour. My gratitude goes to my primary influence Tim Sparrow, for sharing his wisdom and insight into the psychology of human emotions, and for developing with me the EIP theory and questionnaire. Also, to John Cooper, who has grown JCA Global into a business that has Emotional Intelligence and the EIP at the heart of what we do.

There are many others I would like to thank for their contributions to the development of the EIP and this book. To the founding members of the Centre for Applied Emotional Intelligence (CAEI) who provided the original test bed for the first version of the EIP (originally called the Individual Diagnostic Questionnaire). To my colleagues at JCA Global who have helped develop and enhance many of the EIP materials: Maria Clease, John Cooper, Bill Davies, Rob Jones, Dean Pollard, Sophie Seex, and Sarah Speers. To those editors and contributors who have helped make this a better book than it would otherwise have been: Fiona Beddoes-Jones, Jennifer Buttery, Matt Evans, Jo Hennessy, Kay Humphrey, Wendy Lord, and Aaron Wedgbury. To Dan Hughes, Steph Noble, and Poppy Boothroyd for helping to produce the revised EIP questionnaire and reports. To Amanda Jenks for editing several re-writes and supporting and encouraging me throughout this process. Finally, to my son William, who remains a constant source of fun and learning, helping me to develop my own Emotional Intelligence.

PREFACE

Much has been written on the subject of Emotional Intelligence (EI) as a theory and as a way of explaining human behaviour. But what use is psychological theory if the user does not understand how to apply it in order to achieve long-term change and sustainable performance? Those who are reading this book may have already subscribed to the theory that EI is relevant to individual development. But how do they capitalise on this? This book enables the user, in particular the coach, to work with an individual and help them to become the very best they can be.

To help someone develop their EI, the coach needs to know where the person is starting from, which means they need some way of measuring the status quo. The Emotional Intelligence Profile (EIP™) measures current levels of EI and, subject to some level of self-awareness, assumes that development is possible. As such, the questionnaire provides a starting point for the development of a more emotionally intelligent approach to work and life. However, in order to use the results of the EIP to best effect, the user of the tool has to understand the meaning of the scores obtained from the assessment. They also need to grasp how to interpret the results for the individual in such a way that they can use the information to maximum advantage.

This book is designed to help the practitioner use the EIP to its best effect. It will help new users of the EIP convert their theoretical knowledge into good and effective practice with regard to both the measurement of EI and the development of it.

Running throughout this book is the principle that emotionally intelligent behaviour, thoughts, and feelings are underpinned by emotionally intelligent attitudes. Therefore, in order to achieve lasting change and sustainable performance, it is necessary to develop emotionally intelligent attitudes. This is implicit within all aspects of the EIP design and application, including the EIP scales, definition, theory, and framework.

HOW TO USE THIS BOOK

Psychometric tests must clearly define what they measure. There are many measures of EI that vary in terms of their definitions, models, and scales. Therefore, Section One focuses on the definition of EI as measured by the EIP. Readers wishing to broadly understand EI, including its foundations, and how latest brain science underpins the EIP, may find this section of interest.

Section Two explains the construction of the EIP, the different parts of EI as defined by the EIP framework, and describes the 16 EIP scales. Readers looking for a thorough understanding of the EIP and how to measure EI should refer to this section.

Section Three provides a step-by-step guide on how to use the EIP in the workplace, for both assessment and development applications. This section is written largely for the practitioner coach and the assessor, explaining how to develop EI in others, as well as offering more advanced coaching skills for creating change that sticks. The final chapter examines how EI and the EIP are applied in business in relation to leadership, teams, and the organisation.

At the end of each chapter is a summary section which gives the reader a brief overview of the chapter and highlights the key points. For those seeking further information and discussion on the history of EI, and deeper interpretation of the EIP scales, this may be found in the Appendices.

CONTENTS

SECTION ONE
DEFINING EMOTIONAL INTELLIGENCE (EI)

What is Emotional Intelligence (EI) and how is it defined by the Emotional Intelligence Profile (EIP)? How does EI fit into the structure of human personality and what is its relationship with the rapidly developing science of neuropsychology?

EI is concerned with how people manage themselves (their personality, potential, and innate resources) to be both personally and interpersonally effective. How well they do this is largely determined by their attitudes. This approach to EI is strongly supported by neuroscience which explains how attitudes influence feeling, which fuels thinking, and drives behaviour. Therefore, by changing attitudes it is possible to create lasting change in behaviour, thoughts, and feelings.

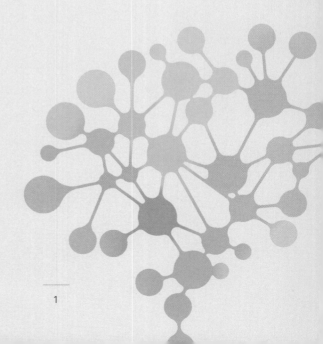

CHAPTER ONE
WHAT IS EMOTIONAL INTELLIGENCE?

INTRODUCTION

The Emotional Intelligence Profile (EIP) measures the building blocks of an aspect of psychological functioning that is referred to as Emotional Intelligence (EI). In order to interpret the results of the EIP, individuals must first understand how EI was defined and conceptualised by myself and Tim Sparrow, the developers of the EIP, as well as the theoretical rationale that underpins the development of the questionnaire.

1.1   Why the need for developing Emotional Intelligence?

The world and society have become ever more complex and demanding. Some of these changes in the working world include greater competition, increased technology, and an exponential growth in information. These changes have been matched by demands and pressures in society including financial insecurity, reduced social responsibility, greater individuality, and a diminished sense of community. Consequently, many of the basic human emotional needs required for individual well-being are not being properly met.[1]

Some of these essential emotional needs include:

— Achievement

— Attention

— Community and status

— Control

— Emotional connection

— Meaning and purpose to life

— Privacy

— Security

The cumulative effect of these factors has put increased emotional pressure on individuals and their ability to cope. In the UK there are some 40 million working days lost every year due to stress, with an estimated cost to the economy of over £7 billion. Up to 60% of employees are reported to suffer from stress at some point during their career,[2] and for those born after 1945 there has been a tenfold increase in depression.[3] Human physiology and emotions evolved to deal with a more stable and less complex 'hunter-gatherer' society, and the human brain and genetics have not kept up with the rate of change in society. However, humans are incredibly adaptive and have specific innate resources to cope, learn, and respond to these challenges. Some of these innate human resources include:

— Conscious self-choice

— Creativity and problem solving (such as IQ)

— Emotional management and relaxation

— Empathy, rapport building, and awareness of others

— Habit formation

— Imagination

— Logical thinking and objectivity

— Sleep and recovery

— Self-observation and emotional awareness

— Reflecting and learning from the past

— Thinking about the future

Possessing these resources is a part of being human; they represent a person's potential and manifest in their personality. When a person's emotional needs are being met they will thrive and be happy. When they are not, they may become anxious, angry, or defensive. Central to EI is learning how to harness and manage these innate resources so as to meet a person's emotional needs (specific examples of how to do this are given in Chapter Eight; Table 8.3).

1.2 A historical perspective of Emotional Intelligence

Despite its recent popularity, EI has roots in many other psychological theories and is not something newly discovered about humankind. EI integrates many of the different historical approaches from psychology: the importance of the unconscious mind, as highlighted by Sigmund Freud; the stimulus-response models of the Behaviourists; the power of experiential emotional encounter used by the Humanists; managing thinking as used in Cognitive Behavioural Therapy (CBT); and the most recent ground-breaking developments in brain science (brain tomography, scanning, and imaging). In addition, EI focuses on the measurement (psychometrics) of effective behaviour (competencies), which has been dominant in business since the 1980s. EI has clear overlaps with everyday language, such as: wisdom, maturity, compassion, sincerity, integrity, tolerance, and understanding. Therefore, EI is an eclectic model that integrates the psychological domains of thinking (cognitive psychology), feeling (humanistic psychology), and behaviour (behaviourism).

The term 'Emotional Intelligence' was first explained by Van Ghent (in 1961)[4] but came to prominence largely through the publications of Daniel Goleman.[5,6,7] The early historical influences before this time are numerous, including Philosopher Renee Descartes,[8] naturalist Charles Darwin,[9] and psychologist David Wechsler.[10] Listed below are some of the more recent and significant publications that have contributed to the field of Emotional intelligence. A more detailed overview on the history of EI can be found in Appendix Two.

Key milestones in EI

1983 Howard Gardner publishes Frames of Mind, differentiating intrapersonal (emotional) intelligence from interpersonal (social) intelligence.[11]

1990 Peter Salovey and Jack Mayer describe an ability-based approach to EI. In 1997 they produce the MSCEIT™, a four-branch measure of EI.[12]

1994 There is a growth in neurological evidence for emotional and social intelligence. Some notable researchers include Antonio Damasio,[13] Joseph LeDoux,[14] and Lane and McRae.[15]

1996 Daniel Goleman[5,7] publishes his bestselling book, 'Emotional Intelligence: why it can matter more than IQ', followed by several other successful publications. This leads to the ECI™ 360,[16] a competency-based measure of EI.

1997 Reuven Bar-On[17] publishes one of the first EI measures: the 'Emotional Quotient Inventory' (EQi™). He describes EI as "an array of traits and abilities that are correlated with personality".

1998 Jo Maddocks and Tim Sparrow[18] define an attitude-based model of EI, describing EI as a verb/doing word and as being "the practice of managing one's personality".

2001 Konstantin Petrides and Adrian Furnham[19] produce the 'Trait EI Questionnaire' (TEIQue™), a measure of "the affective facets of personality".

In 1998, the EIP originated as one of the first models of EI. Since then there has been a proliferation of products for assessing EI, the majority of which are based on personality traits, cognitive abilities, and competencies (refer to Appendix Two). This contrasts with the EIP, which is based on attitudes and how people manage their personality and resources. The EIP attitude-based approach to EI is discussed next.

1.3   Emotional Intelligence as a construct

EI is about how the individual manages their personality.[18] This crucial aspect differentiates EI from other aspects of human personality. People cannot easily change their disposition or IQ but they can learn to manage them in order to maximise the effectiveness by which they apply the raw material they were born with. Personality traits, whether temperamental or intellectual, are the 'what' of a person's identity while EI explains the 'how': how an individual can be more effective through making the best use of their temperament and intellectual traits. The realisation of this crucial distinction was a defining moment for me in my professional career. It was this distinction which made me understand how best to develop people's potential and make it sustainable[20] (through changing attitudes, as will be discussed later), and which led to the development of the EIP.

The EIP is a psychometric test. There are literally thousands of psychometric tests available; together they measure a vast array of attributes relating to typical behaviour, values, motivation, abilities, aptitudes, and more recently competencies. All are aspects of what defines the human personality. Psychometric tests are developed in an attempt to discover and measure what makes one person different from another; they embrace the science of individual differences. But understanding the various characteristics that structure the human personality is only half of the story. It is also necessary to know how effectively the individual manages their attributes, and that is where EI comes in.

Unlike the EIP, which is based on attitudes, most other EI theories and questionnaires define EI as: personality traits (temperaments); a cognitive capacity such as IQ; or as a set of behavioural competencies. However, far from being synonymous with EI, these three aspects of personality are dependent on EI if they are to be applied effectively. The relationship between EI, personality temperament, IQ, and competencies will now be discussed.

1.3.1   Emotional Intelligence and personality temperament

There are two main differences between EI and personality temperament:

1   EI relates to an individual's effectiveness and performance, whereas personality temperament is concerned with predispositions or typical behaviour.

2   EI is changeable and can be developed,[21] whereas personality temperament relates to typical behaviours that are relatively fixed.

The first difference explains why measures of personality are not highly predictive of performance; most personality measures explain a maximum variance of 9% in work performance.[22] In practice, people with different personality temperaments can achieve equally competent results but do so in different ways. What determines whether a person is effective is, to a large extent, down to how well they manage their personality, which is a function of their EI. For example, having an extraverted trait does not make a person effective at doing extraverted things such as communicating with people, just as having an introverted trait does not make someone ineffective at communicating with people. How effectively a person behaves has more to do with their emotional state and underlying attitudes than their personality temperament. For instance, feeling highly anxious before a meeting interferes with an individual's capacity to communicate their thoughts effectively. And holding the attitude, "People don't want to hear what I have to say", inevitably hinders them in being an effective communicator.

The second difference is that EI is changeable and personality temperament is relatively fixed.[23] Personality theories typically focus on measuring enduring and stable characteristics, such as traits and typology preferences, in order to predict how a person will behave in the future. EI is not focused on a person's disposition but rather on their attitudes and habits, both of which are changeable and can be developed; people can adopt attitudes and they can learn habits. Crucially, EI is about how people manage their behaviour by being self-aware in the current moment and making conscious choices about how to behave.

Another important distinction between personality temperament and EI is in how they are applied. Talking someone through their personality profile usually increases self-understanding and knowledge, which tends to happen in their thinking brain (the outer grey matter called the neocortex), but this does not necessarily result in behavioural change. Improving a person's EI occurs in a different part of the brain known as the limbic system (refer to Chapter Two; Table 2.1 for a diagram of the brain's structure). Here, people learn from emotional experience, which is also where changes in attitudes and habits take place. Personality questionnaires are useful for raising cognitive awareness, but this must be followed up by emotional awareness and experience if a person is to change their behaviour. This may also explain why many training and coaching programmes that focus largely on feedback and discussion, rather than taking action, fail to create lasting behaviour change in the workplace.[24]

Standalone personality questionnaires have far more developmental value for the individual when combined with EI. Personality describes 'what' a person typically does and EI explains 'how' they can do this more effectively. Together they provide a powerful combination for self-development. This view of integrating EI with personality is supported by research.[25] Extensive meta-analysis and predictive validity studies on EI and performance have found EI to add significant incremental validity over and above personality and cognitive intelligence measures.[26-29] One researcher, O'Boyle,[26] concludes: "Rather than seeing cognitive intelligence, the Five Factor Model (personality), and EI as competing measures, researchers should focus on developing integrative models that include all three".

1.3.2 Emotional Intelligence and cognitive abilities

Another area that may be differentiated from EI is cognitive intelligence (IQ). Research consistently shows that cognitive intelligence predicts no more than 25% of performance,[30] begging the question: what does the other 75% relate to? Daniel Goleman, in his seminal book 'Emotional Intelligence, why it can matter more than IQ',[5] suggests that much of it is related to EI. Indeed, most competencies or job advertisements are dominated by EI attributes, such as 'good team player', 'copes well with pressure', and 'adapts well to change'. This does not suggest that EI alone accounts for 75% of people's job performance, nor indeed that a questionnaire could measure this, but how effectively people use both their IQ and personality temperament (their performance) is heavily influenced by their EI. (For a summary of performance-related studies on EI, refer to Chapter Nine; 9.1.)

EI is not just about how a person manages their personality temperament; it is also about how they manage their cognitive intelligence. How a person is feeling at a particular moment in time dramatically affects their cognitive performance. This is highlighted by the example of fear activating the fight-flight-freeze mechanism that blocks a person from accessing their cognitive intellectual thinking. A person's ability to think clearly, make sound decisions, analyse information and all the other IQ-related areas, can vary dramatically day to day and moment to moment. When a person feels anxious, stressed, or hurried, their cortical functioning can be severely impaired;[31] but when they are relaxed, alert, and present in the moment they can think more clearly, learn more easily, have more creative insights, and 'see the wood from the trees'. Therefore, enabling a person to become more aware of how their feelings affect their thinking and how to manage their emotional state allows them to make better use of their cognitive intelligence.

One problem with the Intelligence Quotient (IQ) is that it is tested under standardised conditions to assess an individual's maximum performance rather than their typical performance. EI is more relevant to how a person performs in their day-to-day life rather than in controlled conditions. Having a high IQ does not necessarily translate into high performance unless it is backed up by high EI. A 40-year follow-up study of 80 Ph.D. students at the University of California, Berkeley, found that social and emotional abilities were four times more important than IQ in predicting professional success and prestige.[32] If a person does not manage their emotions then it is far more difficult for them to maximise use of their thinking, and therefore their potential IQ. A study by Duckworth[33] found that children's exam results correlated twice as strongly with their self-discipline (emotional control) than with their IQ scores. As with temperament, measuring IQ alone has limited developmental value for the individual, but when combined with EI, becomes a far more potent combination for enhancing clear and accurate thinking.

1.3.3 Emotional Intelligence and behavioural competencies

A third construct that is often confused with, but should be differentiated from EI, is behavioural competence. Many EI measures describe EI as a set of competencies (behaviours and skills). In contrast, the EIP is underpinned by attitudes and feelings. Competencies provide a useful reference point for benchmarking what behaviour is required in a specific context and whether this is being achieved. However, using competencies in isolation does not address how these behaviours may be achieved. Behavioural competencies are only achieved if backed up by congruent attitudes and intentions, so that people are drawn to behave in ways that are consistent with their attitudes.

Changing behaviour is often short-lived if it is not supported by a parallel change in attitude. For example, an organisation introducing customer service competencies is unlikely to succeed if its employees do not want to be of service to others (their attitude). On the other hand, people who do want to be of service to others quickly acquire their own set of appropriate behaviours that are congruent with their attitudes. In practice, behavioural competence is an inevitable outcome of someone who has complementary attitudes, but is a futile endeavour for those with opposing attitudes. EI enables people to understand their own attitudes and align them with their behaviours. When people behave in ways that are inconsistent with their attitudes this creates anxiety and stress (a state known as cognitive dissonance) until they change their behaviour or their attitude. A study (using the EIP) on the EI of prison officers found that those officers who had low regard for prison inmates (their attitude), but who were required to treat inmates with respect (their behaviour), a state known as emotional labour, suffered considerably more stress and burnout than officers who had regard for prison inmates (i.e. their behaviour matched their attitudes).[34] Therefore, the key to developing behavioural competence is to adopt appropriate attitudes through the process of being emotionally intelligent. (For further links between EI and competencies refer to Chapter Nine; 9.2.2.)

1.3.4 The relationship between personality, EI, and competencies

There is a clear relationship between personality, EI, and competencies:

— Personality represents who a person is and includes their temperament and innate resources (such as IQ).

— EI is how well a person learns to manage their temperament and harness their innate resources (their potential).

— Competencies are how this manifests in terms of a person's work performance and behaviours.

EI is therefore the 'glue' or the missing link that turns individual personality (potential) into effective performance and may be summarised as:

PERSONALITY + EI = PERFORMANCE

EI magnifies how well or badly we utilise our potential. For example, a person with low EI may misuse their imagination by anticipating and worrying about all the things that could go wrong, while a person with high EI would learn to manage their imagination to visualise more positive expectations. Consider the analogy of a car (personality) and its driver (EI): the skilled driver listens to the engine, develops a feel for the car, keeps it well maintained and continually improves their handling skills in order to get the best from the car in terms of economy, sustainability, and performance.

The psychological process of turning personality into performance outcomes through EI is described below in the definition of EI and is fully explained by the neuroscience of EI in Chapter Two.

1.4   The definition of Emotional Intelligence

The term EI is not unique and there are several alternative labels that may be used for this concept including:

— Emotional Quotient[35] (EQ): Refers to the measurement of EI. The EIP does not include a single EQ score of EI as the construct is multifaceted and its different components do not necessarily correlate highly with each other.

— Emotional Literacy[36] (EL): Used mostly in counselling and education, EL refers to developing emotional awareness and language skills.

— Emotional Competence[37] (EC): Used mainly in business, EC refers to the development of emotional skills and behaviours.

— Emotional Creativity[38] (ECr): A less commonly used term, ECr is the ability to experience and express original, appropriate, and authentic combinations of emotions.

— Social Intelligence[39] (SI): Refers mainly to the interpersonal aspects of EI and was the precursor to the term Emotional Intelligence.

Alongside these are many other descriptors often used to define EI, such as common sense, empathy, emotional maturity, and wisdom. The term Emotional Intelligence (EI), which is about the intelligent use of emotions (or thinking about feelings), fits closely with the JCA Global definition of EI given below.

Part One   Emotional Intelligence is the practice of managing one's personality, to be both personally and interpersonally effective.

Part Two   This is achieved through the habitual practice of thinking about feeling, and feeling about thinking, to guide one's behaviour.

Part Three   The extent and effectiveness by which an individual does this is determined largely by their attitudes.

The first part of the definition describes 'what' it is to be emotionally intelligent and incorporates the link between personality (which includes IQ and other innate resources) and EI, as discussed previously. It also refers to the two main parts of EI being both 'personal' and 'interpersonal', and forming the two strands of the EIP framework (described in Section 1.6).

The second part of the definition describes 'how' to be emotionally intelligent. It defines EI as a 'habit' that an individual can become better at doing with practice and which becomes easier and more automatic over time. The definition also describes EI as a 'practice', something a person 'does' (a verb) rather than something they 'have' (a noun). This requires being aware of oneself and others in the present by noticing, thinking about, labelling, and interpreting emotions in the body, i.e. 'thinking about feelings'. This in turn helps a person to form their Self Knowledge (an understanding of themselves) and Knowledge of Others, which can be drawn upon when deciding how to behave (as described in Chapter Four; 4.2.1).

Part Two of the definition also includes 'feeling about thinking', which involves recognising intuitive bodily responses, such as feeling uneasy about a decision. Not every feeling and thought is consciously analysed in this way since people quickly form automatic, unconscious, and habitual responses. However, to make sure these habitual responses are effective and remain appropriate it is necessary to engage in the process of 'managing one's personality' (Part One of the EI definition).

The third part to the definition describes 'when' people are emotionally intelligent (when they hold EI Attitudes); 'the extent and effectiveness of their EI being determined largely by their attitudes'. Thoughts and feelings do not occur randomly; they are the response to a stimulus which has been perceived, interpreted, and filtered through their underlying attitudes. It is a person's attitudes that largely influence their thoughts and feelings, which in turn drive their behaviour.[40,41]

The close relationship between attitudes, thoughts, feelings, and behaviours is explained in the next chapter which looks at EI from a psychological and neurological perspective. The attitudes that underpin emotionally intelligent behaviour (as defined by the EIP scales) are described on the next page.

1.5　The attitudes that underpin Emotional Intelligence

Most approaches to examining EI have tended to start at the top, focusing on the outcomes of being emotionally intelligent in terms of behaviour, skills, and competencies and linking these to the importance of feelings. Crucially, however, the EIP was developed from the bottom up, starting with the underlying attitudes of EI.

A metaphor for EI

Consider the metaphor of a tree (Figure 1.1), with attitudes (the roots of EI) that determine feelings (represented by the trunk, or body, which is where feelings are experienced), that then influence thinking (the branches, like the neural networks of the brain), that then translate into behaviours (the leaves in their different shapes, sizes, and colours). Therefore, in order to understand the essence of EI it is necessary to look deeper into the underlying attitudes.

Just as a plant has the innate resources to meet its basic needs (roots to absorb water, leaves to absorb sunlight, and bark for protection), so too, people can harness their innate resources to meet their emotional needs (such as using their imagination to think positively, reasoning to solve problems, and empathy to connect with others).

How well an individual manages to get their emotional needs met throughout their life will largely determine what attitudes they hold towards themselves, others, and the world in general. It is only through developing emotionally intelligent attitudes that people can develop and sustain emotionally intelligent behaviour.

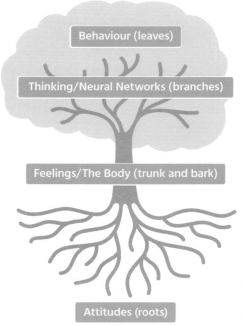

Figure 1.1

Behaviour (leaves)

Thinking/Neural Networks (branches)

Feelings/The Body (trunk and bark)

Attitudes (roots)

The EIP definition of an attitude:

An evaluative position (based largely on
feelings) towards oneself, others, a situation,
an idea, etc. that predisposes the individual
towards certain behaviours or responses

This definition fits closely with theories from most contemporary social psychologists[42-45] such as Azjen (2007) who defines an attitude as "a disposition to respond favourably or unfavourably to an object, person, institution, or event". A defining characteristic of an attitude is that it is evaluative, i.e. emotionally connected.

Drawn from humanistic psychology, such as Transactional Analysis (TA) theory, and underlying beliefs and assumptions about human nature, eight attitudes or mindsets have been defined which help explain the essence of EI. The eight EI Attitudes and their relationship to the EIP scales are described below (also refer to Chapter Three; Table 3.2). The EIP scales are described fully in Chapter Five.

Attitude 1: However you are and others are, is OK

This attitude forms the bedrock to the framework of the EIP, which underpins all of the EIP scales as explained in Chapter Four. The attitude is related to the OK Corral[46] model of Transactional Analysis which includes the first two scales of the EIP: Self Regard (I am OK); and Regard for Others (You are OK). Regard in this sense is focused on accepting and valuing a person for their 'being' (their existence as a person), not necessarily liking or approving of their 'doing' (behaviour). In practice, this attitude may be severely tested; it can be challenging to still have regard for and value someone despite their poor behaviour. Consider the example of a parent who, despite their child's misbehaviour, still retains deep feelings of love and compassion towards them (this does not mean they accept the child's misbehaviour). Note that this attitude applies as much to oneself (however you are is OK) as it does to others.

Attitude 2: Everyone is in control of and responsible for their actions

This is a tough one to accept, as it implies that the buck stops with oneself. When this attitude is adopted it facilitates more empowering and responsible behaviour, but if not adopted a person is more likely to feel helpless and be prone to blaming others. Comments such as, "You made me do it" or "It's not my fault", imply that a person does not have choice or control over their own behaviour. The most relevant scales to this attitude are Personal Power (scale 6, taking responsibility for one's outcomes in life) and Authenticity (scale 10, inviting the trust of others by being reliable, principled, consistent, and known).

Attitude 3: No one else can control our feelings

This may sound obvious, yet everyday comments such as, "You made me angry" or "You upset me", suggest that someone else has control over the other person's feelings. What a person feels is determined by their own internal interpretation of the event, otherwise all people would feel the same about the same situation, which of course they don't. People are different (Attitude 4) and have different emotional responses to the same situation. In confrontation, one person may feel scared and another may feel anger. On losing a job, one person may feel upset and another may feel joy, and so on. This has significant implications on EI, as individuals who believe that others control their feelings are likely to be emotionally Under Controlled (scale 13), Aggressive (scale 14) and Dependent on others (scale 15). Attitude 3 does not discount the reality that people trigger emotions in others. But the trigger (usually an unconscious attitude) and the resulting feelings, belong to the individual and are something they may choose to change through the practice of EI.

Attitude 4: People are different, they experience the world differently, feel different things, and want different things

People often nod sagely at this in agreement yet, in practice, they are surprised, mystified, or annoyed when people do not behave and respond in the way they expect them to. It is very easy to slip into generalisations about people and to assume that other people have the same perceptions as we do. Oscar Wilde had some good advice on this: "Do not do unto others as you would have them do unto you as their tastes may not be the same." Recognising that people are different by raising Awareness of Others (scale 4), rather than forming assumptions about them, helps develop an appreciation of others and their unique value (Regard for Others, scale 2), and increase Flexibility (scale 8) to adapt to people's differences.

Attitude 5: Feelings and behaviour are separate

EI is literally 'the intelligent use of emotions', or as previously defined; the 'practice of thinking about feeling, and feeling about thinking, to guide behaviour'. When people have an 'emotional hijack' (when feelings of anger get the better of them), they go straight from feelings to behaviour without thinking. Comments such as, "I couldn't help it", suggest that the person has not learned to separate their feelings from their behaviour. This in turn can result in emotionally unintelligent behaviour such as poor Emotional Resilience (scale 5), low impulse control (Goal Directedness, scale 7), emotionally Under Controlled behaviour (scale 13), and Aggressive Conflict Handling (scale 14).

Attitude 6: All feelings are justified, acceptable and important

Feelings tell people what they want, like, dislike, need, and fear. Judging feelings as unacceptable or unimportant may lead a person to deny those feelings that are unpleasant or less acceptable to them. If an individual is unaware of their feelings (Self Awareness, scale 3), they are less able to manage them appropriately or respond to their emotional needs. This may result in bottled-up feelings, resentment, hostility, stress, ill-health, inflexibility, defensiveness, and generally less emotionally intelligent behaviour. There are several steps or hurdles to becoming aware of and acting upon feelings:

— The individual must initially notice their feelings. For example, "My tummy tingles",

— then pay attention to them: "This matters",

— then give them significance: "Maybe I feel nervous",

— then think about their feelings: "I want to relax",

— finally, take them into account when deciding how to act: "I will take some deep breaths."

This applies both to the individual's own feelings and to the feelings of others. If a person disregards other's feelings as unimportant (Regard for Others, scale 2) then they are less likely to pay attention, understand, or relate to others effectively (Awareness of Others, scale 4).

Attitude 7: Change is possible

EI is based upon attitudes, habits, and skills – all of which are learned or acquired and are therefore changeable.[47] If something is learned it can be unlearned. It is this attitude which has become the foundation for those working in the field of people development and is of particular relevance to EI. Unfortunately, many EI metrics attempt to justify their scales by correlating them with personality traits. But personality traits differ from EI in two distinct ways: personality traits are more constitutional (innate) and therefore less changeable than EI; and personality traits are not about being effective, which EI clearly is.

Personal development does not require changing personality traits, but rather learning how to 'manage' them, for example, by moving outside of one's comfort zones, changing a long-running habit, or adopting new attitudes. For this reason, personality traits and EI go hand-in-hand, as EI is the practice of making best use of who we are, our resources and potential. This attitude, that change is possible, is particularly relevant to Flexibility (scale 8), and also supports Balanced Outlook (scale 12) and Reflective Learning (scale 16). For methods on how to develop EI, refer to Chapter Eight.

Attitude 8: People have a natural tendency towards growth and health

Everyone can develop their EI – it does not have a fixed or limited capacity. However, much innate human potential is left undeveloped because of people's internal interferences and defences. Aristotle illustrated this concept (which he called Physis, the Greek for 'inherent nature') with a cabbage seed which, if given the right environment, is predisposed to grow and flourish but will also wither in the wrong environment. It is helpful here to apply the self-development formula by Timothy Gallwey[48] 'Performance = Potential – Interference.' In practical terms this means first helping people to recognise their Potential and resources and then to identify and dismantle their Interferences such as limiting beliefs and restrictive habits, and replace them with emotionally intelligent attitudes, habits, and skills. Once the Interferences are removed then people, as with all living things, will naturally develop their Potential and improve their Performance. Personal growth and development is facilitated by Reflective Learning (scale 16).

As well as their theoretical relevance, the eight EI Attitudes also have strong practical implications. It is not intended that people should adopt these eight attitudes as 'truths' but, in practice, when people behave in ways that are not emotionally intelligent they tend to have breached one or more of these attitudes. Therefore, individuals who adopt the EI Attitudes, are more likely to behave with greater EI. For this reason the scales of the EIP were constructed around the eight attitudes and help explain why someone may find it either easier or more difficult to develop any of the EIP scales. For example, a person who has difficulty developing their Flexibility (scale 8) may not endorse EI Attitude 7, that Change is possible. Someone who scores lowly on Personal Power (scale 7) may not accept EI Attitude 2, that Everyone is in control of and responsible for their actions.

When considering the above set of attitudes, the reader is encouraged to distinguish between what they think is true and agree with (reflecting their belief), and what they actually do in practice (reflecting their attitude), since what a person does in practice is often a better indicator of their attitudes, than what they may claim to do. Someone may say they believe in "being honest" (their belief) but in practice they withhold information or tell lies. A person may not be consciously aware of their underlying attitudes that drive their feelings and behaviours, because attitudes are generated in the deeper and usually less conscious emotional centres of the brain (the limbic system). Beliefs on the other hand, live in the higher, usually more conscious thinking parts of the brain (the neocortex). These different areas of the brain and their roles are explained in the next chapter.

1.6   An organising framework for Emotional Intelligence

The EI definition and eight EI Attitudes underpin the development of the EIP and have led to the EIP framework, an organising structure to describe the different parts of EI. A brief description of the EIP framework is given in Table 1.1 and Chapter Four is dedicated to explaining this framework, as it forms the basis to using and interpreting the EIP reports. EI is divided into two streams derived from the work of Howard Gardner.[11] He defined several types of intelligence including Intrapersonal Intelligence (or Personal Intelligence) which is about ourselves, and Interpersonal Intelligence, which is about inter-relating with others. These two streams relate to Part One of the EI definition, to be both personally and interpersonally effective. The two streams are further divided into three levels, which relate to the three parts of the EI definition: What, How, and When.

'What' is EI?

Definition (Part One): 'Emotional Intelligence is the practice of managing one's personality to be both personally and interpersonally effective.' This relates to the Behaviour scales (top level) of the EIP framework that are grouped under the themes of Self Management (personally effective) and Relationship Management (interpersonally effective).

'How' are people emotionally intelligent?

Definition (Part Two): 'This is achieved through the habitual practice of thinking about feeling, and feeling about thinking, to guide one's behaviour.' This relates to the Feeling scales (middle level) of the EIP framework: Self Awareness and Awareness of Others. The complete EIP framework (explained in Chapter Four; 4.2.1) also includes Reflective Learning (thinking about feeling).

'When' are people emotionally intelligent?

Definition (Part Three): 'The extent and effectiveness of an individual's EI is determined largely by their attitudes.' This relates to the Attitude scales of Self Regard and Regard for Others (bottom level), which are derived from the first and primary EI Attitude, However you are and others are, is OK.

The EIP framework

	Personal Intelligence	Interpersonal Intelligence
Behaviour	Self Management	Relationship Management
Feeling	Self Awareness	Awareness of Others
Attitude	Self Regard	Regard for Others

© 1998 ICA Global Ltd.

Table 1.1

It should be noted that the framework has 'arrows of influence' which go from left to right and from the bottom up, so that Attitude (bottom level) influences Feeling (and thinking) (middle level), and this influences Behaviour (top level). It is therefore a person's Attitude that leads to them achieving congruent, consistent, enduring, and desirable Behaviour. With practice, EI becomes more automated, unconscious, and habitual, creating a direct link between Attitude and Behaviour. This in turn frees up consciousness (the middle Feeling level) for further improving EI. The rationale for this model is drawn from the neurological evidence for EI described in the next chapter. The close link between these psychological components, the EIP definition, and the EIP framework is summarised in Chapter Two; Table 2.4.

1.7   Some misunderstandings of EI: What EI is not

Before concluding this chapter on 'What is Emotional Intelligence?', it is worth identifying what EI is not. There are a number of specific misunderstandings which either under-value or over-estimate the potential value of EI, some of which include:

1   EI is something people are born with

Emotional Intelligence is based on attitudes, habits, and skills, none of which people are born with. The great benefit therefore is that EI can be developed by anyone who chooses to develop it. Research on the EIP has shown that many aspects of EI, rather like wisdom, increase with age.[49]

2   EI is a single score

Representing EI as a single scale (such as EQ) can be misleading. EI is not a single construct but is multifaceted. People can be strong in some areas and weaker in others. Reducing EI to a single score detracts from understanding individual differences, strengths, and development opportunities.

3   Women are more emotionally intelligent than men

Research on the EIP has shown that females on average score higher than males on Regard for Others (scale 2), the Awareness scales (3 and 4), Connecting with Others (scale 9), and Reflective Learning (scale 16). Males on average score higher on Self Regard (scale 1), Emotional Resilience (scale 5), and Interdependence (scale 15). Overall there are negligible differences on most EIP scales between genders. Refer to the Technical Manual for more details.[49]

4   EI is a new fad

Although EI was popularised in 1996,[5] it has been used widely within education since 1980 and different terms have been around for similar concepts since the 1920s (refer to Appendix Two for a historical overview of EI). EI is not a fad. Its popularity has continued to grow in business for personal, team, and organisational development. It is well supported by neuroscience (refer to Chapter Two) and there is continued research demonstrating its benefit for individual performance and productivity (refer to Chapter Nine).

5   EI is just naval gazing (self-reflection)

Developing EI requires emotional Self Awareness (scale 3) and Reflective Learning (scale 16) but this is only one element of EI. The EIP framework is made up of six parts (as described in Chapter Four; 4.1) which includes turning Self Awareness (Feeling) into effective Self Management and Relationship Management (Behaviour).

6   EI is just another term for soft skills

Soft or interpersonal skills such as being tactful, showing appreciation, and asking for help are important in developing and maintaining relationships. However, they are unlikely to be sustained if they are not backed up by underlying EI Attitudes (as described earlier in this chapter). For instance, someone who learns assertiveness skills like saying "no" to requests, will soon return to their old behaviours if underneath they do not hold corresponding emotionally intelligent attitudes, such as, However you are and others are, is OK (EI Attitude 1).

7   EI is just about being nice to people

Although EI is about having Regard for Others (scale 2), this does not necessarily mean agreeing with their behaviour. The challenge with Regard for Others is still valuing a person despite disapproving of what they may do. EI also involves being Assertive (scale 14) and being willing to have difficult conversations with people which requires high Self Regard (scale 1). Giving difficult feedback to a colleague, seeking critical feedback from others, standing up to a line manager, being prepared to be in the minority, and risking disapproval from others, are all examples of EI behaviours that go beyond 'just being nice to people'. The scales of Self Regard and Regard for Others are described in Chapter Five; 5.1, and form the foundation to the other 14 EIP scales.

8   EI is about letting out all of your feelings

People who bottle-up emotions until they explode may benefit from learning how to notice and express their feelings sooner while they are more manageable. On the other hand, people who allow their emotions to control them would benefit from learning how to manage their feelings so as not to express them indiscriminately. Many of the EIP scales are about getting the right balance between too much emotional control (bottling-up feelings) and too little (uncontrolled expression of feelings). These are called 'multi-scales' and are described in Chapter Five; 5.4.

9   EI is a panacea

EI has become increasingly popular and is a label often attributed to a wide range of personal development courses, products, and approaches without any clear definition or rationale. Overstating the benefits of EI only devalues it in the long run. Also, some of the existing models of EI are simply repackaging existing personality questionnaires or competency frameworks. Users of the term Emotional Intelligence should be clear as to its definition, understand how it differs from other psychological constructs and recognise the boundaries of where and how it may be applied.

This first chapter has provided a definition and overview of EI. The next chapter discusses the different psychological and neurological aspects that underpin EI and the EIP theory.

SUMMARY POINTS
FROM CHAPTER ONE

The term Emotional Intelligence was popularised in the 1990s, but as a concept has been around much longer with labels such as emotional literacy, maturity, and wisdom.

Traditional psychometric tests focus on what are thought to be stable aspects of psychological functioning, such as personality traits and cognitive abilities. Such tests aim to predict future behaviour and raise the individual's self-knowledge. However, the durability of traits and cognitive abilities has led to a pessimistic view of IQ and personality as destiny and does not allow for the possibility that people can manage their personalities and become more effective, even in situations in which they are naturally less compatible or comfortable.

Humans possess a set of unique resources that enable them to cope with the ever-increasing demands and changes of modern society. It is the individual's ability to harness their innate attributes, (such as using their imagination, thinking through problems, and learning from experience) that enables them to meet their emotional needs (such as the need for security, emotional connection, and meaning) which is what constitutes being emotionally intelligent. Suggestions on how to do this are given in Chapter Eight.

A person's innate resources represent their potential and manifest in their personality. There is a close relationship between EI and personality. EI is the 'missing link' that turns personality (potential, temperament, and innate resources such as IQ) into effective performance (behavioural competence).

EI is reflected by what a person does in the present moment. EI is therefore described as a verb (the practice of managing one's personality) not a noun, and is about 'being' emotionally intelligent rather than 'having' Emotional Intelligence.

EI is defined in three parts

What it is to be emotionally intelligent: Emotional Intelligence is the practice of managing one's personality, including innate resources such as IQ, to be both personally and interpersonally effective.

How to be emotionally intelligent: This is achieved through the habitual practice of thinking about feeling, and feeling about thinking, to guide one's behaviour.

When are people emotionally intelligent? The extent and effectiveness by which an individual behaves with EI is determined largely by their attitudes.

This chapter has described eight underlying attitudes which are the foundation of EI, and upon which the EIP is based. In so far as people adopt these attitudes, they will potentially behave with greater EI.

The definition and attitudes that underpin the EIP have led to the development of the EIP framework and scales (described in Chapter Four; 4.1). The EIP framework shows the arrows of influence that start from the bottom up, where Attitude influences Feeling, and Feeling leads to Behaviour. This psychological sequence, which is supported by neuroscience, is explored in detail in the next chapter.

CHAPTER TWO
THE NEUROSCIENCE OF EMOTIONAL INTELLIGENCE

INTRODUCTION

The phrase Emotional Intelligence (EI) incorporates feeling (Emotional) and thinking (Intelligence), both of which are created and experienced within the brain and the body. The purpose of this chapter is to examine the neurological basis for EI to confirm the definition and theoretical foundation given to the EIP.

The model of EI on which the EIP is based emphasises attitudes as the key determinant influencing feeling, thinking, and behaviour. Other models of EI are based on skills, competencies, personality traits, and cognitive capacities rather than attitudes. As explained below, when judged against the neurological evidence, it is the attitudinal component that lies at the core of what Emotional Intelligence actually is.

2.1   The evolution of the brain

Looking at how the human brain evolved starts to explain, if only crudely, the relationship between the different elements of EI (thinking, feeling, behaviour, and attitude). An early representation of the brain's evolution separated it into three broad stages: reptilian, mammalian, and primate.[1] These brain divisions are present in all vertebrates. The brain evolved by reorganising itself, so that different regions played different primary roles at various stages in evolution.

The earliest reptilian parts of the brain (the central nervous system) enabled the primary survival functions: fight-flight-freeze, and reproduction. As reptiles evolved into mammals they developed more advanced neurological functions, such as the visceral limbic system where emotions were created to reinforce learned behaviour through stimulus-response conditioning. That is, rewards (positive feelings) encouraged any given behaviour, and pain (unpleasant feelings) discouraged any given behaviour. This emotional learning mechanism allowed mammals to learn and adapt rapidly to their environment. Much automatic and habitual human behaviour is largely the result of such conditioning. As mammals evolved into primates, development and access to the neocortex enabled the capacity for thinking and conscious choice. The neocortex (Latin for 'new bark') is the outer part of the brain which is involved in higher level processing such as the interpretation of and deciding how to act upon feelings.

Unlike computer technology, human beings are unable to dispose of and replace outdated software, so many of the earlier primitive neurological programmes have been retained. Much of what is required in people's day-to-day activities, from routine habits to in-depth thinking, is greatly influenced by the early reptilian regions of the brain for instincts and survival, and the mammalian limbic system for emotions, well-being, and motivation. However, this brief explanation is a simplification of the brain's evolution, as natural selection has reprogrammed all parts of the brain to work in combination.[2] For instance, the limbic network, which is heavily involved in forming emotional expectations, draws upon other sensory regions of the brain, such as the visual cortex, to assimilate visual information in forming, and then verifying emotional predictions.[3] As neuroscience advances, the overlap between different brain areas in relation to EI is becoming better understood. For example, the Default Mode Network (DMN), also referred to as the 'social brain', incorporates several brain regions that are instrumental to 'empathic reasoning'.[4] Interestingly these brain regions are separate to the Task Positive Network (TPN) involved in 'analytical reasoning', supporting the notion of there being a separate emotional form of intelligence.[4]

2.1.1 The evolution of the conscious brain

It is worth examining the brain's evolution in a little more detail to consider not only how the brain evolved but why it did so. This helps explain why Emotional Intelligence is necessary to becoming an emotionally healthy and well-adjusted human being.

A chronology of the brain's evolution

YEARS AGO	STAGE IN THE BRAIN'S EVOLUTION
3.5 billion	The first forms of life emerge with single cell organisms
500 million	The first primitive reptilian brainstem appears along with a basic system of nerves for movement
220 million	The late Triassic period saw the start of mammalian life forms
60 million	Earliest primates are recorded
6 million	Early members of the human lineage, Primate Hominids (bipedal, upright, and walking) are recorded
200,000	Earliest recordings of Homo sapiens genetic DNA
60–40,000	The brain's 'big bang'. Human primates develop the capacity for consciousness, creative thinking, and cultural development

Table 2.1

As can be seen from the table above, it is only a fraction (0.0014%) of the brain's evolutionary timescale that separates today's human brain from its earlier lineage. It is fascinating to note how rapidly the brain's evolution has accelerated and to wonder at how soon, and in what form, the brain's next evolutionary leap forward will be.

The first significant step forward in the brain's evolution coincided with the beginning of warm blooded mammalian life. Being warm blooded meant mammals could regulate their body temperature giving them the ability to move around whatever the external temperature,[5] (unlike reptiles and fish which are cold blooded and dependent on the external temperature). The advantages that warm bloodedness gave mammals came at the cost of needing to conserve their energy; a large proportion of a mammal's energy is spent maintaining their internal body temperature.[6] If a mammal responded to every emotional impulse, such as chasing a moving leaf, they would soon exhaust their energy supplies necessary for survival. Nature's answer to this was to evolve the brain (the limbic region in particular) so that mammals could learn from past experience and make energy efficient choices. Rather than simply responding instinctively to every stimulus, mammals' brains were able to draw upon past emotional learning (i.e. positive and negative reinforcement) to determine their response accordingly (albeit at a purely unconscious emotional level).

However, repressing and not acting upon every emotional impulse would in time cause an unhealthy build-up of undischarged emotion (stress) on the autonomic nervous system and eventually result in these instincts (such as to respond to danger or opportunities of food) being dulled or even switched off, which would be catastrophic to survival. Nature's remedy was to allow the unfulfilled emotional expectations to be acted out and expressed metaphorically through the process of dreaming (in REM sleep).[7] Discharging unexpressed emotions through dreaming allowed these instincts to be preserved, and deactivated unresolved anxiety and stress (this is explained in Section 2.5).

The functionality of early mammals' brains is still inherent in today's human brain but over time has developed some powerful upgrades! The second significant step forward in the brain's evolution was the development of the brain's frontal lobes (the prefrontal cortex) and the emergence of consciousness, a mere 40,000 years ago. This is known as the brain's 'big bang' and gave rise to many of the innate human resources (described in Chapter One; 1.1). It allowed humans to develop an awareness of 'self' – a self-concept to make considered decisions and to think about how to respond to their feelings. It also gave conscious access to the higher brain functions of the left and right hemispheres in the neocortex, which for the previous 160,000 years had been relatively underutilised. This conscious access to 'thinking' allowed humans to be creative, consider ideas, reflect on the past, and think about the future. It also led to the development of complex language and so allowed generations to pass on their learning, wisdom, and experience.[8] In essence, having conscious awareness is what makes us human, the results of which are all of humankind's achievements. Giving access to conscious awareness also opened the doorway to human psychological frailties and the need for humans to learn how to manage their conscious thoughts and feelings. Learning how best to use and develop the innate gifts of the human brain is a large part of being emotionally intelligent. The remainder of this chapter describes in more detail how the brain processes feelings, thoughts, and attitudes and why this is integral to being emotionally intelligent. Human well-being falls across a broad spectrum, from being emotionally unhealthy to being emotionally intelligent. The focus of this book is at the top end of this spectrum, although it is useful to recognise that a person can move and inhabit the full breadth of this spectrum during their lifetime.

2.2   How feelings influence thinking

Understanding the brain's evolution provides a useful explanation for how feelings influence thinking. Because the brain evolved outwardly, there are more connections from the deeper limbic system (feeling) to the neocortex (thinking) than there are from thinking to feeling.[9] Therefore, the more primitive, instinctive, and emotional parts of the brain often exert greater influence over a person's thinking. As a result, instinctive drives such as breathing, being startled, and the fight-flight-freeze response are almost irrepressible. This also explains why strong emotional urges (from the limbic area) such as phobias, are difficult to overcome through rational thinking. A person with a phobia of spiders or flying may consciously understand (in their neocortex) that the spider will not hurt them or that the aeroplane is unlikely to crash but they still hold an emotional and debilitating fear. Less extreme emotional states also influence a person's thinking, creating positive thoughts when they feel happy and negative thoughts when they feel sad.[10] Rather than being dominant, a person's thinking is often subservient to and largely influenced by their feeling.

Research has shown that information is sent to and perceived by the limbic region (feeling) momentarily before it reaches the higher thinking cortex.[11] This is consistent with other evidence showing that the decision to act precedes consciousness, in that the brain prepares to take an action 0.3 seconds before the person is aware of choosing to do so.[12] This notion challenges the Cartesian philosophy of thinking being the essence of humanity, "I think therefore I am", which has pervaded western society in general, and can be seen particularly in education (IQ), business (rational decision making), and therapy (cognitive-behavioural). Feelings not only influence thinking but are instrumental in our decision making. Making decisions would be near impossible if people had no emotional attachment to them. Emotions tell a person what they want, like, and desire; without emotional impulse there would be no conviction or confidence in decisions. This has been demonstrated by Antonio Damasio,[13] a neurosurgeon who studied patients with damage to their ventromedial prefrontal cortex, a part of the brain involved in emotional processing. In these cases, the patients retained their ability to think and feel normally but could not combine the two (to think about their feeling and feel about their thinking). As a result, without laborious analysis, they were unable to make even the most basic decisions and were almost entirely lacking in sound wisdom or judgment. Feelings help guide thinking; they provide a sense of conviction to decisions as well as a wealth of deeper intuitive knowing about what is best, right, or wrong (what may be referred to as gut instinct or hunches). Far from being random inconvenient distractions, feelings provide 'intelligent' feedback on how to act (a closer examination of Damasio's research may be found in Appendix Two; Section 2).

The interdependent relationship between thinking and feeling is included in part two of the EI definition (Chapter One; 1.4); 'the habitual practice of thinking about feeling, and feeling about thinking, to guide one's behaviour', which involves noticing, thinking about, labelling, and interpreting feelings in the body. Conscious awareness of feelings helps an individual to develop their self-knowledge and draw upon this when experiencing similar feelings in the future. For example, "I notice myself becoming tired and irritable, and based on past experience I know this is a good time for me to take a break." This process applies as much to others as it does to oneself, by noticing the feelings of others and forming knowledge of others. The EI definition also includes 'feeling about thinking', which involves having feelings about one's thoughts, such as feeling confident about a decision, or feeling excited about a new idea. In summary, there is a co-dependent relationship between thinking and feeling, with each influencing the other and both holding equal status and value.

2.3   How the brain processes attitudes, thoughts, and feelings

Feeling and thinking are the midpoint in the EI process, but what happens before and what happens after the midpoint? Figure 2.1 shows the regions of the brain which are most relevant to EI.

The first part of this process occurs when stimuli are initially received by the brain through the sensory thalamus and instantly scanned by the instinctive and limbic parts of the brain for any potential danger. The instinctive region (the brain stem) contains the natural reflexes for danger, such as to flinch at a sudden movement or jump at a loud bang, whereas the limbic system contains learned responses to danger in a part called the amygdala (Greek for, and in the shape of, an almond).

If the amygdala identifies the stimuli as a serious threat, it sends a powerful emotional response to act upon the perceived danger (the fight-flight-freeze mechanism) and bypasses the higher thinking brain (the prefrontal cortex). The primary function of the amygdala is to keep a person alive and safe. In evolutionary terms, if a person stopped to think through their options while under attack they may be too slow to react and survive. Thus, when a person has a fear response (also termed an 'emotional hijack')[14] the thinking brain is literally incapacitated, and the reactive amygdala takes charge. The amygdala may be likened to a 'security guard' with the power to press the alarm and evacuate the building (flight), lock the doors (freeze), or call the emergency services (fight). Such a lifesaving response is fine if a person is in real danger, but not so useful if the danger is just perceived rather than real. For example, if while making a presentation an individual has an emotional hijack, due to the effects of adrenalin they may start to sweat, experience bodily shakes (preparing for flight), their voice may tremble, and their ability to think clearly is severely impaired. From the day a person is born, they will encounter numerous frightening experiences that become etched onto the amygdala as permanent implicit memories, resulting in the same fear response being triggered whenever a similar stimulus is presented in the future. This may be observed in people's phobias, irrational fears, post-traumatic memories, and excessive emotional reactions.

Although potentially embarrassing, people do not die from fear. The purpose of the brain's fear response is to keep the person alive, which is why it exists as one of the primary emotions. The amygdala is also involved in processing other primary emotions, such as joy, disgust, anxiety, and anger,[15] all of which have their roots in human evolution and survival. Caruso[16] describes the survival purpose of fear as, "Let's get out of here"; sadness as "Help me"; disgust as "Don't eat that"; and anger to give the person energy to fight. Further explanation on the evolutionary basis for emotions is given in Appendix Two; Section One. There does not need to be an extreme amygdala reaction for thinking to be impaired. Too much emotion interferes with clear rational thinking, as 'emotional thinking' is more blunt and categorical (good/bad, right/wrong), thus leading to less refined decision making. Stress has been shown to amplify implicit emotional memories in the amygdala (causing fear) but impair access to explicit event memories in the hippocampus, thus preventing the individual from placing the stressful event into context as a specific past event.[17,18] EI involves getting the right balance between thinking and feeling: enough feeling to guide and inform thinking, but not so much as to be overpowering. More details on how to do this may be found in Chapter Eight; 8.4.

Having gone through 'security checks' by the amygdala for any danger, stimuli are instantly 'pattern matched' with innate templates and past experiences. The pattern matching process might be likened to an internet search engine seeking a match to the stimulus. Past experiences are stored in many deeper regions of the brain, such as the amygdala and the contextual memory stores of the hippocampus,[19] not as literal memories but as metaphorical representations (patterns) that are attached to emotional tendencies. The connection between any particular stimuli, the pattern match and its corresponding emotional 'tag', is referred to in the EIP theory as an attitude, defined earlier as: 'The habitual and evaluative position a person holds towards any given stimuli'. Further explanation of pattern matching is given in the next section, 2.4.

Regions of the brain most relevant to EI

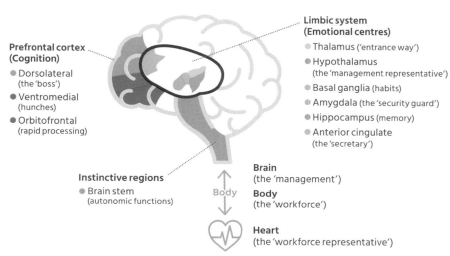

Limbic system (Emotional centres)
- Thalamus ('entrance way')
- Hypothalamus (the 'management representative')
- Basal ganglia (habits)
- Amygdala (the 'security guard')
- Hippocampus (memory)
- Anterior cingulate (the 'secretary')

Prefrontal cortex (Cognition)
- Dorsolateral (the 'boss')
- Ventromedial (hunches)
- Orbitofrontal (rapid processing)

Instinctive regions
- Brain stem (autonomic functions)

Brain (the 'management')

Body (the 'workforce')

Heart (the 'workforce representative')

Figure 2.1

Once the percept (what has been perceived) has been tagged with emotional significance, it is sent to the higher thinking brain (prefrontal cortex) and the hypothalamus, which triggers an emotional experience (feelings) within the body. The hypothalamus may be likened to a 'management representative' that communicates between the 'management' (the brain) and the 'workforce' (the body) through the release of hormones (feelings). The relationship between the brain and body is explained further in Section 2.6.

The percept, with its emotional tag, is also received by the anterior cingulate which communicates with the memory stores of the hippocampus. The anterior cingulate may be likened to the boss's 'secretary' dealing with routine responses, without having to alert the conscious mind (the dorsolateral prefrontal cortex), referred to as the 'boss'. As long as the required action is familiar (a habit), the 'secretary' fires off the necessary neural network that initiates the appropriate behavioural habit without disturbing the 'boss'.[20] The neural networks for habits live mainly within a deeper part of the limbic system called the basal ganglia. Habits free up the higher parts of the brain for conscious thinking.

Thus, much automatic habitual behaviour is the consequence of an initial attitude or pattern match. Even the most mundane behaviours have their roots in emotions and attitudes which usually pass them by unaware, as long as the individual acts upon them and fulfils the emotional expectation. If they do not follow their emotional impulse then feelings steadily increase, often becoming overpowering. This may happen, for example, when a person tries to change a habit, such as changing a routine, going on a diet, or starting an exercise schedule. This can be tremendously difficult as the brain and body continue to send emotional messages to repeat the existing behavioural habit.

Eventually however, through continued repetition, the old patterns will reduce as new neural pathways are formed.

Not all behaviour is habitual and automatic. Humans have the capacity to be self-aware and make conscious choices. The 'boss' (the conscious thinking brain) can choose to become involved and self-observing, such as being aware of feelings, thinking about their behaviour, or deciding to change an automatic habit. The 'boss' is also alerted to pay conscious attention when a person is involved in more complex decision making, is faced with a challenging situation, or when learning something new.

To summarise the entire psychological process from stimulus to response: stimuli are initially connected with their emotional significance through a pattern matching process in the emotional-based region of the brain (the limbic system) and checked for possible danger in the amygdala (the 'security guard'). A pattern match will attach an emotional tag to the percept and send this direct to the hypothalamus, triggering an emotional experience in the body, and sending a message to the anterior cingulate (the 'secretary') to initiate a response. From here it is either processed unconsciously by the basal ganglia as an automatic habit, or consciously through the prefrontal cortex (the 'boss') where the individual chooses how to respond/behave. Their behaviour delivers a certain outcome (positive or negative) either reinforcing or discouraging their behaviour, as illustrated in Table 2.2.

The six psychological stages of EI

STAGES	EXAMPLE PROCESS
Stimulus	A colleague criticises their work
Attitude/ Pattern match	This triggers their underlying attitude of, "I am incompetent"
Feeling/ Emotion	This is experienced in their body as feeling deflated
Thought	Their conscious self-talk is, "Why should I bother?"
Behaviour/ Habit	Their automatic response is to withdraw
Outcome	Their performance gets worse and they communicate less

Table 2.2

Understanding the six stages of the psychological process helps explain the different ways in which EI can be developed. For example, if a person is too passive in conflict they could address it at any stage in the process as shown in Table 2.3.

Examples of EI development

STAGES	EXAMPLE APPLICATION: BEING IN CONFLICT
Stimulus	Rather than avoid difficult conversations they could address issues sooner
Attitude/ Pattern match	They could replace negative attitudes such as, "People won't like me if I disagree", with helpful ones such as, "People's differences are valuable"
Feeling/ Emotion	They could practise breathing techniques to stay calm before, during, and after confrontation
Thought	They could challenge their negative or passive self-talk with positive affirmations, such as, "What I think does matter"
Behaviour/ Habit	They could repeat useful habits or phrases, such as, "Please give me a moment to think about that", before agreeing to do something
Outcome	They could visualise or role-play acting assertively with a person who is behaving aggressively towards them

Table 2.3

How to develop EI in each of these stages is discussed in more detail in Chapter Eight.

Although this explanation of the brain may seem sequential and reductionist, in practice many of these processes are happening simultaneously, instantaneously, interdependently, and continuously, with the different parts of the brain being interlinked and multifunctional. The brain has been likened to a quivering web with millions of synaptic connections firing at every moment. The three regions of the brain (instinctive, limbic, and prefrontal cortex) are inter-connected by the orbitofrontal cortex, which contains super-fast neuronal transmitters (spindle cells), which instantly link instinct, emotion, and thought. This explains why people can make snap decisions on whether they trust someone from first impressions. Furthermore, the relationship between thinking and feeling is more cyclical than sequential. Feelings trigger thinking as much as thinking fuels feeling. However, it is useful to separate out these psychological functions as they offer different doorways into personal development.

The six stages may be more accurately represented as a cycle with a connection between each of the psychological facets. Each facet has a primary link in the order of the cycle (such as Behaviour leads to an Outcome), but also has a secondary influence on each of the other four facets (such as Behaviour influences Feeling) as shown in Figure 2.2. For example, by standing upright and talking assertively (Behaviour) a person may start to feel more confident (Feeling) or by making a positive facial expression this may elicit positive feelings.[21] There is also a strong direct relationship between Attitude and Behaviour, which may largely bypass conscious feeling and thinking.[22] One meta-analytic study found a high correlation of .38 between 'attitude opinion' and 'behavioural action', and concluded that attitudes significantly and substantially predict future behaviour.[23] The relationship between the six psychological facets may be abbreviated by the acronym SAFE-TBO. A helpful reminder for this acronym is 'SAFE To Be Oneself', which fits with the premise of EI being about Self Regard and unconditional self-acceptance.

The SAFE-TBO model

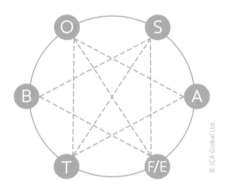

S	Stimulus
A	Attitude/Pattern match
F/E	Feeling/Emotion
T	Thinking
B	Behaviour/Habit
O	Outcome/Performance

Figure 2.2

© JCA Global Ltd.

The SAFE-TBO model has direct relevance to the construction of the EIP. It highlights the importance of attitudes in influencing feelings, thoughts, and behaviour, and supports the rationale for the EIP being underpinned by eight EI Attitudes (described in Chapter One; 1.5). The SAFE-TBO model is also represented in the three-part definition of EI: 'What', 'How', and 'When', and in the EIP framework (refer to Chapter One; 1.6). The relationship between these three models is shown in Table 2.4.

Links between the EIP definition, framework, and SAFE-TBO model

EIP definition of EI	EIP framework	SAFE-TBO model
		Outcome/Performance
What: ... to be both personally and interpersonally effective	Behaviour	Behaviour/Habit
How: ... EI is the habitual practice of thinking about feeling, and feeling about thinking	Thinking	Thinking
	Feeling	Feeling/Emotion
When: ... EI is determined largely by a person's attitudes ...	Attitude	Attitude/Pattern match
		Stimulus

Table 2.4

At the heart of the psychological model and EIP is a pattern matching process reflecting a person's attitudes. Attitudes are one of the key features that differentiate the EIP from other personality (temperament/trait), cognitive, and competency-based models of EI. The next section looks in more detail at how patterns and attitudes are formed.

2.4   How attitudes form in the brain

The term 'pattern matching' was used by Joe Griffin,[24] a dream researcher, to explain his theory of how the brain perceives, interprets, and gives meaning to stimuli. A pattern match occurs when stimuli are recognised by the brain as belonging to a previously identified class of stimuli. The brain is highly efficient. Rather than having to interpret millions of bits of sensory information it simply matches these with pre-existing templates (patterns). A 'pattern' is effectively an internal representation of external and internal stimuli. Patterns can be either innate (instinctive templates, such as the capacity to learn language) or developed through experience. They are stored as metaphorical representations rather than literal memories. Each pattern is tagged with an emotional significance that is released once a pattern has been matched. The emotional tag takes the form of a neurochemical messenger which stimulates a response in the higher parts of the brain, forming a connection between the feeling (limbic) brain and the thinking (prefrontal cortex) brain. The emotional tag may also bypass the thinking brain, such as in a perceived emergency, triggering an immediate physiological and emotional reaction (fight-flight-freeze).

A pattern and its emotional tag may be seen as the neurological equivalent of an attitude. As defined earlier, an attitude is: 'An evaluative position (based largely on feelings) towards oneself, others, a situation, an idea, etc. that predisposes an individual towards (or away from) certain behaviours or responses'. Patterns are certainly 'evaluative' in that they have an emotional response, such as like, want, dislike, fear, and they are 'towards/away from' (or in response to the perception of) any given stimuli. In this sense the emotional tag 'predisposes an individual', directing them to think and behave in a certain way. In effect, through pattern matching, the individual has both the stimulus and the response within them. Using the previous example (Table. 2.2), the individual has a pre-existing pattern (and therefore expectation) of the stimulus ('being criticised'), which connects with their attitudinal response, "I am incompetent", and their emotional response of feeling 'deflated'.

The brain is essentially a pattern matching organ, constantly scanning external and internal sensory inputs (visual, auditory, and kinaesthetic) for a potential match with past experiences. Lisa Feldman-Barrett[25], a psychologist and neuroscientist, describes this as a four-stage process: predict, stimulate, compare, and resolve errors. The brain does not simply react to sensory inputs; it anticipates and aims to predict them through searching past sensory experiences to form simulations (rather like a weather forecast).

Simulations are then compared with incoming sensory data, which if they match become the person's perceived experience (emotions, thoughts, movements etc.). This process takes place instantaneously and continuously with billions of neurons firing in parallel to create simulations. Consider the experienced fell runner who can descend a rock-strewn mountain at great speed, instantly comparing simulations with visual and kinaesthetic feedback to make micro-adjustments to the position and pressure of each stride. Where predictions don't match incoming sensory data, the simulation error is revised and stored to inform future predictions.

Griffin proposed that people form and adapt their patterns (attitudes) in the dreaming phase of sleep (indicated by rapid eye movement, REM sleep). He termed this the 'expectation fulfilment theory' of dreaming,[7] whereby any unfulfilled emotions/expectations from the previous day are metaphorically acted out in their dreams. He concluded that this both preserves the integrity of the existing patterns and allows new patterns to be formed or reconfigured.[26,27] Patterns (attitudes) are formed throughout a person's life. New-born babies, for example, form new patterns as they make sense of the world, spending up to 70% of their sleep time in the REM state compared with 25% for adults.[28] People also drift in and out of the REM state to varying degrees during the day, such as when daydreaming, using their imagination, or in a focused state of attention. In this way, patterns are formed and adapted throughout life, influencing how people respond to events in terms of their feelings, thoughts, and behaviours, and are therefore an integral part of Emotional Intelligence.

2.5 How the brain helps regulate feelings

Apart from pattern formation, REM sleep has another essential purpose which is to deactivate unresolved emotions and anxiety from the previous day.[29-31] This is vital to Emotional Intelligence as sleep cycles are part of emotional management, enabling the individual to recover emotionally and physically from the previous day. Leaving emotions unresolved would interfere with the individual's capacity to think clearly, resolve problems, and generally cope with day-to-day life. By metaphorically acting out emotional expectations through dreams, the individual discharges their unfulfilled wishes and emotions. Dreaming may be seen as nature's therapist and a natural coping mechanism ... up to a point. REM sleep can only manage so much excess emotion before a person suffers negative consequences. Someone who experiences a lot of anxiety or stress will need to spend more time in the REM sleep state to work through their built-up emotions. The REM state is initiated by a firing of the orientation response, which has the purpose of focusing a person's attention and activating their imagination, enabling the individual to dream.[32] Because of this alerting orientation response, dreaming sleep is not restful and can leave a person feeling tired if they do not get sufficient recuperative non-REM sleep. This is why a person who is anxious or depressed and sleeps for a long time (engaged mostly in REM sleep in order to process unresolved emotion)[33] still feels tired when they wake up. Also, because their orientation response is exhausted (from continuous firing) they find it difficult to focus their attention while awake. This becomes a downward spiral; if a person feels tired in the morning, they will be less able to cope with the following day's stressors, which will build-up more unresolved anxiety, requiring more REM sleep the following night, so perpetuating the cycle. This will eventually lead to extreme tiredness with high levels of unresolved anxiety, sleep problems, general exhaustion, and depression.

If the person's anxiety continues, then they will require so much REM sleep that they may wake up still in the REM trance. In this state of 'waking sleep' the person is still sleeping but with their eyes open, that is, having to perceive the external stimuli of the outside world through their dreaming brain. They may be unable to distinguish dreaming from waking reality and suffer psychotic symptoms including hallucinations (dreaming while awake), hearing voices (the left brain's language system linking with the right brain's imagination centres), and catatonia (a natural occurrence during REM sleep of numbing the senses and paralysis to avoid physically acting out one's dreams).[34]

The key to recovery and avoiding stress-related problems is for the individual to manage their level of arousal during waking hours, thus allowing their innate coping mechanism (REM sleep) to pick up the slack and support them while they sleep. Some ways to do this are: noticing early signs of anxiety, taking time out for rest and recovery, learning relaxation exercises, and allowing sufficient time for sleep (specific information on managing and reducing stress is given in Chapter Eight; 8.4). The importance of this is not just for an individual's mental health but for maximising day-to-day performance in work and life in general. People who are better able to manage their daily emotions through EI will recover more quickly from stress, feel more energised in their life, and be more productive in what they do.

2.6   Body-brain interaction

This chapter has so far explored the neurological foundations of Emotional Intelligence. However, it would be naïve and remiss not to consider the brain as part of a single system within the body. Extending the organisational metaphor for parts of the brain (the 'security guard', the 'boss', and the 'boss's secretary'), the whole brain may be seen as the 'management' and the body as the 'workforce'. Both must work in harmony together. This is highlighted by the strong influence thoughts and feelings have on a person's physical health (a field of research known as psychoneuroimmunology – PNI). Certain emotions such as prolonged stress, anxiety, grief, hostility, suspicion, pessimism, and their associated hormones can double the risk of many diseases including: heart disease, asthma, arthritis, skin diseases, ulcers, and headaches.[35] Chronic stress in particular is known to weaken the immune system, accelerate the onset and development of ill-health, and slow down recovery from illnesses such as viruses, diabetes, bowel disease, and cancer.[36]

Communication between the brain and the body is a two-way process, i.e. a continuous loop. The body responds to messages sent from the brain (through the activation of neural pathways and the release of hormones, see Section 2.8), and the brain responds to feedback from the body (through changes in heart rate, blood pressure, muscle tension, facial expression, and so forth). Barrett describes this process as 'interoception'[37] – the brain's assimilation, integration, and representation of all sensations from the body's internal organs and tissues. The interoceptive network forms predictions about the body (that include emotional predictions) in the form of simulations (patterns), which if matched against sensory inputs from the body, present as emotional experience. The reciprocal relationship between the brain and the body is illustrated by the heart and brain relationship, with as much information being sent from the heart telling the brain what to do as there is in reverse. This is done neurologically (through the nervous system), biochemically (through hormones and neurochemicals), mechanically (through the blood vessels), and intrinsically (through electrical conduction).

The heart communicates with different parts of the brain, including: the amygdala (triggering positive and negative memory patterns), the thalamus (a pathway to decision making and mental clarity), and the medulla (influencing the autonomic nervous system, such as blood pressure). Far from being a purely mechanical pump responding to the brain's requests, the heart is to some extent self-determining and there is ongoing research into how the heart influences both emotions and thinking. Techniques have been developed that enable a person to self-regulate heart rate rhythm and in so doing influence a range of brain functions.[38,39] Key findings from this research show that getting the heart and brain synchronised (through creating a regular heart rate rhythm) is beneficial to body and brain functioning. This balances the parasympathetic nervous system (which slows down heart rate) with the sympathetic nervous system (which increases heart rate), rather like getting the correct balance between the brake and the accelerator in a car.

2.7   The importance of feelings

Feelings and emotions are the main form of communication between the body and the brain. The words 'emotion' and 'feeling' are often used interchangeably but feeling may be seen as a person's subjective experience (conscious awareness) and labelling of their emotional or physiological state. Feelings that are experienced for a prolonged period of time are called 'moods'. There are three main sources of feelings:

Physiological	Hunger, thirst, nausea, pain, heart rate, etc.
Emotional	Anger, fear, happiness, guilt, pride, envy, desire, etc.
Intuitive	Gut feeling, instant judgments, and inner-knowing

Underlying feelings and emotions is a person's 'affect'.[40] This is composed of two features: valence (how pleasant or unpleasant a person feels), and arousal (the level of energy or intensity of a person's feelings), illustrated in Chapter Nine, 9.4. Combining these two dimensions reveals some of the primary or basic feelings that are broadly common to all people, such as anger, joy, fear, sadness, disgust, and anxiety. These blend into multiple combinations and finer granularity,[41] such as envy, embarrassment, jealousy, and guilt, rather like a colour palette which has infinite variations on the primary colours. Some emotions are present very soon after a child is born and most emotions are present after the first few years of life.

0-3 months	Babies show the emotions of happiness, interest, sadness, and disgust
4-6 months	Emotions of anger and surprise develop
18-24 months	Emotions related to conscious awareness of oneself appear, such as embarrassment, empathy, and envy
30-36 months	Emotions related to self-awareness in a social context appear such as pride, shame, and guilt

Although specific emotional responses appear at different ages in a child, this does not assume that people are genetically hardwired with specific emotional 'fingerprints'. Evidence is mounting for the constructionist view that emotional concepts are constructed through past and present experience so as to organise and provide meaning to our social, cultural, and internal sensory experiences.[41] For instance, historians tell us that in the 16th century sadness rather than happiness was seen as a virtue to be cultivated, and that 'boredom' only become a word in 1852 in response to greater leisure time in Victorian Britain.[42]

Feelings have their origins in survival and keeping people safe, such as anger to fight, anxiety to pre-empt risk, and disgust to avoid dangerous food. They tell a person when their emotional needs are not being met, such as jealousy/envy to meet the need for status, and guilt to meet the need for connection. Feelings also reward people when their emotional needs are met, such as feeling pride in a meaningful achievement. Feelings are neither good nor bad in themselves; what matters in EI is how the individual learns to interpret, respond to, and manage their feelings. If feelings are not managed effectively they can:

— Cause prolonged distress

— Interfere with clear thinking

— Distract attention

— Cause inappropriate behaviour

— Interfere with sleep

— Impair health

— Deplete energy

— Create unpleasant feelings

On the other hand, if feelings are managed effectively they can:

— Improve empathy with others

— Guide decision making

— Provide intuitive awareness

— Alert us to danger

— Focus our attention

— Create positive feelings

Focusing attention on feelings provides valuable feedback about a person's attitudes. For example, if a person feels angry when people ignore them, this may indicate that they have a strong need for attention. People sometimes choose to deny their feelings particularly when they are painful, such as when feeling humiliated, ashamed, or upset. Feelings do not just disappear but will manifest in other ways, such as becoming stressed and unwell, being rigidly defensive, and having sudden emotional outbursts. (For examples of defensive behaviour refer to Chapter Four; 4.3.2.) It is important therefore to accept all feelings as messages from the body and try to understand their origins (as described in EI Attitude 6: All feelings are justified, acceptable, and important). In an organisational context, it is rather like the board of directors (the brain) ignoring the concerns of the workforce (the body) which will sooner or later lead to strike action (becoming ill). If a person's feelings are unpalatable then they need to look at the internal cause of their feelings (their attitudes) and not ignore the feedback they are providing. Advice on how to pay attention to and manage feelings is given in Chapter Eight; 8.4.

2.8   How hormones create feelings

It is worth considering some of the key hormonal neurochemicals that create feelings. There are two primary chemical motivators in life: one is dopamine which gives a feeling of desire or the need for something, and the other is serotonin which gives a feeling of reward or pleasure from doing something or getting these needs met. Naturally, a person receives less reward each time they repeat an action. Therefore, a person needs to increase the level of what they do in order to get the same level of satisfaction. If this wasn't the case then humans would be perfectly content repeating the same action over and over again (rather like most other species on the planet) and would not have developed the desire for learning, creativity, and setting new challenges. The catch to this, however, is that people can just as easily become motivated towards, or addicted to, negative rewards such as unhelpful habits, defensive behaviours, and physical addictions, as they can to positive rewards.

There are many other chemicals relevant to Emotional Intelligence that form part of the dynamic endocrine (hormonal) system, such as oxytocin and vasopressin, which are involved in relationships and feelings of caring, bonding, empathy, trust, and love. Another important chemical that influences Emotional Intelligence is the steroid cortisol. This, along with noradrenaline, is released during times of stress and anxiety.[*] These in turn stimulate the amygdala (the fight-flight-freeze response) and prepare the body for action, which can be useful in small doses, but in the long run will deplete the immune system making a person more susceptible to ill-health. Learning how to manage the body's emotional system so as to minimise prolonged stress, maximise positive motivation, and reinforce useful habits is discussed further in Chapter Eight; 8.6.

Löveheim[43] provides a useful model that summarises the relationships between three of the main neurotransmitters and Silvan Tomkins'[44] eight basic emotions. According to the model, fear is produced by the combination of low serotonin, high dopamine, and low noradrenaline (Table 2.5).

[*] Cortisol is not exclusively a stress hormone; its purpose is to flood the bloodstream with glucose whenever the body needs energy.

Relationship between neurotransmitters and emotions

BASIC EMOTION	SEROTONIN	DOPAMINE	NORADRENALINE
Shame/humiliation	Low	Low	Low
Distress/anguish	Low	Low	High
Fear/terror	Low	High	Low
Anger/rage	Low	High	High
Contempt/disgust	High	Low	Low
Surprise	High	Low	High
Enjoyment/joy	High	High	Low
Interest/excitement	High	High	High

Table 2.5

Neurotransmitters, neurochemicals, and hormones are made up of peptides which are in themselves made up of amino acids. Peptides act as information messenger molecules, able to reach all tissues within the body and brain via the bloodstream and cerebrospinal fluid by locking onto their matching receptors, acting as a type of remote communication system between the organs of the body. Candace Pert describes peptides as the 'molecules of emotion'.[45] Peptides bind with their specific receptors and start off a long chain of physiological and neurological reactions that produce emotions and influence behaviour. In this way emotions, whether conscious or unconscious, are created at a chemical level within the body and brain.

An important feature of peptide receptors is that they have the potential for change in terms of their quality, quantity, and biochemical composition.[45] This is determined by all of a person's experiences, such as what they eat, their physical activity, and emotional experience. The emotion-carrying peptides and their receptors contained throughout the body have far-reaching effects in filtering a person's perception, directing their attention, informing actions, and influencing decisions. In this regard, the body has an 'innate intelligence' that learns, develops, and has an emotional memory.

One group of peptides relevant to emotional experience is neuropeptides. Along with their receptors, they have a particularly high concentration in the limbic (emotional) region of the brain. About 85% of them are located here,[45] and most of these are contained within the hippocampus (the main memory centre). Neuropeptides (the information carriers) and their receptors extend outside of the limbic region to other parts of the body joining the brain, glands, and immune system in a network of remote communication. The complex interaction between the body's organs is coordinated into a single web by peptides and neuropeptides. Pert uses a helpful metaphor of the body being like an orchestra that follows the information on a musical script (peptides) to produce music (emotions). To extend this metaphor, the orchestra includes many leading roles (organs) such as the conductor (the brain) and the lead violinist (the heart).

This chapter has described the neuroscience behind Emotional Intelligence, and how this strongly influenced the construction of the EIP, which is the focus of the next chapter.

SUMMARY POINTS
FROM CHAPTER TWO

A major step in the brain's evolution came about relatively recently (40,000 years ago) with what is known as the brain's 'big bang'. This gave humans greater access to their prefrontal cortex and with this the capacity for self-awareness, self-choice, and consciousness.

Consciousness and self-awareness also gave rise to human emotional vulnerability and the need to learn how to consciously manage the different faculties of the brain (that is, to be emotionally intelligent), for example, learning to use imagination for positive thinking rather than for excessive worrying.

Emotional Intelligence may be separated into several psychological stages summarised by the acronym SAFE-TBO; Stimuli are initially pattern matched with Attitudes that initiate Feelings (Emotions) that fuel Thinking, and drive Behaviour, which in turn leads to Outcomes. These psychological stages are integral to the EIP and are mapped onto the EIP definition and framework (see Table 2.4).

Understanding the various psychological and neurological processes that influence behaviour (SAFE-TBO) has helped identify the different aspects of EI and how each of these may be developed (as presented in Chapter Eight).

An important aspect of EI is achieving the right balance between thinking and feeling, as too much emotion can interfere with a person's capacity to think clearly and problem solve, i.e. their IQ. For example, a perceived threat may trigger the survival response (fight, flight, or freeze) in the amygdala, which can disengage a person from their higher-level thinking neo-cortex.

One of the brain's innate resources is the capacity to deactivate unresolved emotion during the dreaming (REM) stages of sleep. This works effectively as long as a person is not over-burdened with excessive amounts of emotional arousal. It is therefore important that a person learns to manage their emotions (using EI) during the waking day.

The brain is one part of a single system, the body. For the whole system to work in harmony it is vital that the brain listens and responds to sensory feedback (feelings) from the rest of the body. Feelings not only tell a person what they need and want, they also provide intelligent feedback to inform decision making. Developing emotional self-awareness enables an individual to respond, think, and act appropriately and is the cornerstone to Emotional Intelligence.

SECTION TWO
INTERPRETING THE EMOTIONAL INTELLIGENCE PROFILE

Having read Section One you will be familiar with the definition, theory, psychology, and neuroscience of EI, and how these underpin the EIP. Section Two describes the construction, structure, and interpretation of the EIP scales.

Before going on to use the EIP, the user must be satisfied with the psychometric properties of the instrument, the construction of the items and scales, and evidence for its validity and reliability. Following this, they need to understand the core meaning of the scales and how to interpret these. Having gained the necessary knowledge and understanding of the EIP, the user will be ready to progress on to Section Three, which explains how to apply the EIP in a coaching and selection context.

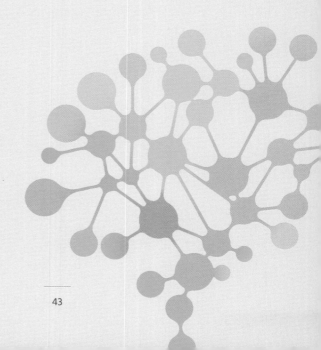

CHAPTER THREE
HOW THE EIP WAS CONSTRUCTED

INTRODUCTION

Before using any psychometric instrument, it is important to become familiar with the theory and rationale behind its development and the statistical properties that qualify it to be a psychometric product. Only by doing this is it possible to understand where it may be appropriately applied and to evaluate the validity (accuracy) and reliability (consistency) of the tool. In this chapter the rationale for the EIP, its technical construction, psychometric properties, and the EIP scale definitions are explained. A separate EIP Technical Manual[1] is available from JCA Global for anyone wishing to examine the statistical data behind the EIP construction.

3.1   Rationale for developing the EIP

The EIP reflects the different backgrounds of its creators: myself, an occupational psychologist with expertise in behavioural measurement, and Tim Sparrow a psychotherapist with expertise in emotions. The EIP combines the elements of hard objective empirical assessment with a humanistic, people-centred understanding – an essential balance for any measure of EI. The humanistic side of the product emphasises that people can change, gives respondents their item responses to explore, and addresses deeper areas such as Self Regard. On the assessment side, the EIP provides standardised scale scores, normative comparison results and predictive scale interpretations. This unique aspect of the EIP means it appeals to a wide spectrum of users – to the analytical thinker who takes a more 'scientific' approach, and to the holistic thinker who takes a more 'humanistic' approach.

An objective in producing the EIP was to fill the diagnostic gap between personality and behavourial competence. Personality questionnaires help individuals understand their behavioural tendencies and potential but not necessarily how to change their behaviour. Competencies shine a light on what behaviours a person may aim for, but not how to make this happen. EI is the 'how to' part, that explains how a person can manage their personality to become personally and interpersonally competent. Placed together, personality, competencies, and EI provide a very powerful triad for personal development.

This realisation, that there was a missing link between personality and competencies, came about from my experience of using personality questionnaires in coaching. This often resulted in what may be called the 'so what' factor. Having identified the individual's characteristics, the question still remained as to what the individual could do to change or develop their behavioural competence. Inevitably I would find myself drawn down the path of discussing the client's attitudes and feelings as the route to changing their behaviour.

The attitudinal basis for the EIP also has its origins in earlier work I conducted while working with teenagers who were perceived as being hard to help, demotivated, and having low self-esteem. Having spent some years developing behavioural change programmes for this client group, I observed that all too frequently they would return to their old negative and unhelpful behaviours. This was demonstrated by the high percentage of young people who began apprenticeships but did not complete them. After interviewing the teenagers, parents, training providers, and employers it became apparent that beneath the behavioural challenges were a clear set of attitudinal blocks. These attitudes included: a lack of enthusiasm towards opportunities (motivation), a resistance to forego short-term gratification for longer-term gains (ambition), an inflexibility to change their behaviour (adaptability), an unwillingness to persevere when things went wrong (perseverance), and negative expectations and aspirations (low self-esteem). It was decided to create a set of activities to assess the teenagers attitudinal blocks and their readiness for completing an apprenticeship. Alongside the assessment were programmes to encourage changes in attitudes to a more constructive position, which resulted in a marked improvement in retention and ultimately employability. This became known as MAPS[2] (Motivation, Ambition, Adaptability, Perseverance, and Self-esteem). These were the key attitudinal blocks that initiated the development of the EIP scales.

The success of these programmes led to my conviction that attitude change was important for subsequent and sustainable behavioural change, which is supported by a long history of psychological research, carried out by: LaPierre,[3] Festinger,[4] Eagly,[5] Huczynski,[6] and Makin.[7] At this time, there was also a growth in neurological research highlighting the importance of feelings,[8–10] providing a clear rationale for how attitudes influence feelings, which impact on decision making and behaviour. As described in Chapter Two, this research has strongly influenced the theory and design of the EIP.

We also drew upon our experience and expertise in three psychological models of human development: FIRO® theory,[11] Transactional Analysis (TA),[12] and The Human Givens.[13] FIRO® theory provides a proven method and model for developing behaviour and relationships, through understanding feelings and attitudes. In my view, the work of Will Schutz was well ahead of its time and closely resembles what has since become known as Emotional Intelligence. Another key influence on the EIP was TA theory which is represented in the EIP framework, the underlying EI Attitudes, and the Attitude Matrix that links together all of the EIP scales (refer to Chapter Four; 4.3). The third key influence on the EIP is the work by Griffin and Tyrell from the Human Givens Institute. Their clear explanation of human emotional needs and innate resources provides a strong foundation for EI.

Also, their description of the brain's processes helped inform the development of the SAFE-TBO model (see Chapter Two; Figure 2.2). This model explains how attitudes influence feeling, thinking, and behaviour, and is represented in the EI definition and the EIP framework (refer to Chapter Two; 2.3 and Table 2.4). Since its inception 20 years ago, the EIP questionnaire and framework have been rigorously examined and refined, through a combination of my doctoral research, feedback from many thousands of EIP users, and the statistical analysis conducted by JCA Global.

3.2   Features of the EIP

There are several unique features of the EIP that differentiate it from other approaches. Perhaps the most salient feature is that the EIP is an attitude-based model focused on sustainable change.[14] This runs through all aspects of the EIP, including the rationale and definition of EI, the theoretical basis for the EIP, and the EIP Report itself. These features are listed below.

3.2.1 The EIP theory

— EI is based on attitudes. Other approaches view EI as personality traits, a set of competencies, or an aspect of cognitive intelligence.

— EI is about being in the moment. It is a verb or a 'doing' word. Other models of EI see it as being relatively fixed, or more constitutional and therefore less developable.

— EI is multifaceted, in that most people have strengths and development areas. Other approaches describe EI as being reduced to a single construct or 'EQ' score that people have more or less of.

— EI is described as the practice of managing one's personality. Other definitions of EI describe it as an aspect of personality without making the distinction between personality and EI explicit.

3.2.2 The theoretical basis

— The EIP framework provides an organising structure for different aspects of EI, which includes:
    – A six-part framework which is unique to the EIP
    – Personal and Interpersonal forms of intelligence
    – Three levels of EI: Behaviour, Feeling, and Attitude

— The Attitude Matrix (described in Chapter Four; 4.3) combines Self Regard and Regard for Others. This gives a theoretical structure and underlying rationale for each of the 16 EIP scales.

— The 16 EIP scales are underpinned by a philosophical approach in the form of eight EI Attitudes (described in Chapter One; 1.5). In essence, when people behave in ways that are at odds with being emotionally intelligent (as defined by the 16 EIP scales) they are breaching one or more of these attitudes. Few other EI products have such a strong theoretical foundation which underpins the scale construction.

— The EIP is consistent with evidence from current neuroscience (described in Chapter Two). There are direct parallels between the neuropsychological stages of processing attitudes (SAFE-TBO), the EI definition, and the EIP framework (refer to Chapter Two; Table 2.4). Other approaches to EI focus mainly on behaviours without consideration to their antecedents.

3.2.3 The EIP Report

— Particular to the EIP Executive Report is a list of all item responses and their scores. This provides the reader with ownership of, and the information to understand, their scores. Ultimately, only the respondent knows why they gave the answers they did. Very few psychometric measures do this, and the item responses are usually kept hidden.

— The EIP multi-scales (explained in Chapter Six; 6.3.1) show variations in patterns of behaviour. For example, a person who is Over Trusting (scale 11) may also become Mistrusting if they are constantly let down by people. Identifying behavioural and emotional patterns in this way is essential to EI yet unique to the EIP.

— The multi-scales also give rise to another specific feature of the EIP reports – Defensive Habits (described in Chapter Seven; 7.3.1). There are nine Defensive Habits that indicate the overuse and underuse of specific behaviours which can impact negatively on performance. These Defensive Habits are often referred to in workplace literature as 'derailers'.

3.2.4 Differences between the EIP framework and other models

Emotional Intelligence (EI) is commonly separated into two models known as the 'ability' and 'mixed' models (also see Appendix Two; Section 4). The ability model is measured as maximal performance with IQ-like performance tests and refers to the conscious processing of thoughts and feelings. The mixed model is measured as typical performance with self-report or 360 degree questionnaires[15] and refers to behavioural traits and competencies. In relation to the EIP framework and definition, the ability model relates most closely with the middle Feeling and Thinking levels, and the mixed model relates most closely to the top Behaviour level. One key part of the EIP framework and definition that is not referred to by either of the two models is the bottom level of Attitude. There are several benefits to including the underlying attitudinal layer in a model of EI, as summarised next:

1   The attitude-based EIP definition and model of EI provides an alternative approach to the established ability and mixed models of EI, helping to address some specific criticisms levelled at these established approaches. For example, ability models are shown to be weaker predictors of job performance,[16] while mixed models are widely criticised for their theoretical under-development[17] and for being a 'grab bag' of mixed constructs.[18] In contrast, the EIP framework and Attitude Matrix (see Chapter Four; 4.3) provide a clear theoretical structure and organising relationship for the 16 EIP scales.

2   Another concern about other EI models and measures is a lack of ethical principles[17] suggesting a 'dark side' to EI,[19] such as manipulating others for personal gain,[20] or the organisation setting an agenda for what constitutes acceptable emotions and behaviours.[21] These scenarios would be incompatible with holding attitudes of high Self Regard and Regard for Others, or with the eight humanistic and ethical principles on which the EIP was founded.

3   The ability model describes EI largely as a conscious process. However, much of EI is about developing automated processes and habits that do not require constant awareness and attention. The act of practising EI (thinking about feelings to guide behaviour) allows EI processes to be consolidated as automatic procedural processes in the form of attitudes and habits. This is shown on the EIP framework where Attitude has a direct link to Behaviour,[22] which may bypass conscious processing and Awareness.[23-25] This in turn frees up space for a person to consciously process and attend to more demanding events and continue to create and embed new attitudes and habits. The EIP framework therefore represents a dual-processing model* of EI that includes both the conscious (Awareness) and automatic (Attitude – Behaviour) pathways of EI (see Table 3.1).

4   It is further proposed that the inclusion of attitudes within the EIP framework provides a broader context for understanding the inputs and outputs of EI (see Table 3.1), something that is yet to be demonstrated by either ability or mixed models independently.[26-28] The EIP framework is a hierarchical model of EI where attitudes are the antecedent inputs of conscious feelings and thought (ability EI) that manifest as mixed behavioural traits and competencies, i.e. the outputs of EI. The Attitude Matrix (described in Chapter Four; 4.3) provides an explanation of how the attitudes of Self Regard and Regard for Others (inputs) are antecedent to the behavioural output of EI (i.e. the linear and multi-scales).

An input-output model of EI

EI PROCESS	EI MODEL	EIP PSYCHOLOGICAL FACETS
EI outputs	Mixed EI	Behavioural traits and competencies
EI	Ability EI	Emotional and cognitive processing
EI inputs	Antecedents of EI	Attitudes

Table 3.1

*A dual-processing model of EI; conscious processing is indicated by the solid arrow and automated processing is indicated by the dotted arrow.

3.3   Technical construction of the EIP

The EIP has its origins in the MAPS attitude indicator (1997),[2] described previously in Section 3.1, and the JCA Global model of EI (1998), which was later represented in the EIP self-report questionnaire (2003).[1]

The first phase of development involved a comprehensive review of the existing theories of EI and assessment products. At this time, there were relatively few other EI models and an absence of any team measures of EI, so it was decided to develop two products, one for team EI and a second for individual EI. Both products share the same EI principles, with clear links between the two approaches (described in Chapter Nine; 9.3). The description below refers to the individual EIP, although both products were developed concurrently using similar methodology.

Following this review, we defined the scale constructs and theoretical rationale for both instruments. This was drawn from our experience across several, mostly humanistic, theories of development, including:

— FIRO® theory[11]
— Gestalt[29]
— The Human Givens approach[13]
— Neurolinguistic programming[30]
— The neuroscience of emotions[9]
— Personality trait theory[31]
— Psychometric theory[32]
— Psychological type theory[33]
— Transactional Analysis[12]

These theories helped us devise the foundations for our model of EI and the EIP questionnaire which included:

— A premise for EI, based on emotional needs and innate resources
— A three-part definition of EI
— Eight humanistic attitudes that underpin EI
— A six-part neuropsychological process for EI (SAFE-TBO model)
— An organising framework and model of EI
— A set of matrices for exploring attitude, feeling, and behaviour
— 16 scale constructs of EI

Item production and trialling was carried out over a two to three-year period, producing three versions of the items, norms, and product. The individual tool was originally called the Individual Diagnostic Questionnaire (IDQ), then changed to Individual Effectiveness and subsequently to the Emotional Intelligence Profile (EIP). The team tool was originally called the Team Diagnostic Questionnaire, then Team Effectiveness (TE), and was updated in 2013 to the Team EIP. Each iteration of the EIP has included enhancements to the report narrative and design, however the founding models, scale structure, and items remained unchanged.

Items were designed to be 'diagnostic' rather than just a means of generating scores. This meant that they needed to be relevant, meaningful, and provocative so they could be shared with the client when exploring their EIP scale scores. Item test development included 'empirical keying' of items (a process by which items are defined and agreed by experts in the field). The experts were individuals who had attended a nine-month part-time programme in EI and were all qualified EI practitioners with the CAEI (Centre for Applied EI). At that time, the CAEI was the only UK organisation that gave formal diploma-level training in EI. The first two editions of the questionnaire were trialled by 15 EI practitioners as part of their own applied diploma projects. Further quantitative and qualitative feedback on the items and scales was also collated and analysed which led to the third and final set of items. Subsequent research on the EIP included 11 criterion-related validity studies, five construct validation studies, and a normative database of over 30,000 participants, available in the EIP Technical Manual (2013).[34]

3.3.1 Latest evolution of the EIP

Since the creation of the EIP in 1998, there has been strong evidence that EI is a significant predictor of workplace performance,[28,35] leadership effectiveness,[36] and job satisfaction.[37] The origins of the EIP were in personal development, however, a high level of interest and demand from clients to use the EIP for selection and assessment led JCA Global to conduct a thorough revision of the EIP, to make it relevant for both assessment and development applications.

These revisions gave JCA Global an opportunity to make enhancements to the EIP, based on over 15 years of data collection, research, and applied experience. Included in this were updated items, analysis, revised scoring, and new assessment reports (see Chapter Seven). It should be noted that the revisions did not include any changes to the EIP fundamentals such as the definition, framework, attitudes, and scales. In 2017, JCA Global launched the revised version of the EIP, known as the EIP3, which included several psychometric improvements described in the EIP3 Technical Manual.[1] As the underpinning EIP theory and scale definitions remain the same as previous versions of the EIP, for simplicity, I will continue to refer to 'the EIP' when discussing the current version of the EIP tool.

3.3.2 Scoring the EIP scales

The majority of naturally occurring factors in life such as height, shoe size, ability, personality, and EI are 'normally distributed' among the population. That is, if you were to measure the shoe size of everyone in the world and then draw a frequency graph, you would end up with a symmetrical bell-shaped curve, i.e. more people fall into the centre and fewer fall towards the extremes of the scale. This natural spread of scores, known as 'the normal distribution', holds certain mathematical properties that allow us to create standardised scale scores beneath it. One of these types of scales is referred to as a Sten (standard ten), which is a standardised score from one to ten relative to a comparison group. This is the scale used to represent scores on the EIP.

Sten scores are calculated by comparing an individual's raw score with a mean average raw score of the comparison group. Using the mathematical properties of the normal distribution this can then be transformed into a one to ten Sten score. It has the practical advantages of being easily understood by respondents and also provides sufficient differentiation without being too granular (which can lead people to over-interpret small score differences). Sten scores make it possible to compare a single scale score between individual candidates, or to compare different scale scores for the same individual, so as to identify their relative strengths and development areas.

A mid-range score of five or six indicates that an individual is in the average band of the comparison group (within half a standard deviation either side of the mean score for the group). Scores further away from the mid-point indicate the individual is higher or lower than the average band. As a general guide, Sten scores can be interpreted in the following way:

Sten 1	Extremely low	Sten 7	Fairly high
Sten 2	Very low	Sten 8	High
Sten 3	Low	Sten 9	Very high
Sten 4	Fairly low	Sten 10	Extremely high
Sten 5 or 6	Average		

Clearly, an individual's Sten score may differ depending on who they are being compared against. The comparison group is known as the 'norm group' (a normally distributed, representative sample of people from that population, e.g. 500 senior managers). Users should choose the norm group that is most relevant to the context in which the EIP is being applied. For self-development, they may choose a norm group from an occupational level that the individual aspires to be at, such as when progressing from 'middle' to 'senior' manager level. For assessment, the selected norm group would normally reflect the job level or job role that is being assessed. The latest EIP norm groups available are given in the Technical Manual.[1]

Sten scores and the normal distribution curve

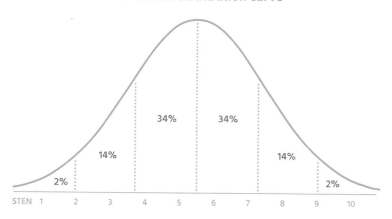

Figure 3.1

3.3.3 Structure of the EIP scales

The 16 scales of the EIP are structured within a six-part framework. This separates the scales into either Personal or Interpersonal aspects of EI. It also splits them into three levels:

Behaviour: Self Management and Relationship Management scales

Feeling: Self Awareness and Awareness of Others scales

Attitude: Self Regard and Regard for Others scales

There are two types of scale within the EIP: linear scales (scales 1-10 and 16) and multi-scales (scales 11-15). The linear scales (see Figure 3.2) are scored so that higher scores represent higher levels of Emotional Intelligence. For example, high Self Awareness is preferable to low Self Awareness. For multi-scales (see Figure 3.3) the most emotionally intelligent score is represented by the middle green bar and the least emotionally intelligent scores are at the extremes (the two enclosing red bars). Therefore, multi-scales are made up of three separate sub-scales. With Trust (scale 11), for example, it is better to score high on Carefully Trusting (the middle scale) and low on Mistrusting and Over Trusting. (An explanation on how to interpret multi-scales is given in Chapter Six; 6.3.1).

The multi-scales are summarised by a blue bar* which shows the overall balance between all three sub-scales. High scores on the blue bar indicate that the client has a good overall balance on this scale, i.e. more green than red on the sub-scales. Low scores on the blue bar indicate the client has a poor balance on the scale, i.e. more red than green. In this case, they may choose to examine the sub-scales to identify where specifically they are out of balance.

Figure 3.2

Example linear scale

Self Awareness

Example multi-scale

Trust
Mistrusting
Carefully Trusting
Over Trusting

Response options for the EIP range from 1-5 (Strongly disagree = 1, Disagree = 2, Neither agree nor disagree = 3, Agree = 4, Strongly agree = 5). There are 158 items in total with 7-8 items per linear scale and 15-16 items for the multi-scales (five to six items for each of the three sub-scales). Items are presented in a mixed order in the questionnaire. For the linear scales, approximately 40% are negatively phrased (where high scores represent low EI) and 60% are phrased positively. Varying between positive and negative items helps to minimise 'response set', where a respondent may always give the same answer to questions or not think about the answer they give. For the multi-scales, the items for the two red sub-scales are phrased negatively, (as with Mistrusting and Over Trusting), and the items for the green sub-scale, (Carefully Trusting) are phrased positively.

*The blue bar is calculated by subtracting red from green. Red scores are divided by two because there are two of these scores. Note that this calculation is done using standardised 'Z scores', not Sten scores, because they are more granular. The result from this calculation is then compared normatively to derive the blue bar as a Sten score.

3.4 Psychometric properties of the EIP

The EIP is a psychometric test* meaning it conforms to principles of measurement that quantify the precision and accuracy of its scales in differentiating between people. It also provides a facility for predicting how the individual's responses to the questionnaire relate to how they are likely to behave in real life situations. Accurate interpretation not only depends on the robustness of the measuring tool, but also on the respondent's accuracy of self-reporting and the user's understanding of the psychometric test. Understanding the psychometric properties of a test will advise the user on how much confidence to place on a scale score, the likely margin of error, and how closely it correlates with other scales.

There are five key properties that distinguish a psychometric test:

1 **Reliability** How consistent the test is
2 **Validity** How accurate the test is
3 **Objectivity** To what extent personal subjectivity is minimised
4 **Standardisation** To what extent any influences on test conditions are kept constant
5 **Discriminating** How well the test discriminates between scale scores

The main indicators of a test's quality are its reliability and validity:

— Reliability looks at how consistent a test is in measuring the same aspect. There would be little use in developing a measure of EI if it measured something different every time it was used.

— Validity looks at whether the test measures the construct it claims to measure. Again, there is little point in a test that measures something if the user does not know what it is measuring or if it is not measuring what the user intended.

The psychometric properties of the EIP are fully explained in the EIP3 Technical Manual.[1] Research studies conducted on the EIP show that it has good levels of reliability, it correlates with related constructs measured in other psychometric questionnaires, and it predicts job performance (based on external manager ratings).

* 'Test' is the conventional term for a questionnaire developed from psychometric principles.[32] When working with clients, users are advised to use the term 'questionnaire' as opposed to 'test' which may infer the EIP is being used as a 'pass/fail' score, without interpretation or interview.

3.5 The core meaning of the EIP constructs

It is important to clearly understand the core meaning at the heart of each of the scales and not to go beyond the meaning of the data. The core meaning of a test scale is defined here as: 'the essential aspect of what is being measured by a scale and what differentiates it from all other scales in the test'. In the EIP, each of the scales measures an attribute that has a unique influence on an individual's overall Emotional Intelligence. Test users can understand the nature of that unique influence by initially learning the core definitions of the 16 EIP scales presented in Table 3.2.

The EIP scale definitions

Table 3.2

EIP FRAMEWORK	EIP SCALES	CORE MEANING OF THE EIP SCALES	RELATED EI ATTITUDES*
Attitude	Scale 1 Self Regard	The degree to which an individual accepts and values themselves	1
	Scale 2 Regard for Others	How much a person accepts and values others (as distinct from liking or approving of what they may do)	1 4
Feeling	Scale 3 Self Awareness	The degree to which a person is in touch with their physiology, feelings and intuitions	6
	Scale 4 Awareness of Others	The degree to which a person is in touch with the feelings of others	4 6
Behaviour: Self Management	Scale 5 Emotional Resilience	The degree to which an individual is able to pick themselves up and bounce back when things go badly for them	5 1
	Scale 6 Personal Power	The degree to which a person believes that they are in charge of and take sole responsibility for their outcomes	2 3
	Scale 7 Goal Directedness	The degree to which a person's behaviour is aligned with their long-term goals	5
	Scale 8 Flexibility	The degree to which a person feels free to adapt their thinking and behaviour to changing situations	7 4
	Scale 9 Connecting with Others	The extent and ease with which an individual makes significant connections with other people	1 8

EIP FRAMEWORK	EIP SCALES	CORE MEANING OF THE EIP SCALES	RELATED EI ATTITUDES*
	Scale 10 Authenticity	The degree to which an individual invites the trust of others by being principled, reliable, consistent, and known	2
Behaviour: Relationship Management	Scale 11 Trust	The tendency for a person to place the right amount of trust in others	1 8
	Scale 12 Balanced Outlook	How effectively an individual balances optimism with realism	7
	Scale 13 Emotional Expression and Control	The degree to which an individual achieves appropriate balance in the expression and control of their emotions	3 6 5
	Scale 14 Conflict Handling	How well conflict is handled; how assertive a person is	5 1
	Scale 15 Interdependence	How well an individual manages to balance taking themselves and others into account	3 2
Developing EI	Scale 16 Reflective Learning	The degree to which Emotional Intelligence is enhanced by the individual reflecting on what they and others feel, think, and do, noticing the outcomes these produce and altering their patterns accordingly	8 7

* The eight EI Attitudes are described in Chapter One; 1.5, page 13. Note that all of the EI Attitudes have some influence on all of the scales, in particular EI Attitude 1: However you are and others are, is OK. The EI Attitudes listed for each scale are those with the most specific relevance.

Having learned the core definition of the 16 EIP scales, the user may go on to enrich their understanding by reading Chapter Five, which explains the meaning of the scales and their relationship to each another. For those seeking further insight and wider knowledge of the scales, they may refer to the scale interpretations given in Appendix One.

SUMMARY POINTS
FROM CHAPTER THREE

The key reason for developing the EIP was to produce a product that would facilitate change in attitudes, leading to a sustainable change in behaviour. This was brought about by my experience of working with young people to raise their motivation and self-esteem. I found that by shifting their attitudes towards a more positive mindset they were far less likely to revert back to their old negative behaviours.

A second key influence was my experience of coaching with personality questionnaires and 360 behaviour measures. I perceived there to be a 'missing link' between the two: how to transfer personality and potential into behaviour change and performance. This I defined as Emotional Intelligence – the practice of an individual managing their personality to be both personally and interpersonally effective.

There were a number of other key influences in developing the EIP theory, including the application of FIRO®[11] theory for improving self-awareness and relationships, the practical relevance of TA theory[12] for personal development, and the application of neuroscience for self-development as used by The Human Givens Institute.[13] All of these approaches have their foundations in the application of attitudes and feelings for personal development.

The EIP has several unique features that distinguish it from other models of Emotional Intelligence. These include:

— The definition of EI as a process (a verb).

— The theory of EI – to manage one's personality (their innate resources and potential).

— A strong underpinning rationale for the EIP, which includes a set of eight EI Attitudes and a grounding in neuroscience.

— The six-part EIP framework that explains the relationship between the different facets of EI.

— A set of multi-scales that measure emotional and behavioural patterns.

— The most significant difference between the EIP and other models of EI is the inclusion of attitudes. In contrast to other approaches, this provides an ethical platform for EI, a rationale for the antecedents of EI, and an explanation of how, with practice, EI may become automated and habitual.

Over a period of two years, and after extensive review and statistical analysis, in 2017 JCA Global launched the revised version of the EIP, relabelled as the EIP3, which included several psychometric improvements.

The EIP scales are standardised and scored using a Sten scale from one to ten, indicating how the individual compares to various norm groups.

Before using the EIP it is important that the coach or assessor is well grounded in the psychological theory of EI and has a clear grasp of the core meaning for each of the 16 EIP scales.

Those wishing to examine the statistical properties of the EIP, normative data, and other research, can refer to the EIP3 Technical Manual,[1] which is frequently updated.

CHAPTER FOUR
INTERPRETING THE EIP FRAMEWORK

INTRODUCTION

The EIP consists of 16 scales of Emotional Intelligence that were derived from the EI Attitudes and theories described in Chapters One and Two. The EIP scales are organised and structured within a framework of EI that is easy to understand and practical to apply for coaching and assessment. The framework consists of six parts separated into three paired matrices: Attitude, Feeling, and Behaviour. This chapter explains how to interpret the framework and the EIP matrices.

4.1 The EIP framework

Emotional Intelligence is a combination of skills, attitudes, and habits that distinguish superior from run-of-the-mill performance, both in life as a whole and at work. The different parts of EI are brought together and organised by the EIP framework which consists of two streams:

1 Personal Intelligence:

The individual being intelligent in noticing what is going on inside themselves (Self Awareness) and acting on these feelings and notions (Self Management). This includes aspects such as:

— The individual knowing what they want and motivating themselves to achieve their goals

— Dealing with challenges and setbacks

— Maintaining their physical and emotional well-being

— Being confident in their decisions and actions

— Having clarity of thinking

— Adapting to new situations

2 Interpersonal Intelligence:

The individual being intelligent in noticing what is going on for other people and also between people (Awareness of Others) and doing what they need to do to manage this (Relationship Management). This includes aspects such as:

— Knowing what others want

— Building trusting relationships

— Leading and managing others

— Helping to motivate others

— Working in a team

— Coaching people

— Managing confrontation constructively

There are three levels to the EIP framework. At the deepest level Emotional Intelligence is influenced by the individual's attitudes, in particular their attitude towards themselves (Self Regard) and their attitude towards other people (Regard for Others). This in turn influences (and may distort) their Self Awareness and Awareness of Others (Feeling), which then manifests in their Behaviour (Self and Relationship Management). In summary, an individual's Attitude (the deepest level) creates their Feeling (the middle level) that manifests in their Behaviour (the top level). The relationship between the six parts of Emotional Intelligence is shown in the EIP framework below.

The EIP framework

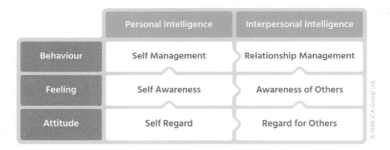

Table 4.1

4.2 How the six parts of the EIP framework relate to each other

The arrows on the framework indicate the predominant direction of influence between the six parts of the framework. These move from left to right and from the bottom upwards, although there is also an influence, to a lesser extent, in the opposite direction. The left to right arrows indicate that Personal Intelligence impacts on Interpersonal Intelligence. People who are low on Personal Intelligence but high on Interpersonal Intelligence may focus so much attention on the welfare of others that they fail to take care of their own needs and eventually become too unwell or exhausted to be of any help to others. It is difficult for someone to look after others if they do not look after themselves. This is why on an aeroplane, passengers are instructed to place their own oxygen masks on first, before aiding others, including their children.

The left to right arrows of influence also apply to each of the three levels. At the Attitude level, if an individual feels bad about themselves (low Self Regard) they are more likely to become critical towards others (low Regard for Others). At the Feeling level, if an individual is unaware of their own feelings (low Self Awareness) they are less able to empathise with the feelings of others (low Awareness of Others). At the Behaviour level, if an individual does not manage their own feelings, such as feeling angry (low Self Management), this is likely to impact upon how they handle conflict and their relationships (Relationship Management).

The arrows also move from the bottom upwards. On the left side of the framework (Personal Intelligence), if an individual has high Self Regard (Attitude) they are more open to all of their positive and negative feelings (high Self Awareness), which helps them to manage their behaviour appropriately (high Self Management). On the right side of the framework (Interpersonal Intelligence), if an individual has low Regard for Others (Attitude) they may negatively distort their perceptions of others (low Awareness of Others), which may cause them to be more guarded or hostile towards people (low Relationship Management). Consider these further examples:

Example 1

It is possible to have high Self Awareness and Awareness of Others (the middle layer) but fail to put this into action, i.e. to have low Self Management and Relationship Management (the top layer). Consider the 'navel gazer', who is full of self-understanding but fails to take action, or those who engage in a lot of personal development but don't actually change their behaviour, and people who 'talk the talk' but don't 'walk the walk'. Awareness is an important basis for development but is only useful if a person chooses to consciously apply it.

Example 2

An individual can have high Self Management but low Self Awareness. This may suggest a tendency to follow learned patterns of behaviour, rather than being in touch with what they want for themselves and what makes them happy. For example, living out their parents' dream, doing what is expected by others, or cruising through life waiting for something to happen. This is a common issue often dealt with in coaching, where an apparently successful and capable individual is feeling unfulfilled and dissatisfied with their life. From time to time it is necessary for the individual to 'check in' with themselves to find out if what they are doing is still satisfying or whether their wants and needs have changed. If an individual leaves it too long then they may lose touch with their essence and their sense of purpose; living their life on 'autopilot'. It may take a significant life event such as retirement, divorce, ill-health, redundancy, or bereavement to give them a 'wake-up call', and prompt them to re-engage with what they want through developing their Self Awareness.

Example 3

A person with strong Relationship Management and low Awareness of Others may appear to others as being rehearsed and artificial. If an individual does not show Awareness of Others they may be seen as inauthentic despite having good communication and interpersonal skills (Relationship Management). For instance, a leader may deliver a well prepared and slick presentation but fail to engage or motivate people if they do not empathise with and understand their audience.

There is also a strong link between the top and bottom levels of the framework: Attitude and Behaviour. People's behaviour tends to be consistent with, and is a good indicator of, their attitudes. This is illustrated below with an example for each of the EIP scales.

Example attitude and behaviour links for each EIP scale

Table 4.2

EIP SCALE	EXAMPLE ATTITUDE	EXAMPLE BEHAVIOUR
1 Self Regard	I am OK	Accepting positive feedback
2 Regard for Others	Others are OK	Praising people
3 Self Awareness	Feelings are important	Noticing early signs of stress
4 Awareness of Others	People's opinions matter	Listening to others
5 Emotional Resilience	Problems are only temporary	Persevering after a setback
6 Personal Power	I am capable and competent	Taking responsibility
7 Goal Directedness	I have a clear sense of purpose	Not being easily distracted from their objectives
8 Flexibility	Failure is useful feedback	Trying out new experiences
9 Connecting with Others	People are mostly okay when you get to know them	Initiating conversation with others
10 Authenticity	It is important to follow your principles	Being consistent regarding their values
11 Trust	Everyone has potential	Delegating work to others without 'micro-managing'
12 Balanced Outlook	There are many things to look forward to	Being motivated and enthusiastic about the future

EIP SCALE	EXAMPLE ATTITUDE	EXAMPLE BEHAVIOUR
13 Emotional Expression and Control	People are interested in what I think and feel	Communicating openly and appropriately about themselves
14 Conflict Handling	My thoughts and opinions are valuable	Speaking up for themselves without being aggressive
15 Interdependence	Teamwork is useful	Collaborating with colleagues
16 Reflective Learning	Past experiences provide valuable learning	Keeping a self-development journal or reflective diary

4.2.1 Reflective Learning and Self Knowledge

The EIP framework shows that Self Awareness links to and enables Self Management, and Awareness of Others links to and enables Relationship Management. However, this is a simplification; between awareness and management lies Self Knowledge and Knowledge of Others. A person may be acutely aware of their own and others' feelings yet not know what to do about it. For that, they also need to draw upon experience about themselves (Self Knowledge) and about others (Knowledge of Others). Knowledge of self and others is developed through the process of Reflective Learning or thinking about feeling which is one part of the EI definition.

For example:

1 An individual notices themselves becoming very excited by a new idea (Self Awareness)

2 They reflect on past experiences in similar situations (Reflection/Thinking)

3 This has taught them that they can be over-optimistic (Self Knowledge)

4 They therefore decide not to rush into making a decision (Self Management)

This process, which includes Thinking (Reflection) and Knowledge, extends the EIP framework as shown on the following page. (More detail on the process of Reflective Learning, scale 16, may be found in Appendix One).

The extended EIP framework

	Personal Intelligence	Interpersonal Intelligence
Behaviour	Self Management	Relationship Management
Knowledge	Self Knowledge	Knowledge of Others
Thinking	Self Reflection	Reflecting on Others
Feeling	Self Awareness	Awareness of Others
Attitude	Self Regard	Regard for Others

© 1998 ICA Global Ltd.

Table 4.3

The reader may recall from Chapter Two, Table 2.4, that the complete EIP framework (including the Thinking stage) is derived from, and maps onto, the definition of EI and the psychological stages of EI (SAFE-TBO).

Rather than interpret the whole framework in one go, it is more manageable to first consider each of the three main tiers of the framework (Attitude, Feeling, and Behaviour) separately. This is done by looking at how the pair of scales within each tier combine to form a 2x2 matrix.

4.3   The Attitude Matrix

The first matrix shows the balance between the Attitude scales of Self Regard and Regard for Others. These scales form the bottom layer of the EIP framework. Taken together, they constitute a person's Core Attitude or 'Life Position'[1] which is extremely powerful in determining not only their Emotional Intelligence but also their perception of themselves, others, and of life in general.

The concept of Life Positions (Core Attitudes) comes from TA (Transactional Analysis). It is based on the idea that when babies arrive into the world they are confronted with two life questions: "Who am I and am I OK?", and "Who are all these other people and are they OK?" A baby's conscious thinking is largely undeveloped, so the response is at an unconscious, emotional, and evaluative level, i.e. "I am and people are, either OK [good, valuable, trustworthy, to be respected, and safe] or Not OK [bad, worthless, unreliable, unworthy of respect, and dangerous]." These form the individual's initial Core Attitudes on life, which may be consolidated or modified depending on the individual's experience throughout life.

Originally described in TA as the 'OK Corral',[1] the Attitude Matrix provides a simple shortcut for the Core Attitudes. In brief, the top right of the matrix is the "I am OK" (Self Regard) and "You are OK" (Regard for Others) position, often shortened to I+ U+, or the Ideal box. This is the emotionally intelligent and mentally healthy attitude to maintain.

Links between the Attitude Matrix and the EIP scales

	LOW SELF REGARD	HIGH SELF REGARD
HIGH REGARD FOR OTHERS	Submissive position "I'm Not OK, You're OK" Get away from ('flight') EIP scales: Low Self Awareness Low Personal Power Low Goal Directedness Over Trusting Pessimistic Emotionally Over Controlled Passive Dependent	Ideal position "I'm OK, You're OK" Get on with ('healthy') EIP scales: High on all EIP scales
LOW REGARD FOR OTHERS	Blocked Potential position "I'm Not OK, You're Not OK" Get nowhere with ('freeze') EIP scales: Low on all EIP scales	Critical position "I'm OK, You're Not OK" Get rid of ('fight') EIP scales: Low Awareness of Others Low Flexibility Low Connecting with Others Mistrusting Over Optimistic Emotionally Under Controlled Aggressive Over Independent

Table 4.4

The bottom left refers to the "I am Not OK" and "You are Not OK", or Blocked Potential attitude. The bottom right refers to the "I am OK" and "You are Not OK", or Critical position. The top left is the "I am Not OK" and "You are OK", or Submissive position. Because attitudes underpin feelings and behaviour, all of the other EIP scales can be mapped onto the Attitude Matrix. Someone whose attitude is Critical (I'm OK, You're Not OK) is more likely to display low Flexibility, low Awareness of Others, be Mistrusting, Over Independent, and Aggressive. In comparison, someone from the Submissive position (I'm Not OK, You're OK) is more likely to be low on Self Awareness, Personal Power, and Goal

Directedness and be Over Trusting, Passive, and Dependent on others. A description of how the Core Attitudes are linked to each of the scales is given in Chapter Five; 5.1 and Appendix One.

4.3.1 How to interpret and explore the Attitude Matrix

Self Regard and Regard for Others are in some ways the most difficult scales to measure accurately as they represent deeper, underlying, often unconscious attitudes rather than specific observable behaviours. The scores on the EIP give an indication of what an individual's pervading Core Attitude may tend to be, but it may also be influenced by how an individual was feeling about themselves at the time of completing the questionnaire. In fact, people can move between positions quite readily in response to their current circumstances and specific environmental factors, such as their current work situation, the state of their personal relationships, how their day has been, and how they are feeling at any particular moment. The EIP coach should therefore look to distinguish the following, through discussion with their client:

— What is their pervading Core Attitude/Life Position?

— Where are they on the matrix currently in their life?

— How do they feel about themselves at that specific moment in time?

When using the Attitude Matrix during exploration of the EIP, it is important to emphasise that holding a Core Attitude does not mean an individual always behaves in this way. Core Attitudes explain where a person tends to return to and feel most familiar. During a stressful period, a person is likely to fall out of the Ideal position and into a more defensive position. How easily this happens depends on how strong their Self Regard and Regard for Others are. Where these are both strong, an individual is likely to spend more time in the Ideal position.

There is an interesting pattern in how a person may move between the Attitude positions from Blocked Potential to Critical to Submissive to Ideal. The least effective position is Blocked Potential. One way for a person to progress from this position is to become slightly more selfish and self-focused – to look after themselves (even if this is at the expense of others), so moving themselves into the Critical position. The Critical position can help people feel more energised and able to take control over their circumstances. However, the Critical position of low Regard for Others is also masking low Self Regard, as illustrated by the defensive descriptions in Table 4.5. A natural development from here is to become aware of this low Self Regard and therefore move into the Submissive position. Often, when people have finished blaming and criticising others they recognise the futility of this and how their complaining had more to do with their own mood and feelings than about those they were criticising. From the Submissive position an individual is ready to progress to the Ideal position and accept themselves more fully despite their imperfections.

4.3.2 The defensive positions

Any time a person falls out of the Ideal position, they are falling into a defensive position (Critical, Submissive, or Blocked Potential). A defence may be a temporary measure to protect a person from more negative and uncomfortable feelings they may have about their self-concept (reflecting a low Self Regard). They are usually unconscious attitudes that a person has formed about themselves and how to get on in the world. Defences or coping mechanisms work by distorting a person's perception of reality to fit with the kind of self-concept that allows them to feel better about themselves, such as pretending that everything is fine when it is not (denial). The problem is that by distorting reality someone is reducing their Self Awareness, which means they are less able to identify and resolve the underlying causes of their defensive behaviour. Also, because defensive behaviours provide temporary relief to negative feelings (therefore providing a 'pay-off'), they can become habitual, insatiable, and addictive.

Defensiveness is characterised by rigid and inflexible behaviour. For example, a person may feel the need to 'be perfect' in everything they do in order to feel OK about themselves, known in TA as a 'condition of self-worth'. However, high Self Regard is about having unconditional self-acceptance, meaning that a person still feels OK about themselves despite not being perfect in what they do. Some of the classic defence mechanisms and conditions of self-worth within each of the Attitude Matrix positions are described in Table 4.5, 4.6 and 4.7. Some of the defences are also included in the EIP reports as described in Chapter Seven; 7.3.1.

Defences linked to the Critical position

(High Self Regard and low Regard for Others)

DEFENCE	DESCRIPTION (ATTITUDE/PAY OFF)	MOST RELATED EIP SCALES
Blaming	"By blaming others I avoid having to look at what I do not like about myself"	Defensive blaming reflects low Regard for Others masking low Self Regard
Anger	"By being angry with others I can dominate them. Being right makes me better than the other person"	Being angry reflects aggressive Conflict Handling and low emotional control
Helping/ Rescuer	"If I focus on helping others with their problems then I can avoid looking at my own problems"	The Rescuer views others as unable to cope (low Regard for Others). Others may therefore become Dependent on them

Table 4.5

DEFENCE	DESCRIPTION (ATTITUDE/PAY OFF)	MOST RELATED EIP SCALES
Be Perfect	"Through experience I have learned that I am not OK if I am ever wrong or make a mistake, however small"	This may affect a person's willingness to learn through trial and error (Flexibility) or allow others to do the same (Trust), or to express themselves openly and freely without self-criticism (Emotional Expression and Control)
Be Strong	"My upbringing has taught me that I am only OK if I do not have or express feelings, needs, or signs of weakness"	A 'Be Strong' defence leads to low Self Awareness (of one's feelings), being emotionally Over Controlled and Over Independent
Railroad (I win, you lose)	"By bullying, shouting, and being aggressive I can railroad others so that I get what I want, at least for now"	Bullies are likely to be Aggressive (Conflict Handling) and have low Flexibility
Get rid of/ Move against	"If I move against others and get them out of my way they will no longer be a threat to me"	Feeling threatened by others may lead to being Mistrusting, Aggressive, Over Independent, and having low Flexibility

Defences linked to the Submissive position

(Low Self Regard and High Regard for Others)

DEFENCE	DESCRIPTION (ATTITUDE/PAY OFF)	MOST RELATED EIP SCALES
Self-blaming	"The pay-off from criticising myself is that I avoid having others criticise me first. It also gets others to reassure me that I am OK and people will expect less of me"	Self-blaming indicates low Personal Power and may result in low Goal Directedness and low Emotional Resilience
Guilt/Shame	"I know what I have done is wrong, but horrible people wouldn't feel remorse, so I must be an OK person"	Guilt occurs when a person behaves in a way that contradicts their values, so is related to Authenticity

Table 4.6

DEFENCE	DESCRIPTION (ATTITUDE/PAY OFF)	MOST RELATED EIP SCALES
Worrying	"Because I worry about other people and situations I am not selfish and must be a caring person"	People who worry about but do nothing to change the situation are likely to be low on Personal Power
Demanding	"By repeatedly requesting that others tell me that I am OK, I get others to do for me what I do not do for myself, that is, to like myself"	Demanding reassurance from others indicates low Emotional Resilience, low Personal Power, and being Dependent on others
Please Others	"My experience has taught me that I can only feel OK about myself if I always put others first and keep them happy"	May result in low Goal Directedness, being Over Trusting, Passive, emotionally Over Controlled (especially if they also have a 'Be Strong' defence), and Dependent
Hurry Up	"I have learned through experience that I must not relax or take my time over things if I am to be OK"	May lead to unrealistic expectations (lack of Balanced Outlook), exhaustion (low Emotional Resilience), impatience with others (Over Independent), and a lack of time for Reflective Learning
Get away from others	"One way I cope with feelings of inferiority is to move away from others and avoid the risk of being humiliated"	Avoiding others reduces Awareness of Others, Connecting with Others, Trust, and Interdependence
Seek harmony (I lose, you win)	"If I am willing to forgo my own interests I will avoid conflict and being criticised by others"	Seeking harmony in this way reflects low Goal Directedness, low Authenticity, and poor Conflict Handling (Passive)

Defences linked to the Blocked Potential position

(Low Self Regard and low Regard for Others)

DEFENCE	DESCRIPTION (ATTITUDE/PAY OFF)	MOST RELATED EIP SCALES
Victim	"Whatever I do is not good enough for others; people have got it in for me. It is not my fault and I am not responsible for my problems"	The Victim attitude represents low Personal Power and results in low Emotional Resilience and low Goal Directedness
Disappointment	"I am a good person (better than other people) and despite trying my best for others, people let me down, which is also why I don't succeed"	Disappointment in others may be caused by Over Trusting people and being Over Optimistic
Denier	"There are no problems, and everything is OK." By ignoring any problems and pretending that everything is OK the Denier does not have to face the painful reality of their own negative feelings	The Denier distorts reality by being low on Self Awareness, Over Optimistic, Mistrusting, and less inclined to learn from experience (Reflective Learning)
Try Hard (but don't succeed)	"The message I received during my upbringing was that suffering is good and that I am OK so long as I try hard. It's the trying that counts not the achievement"	May impair their Personal Power as they do not allow themselves to experience success, and in the long-term affects their Emotional Resilience as they are unlikely to allow themselves sufficient rest
Withdrawal/ Passive-Aggressive (I lose, you lose)	"There is nothing I or anyone else can do to help me or to change my situation so I will give up trying and stop making any effort. By withdrawing from situations I can also avoid conflict without giving in to the other person"	Passive-aggressive behaviour reflects poor Conflict Handling and reduces collaboration (Connecting with Others and Interdependence)

Table 4.7

Defences are formed as attitudes, experienced as feelings, and expressed as rigid behaviours. Defensive behaviours are therefore the manifestation of defensive attitudes and their associated feelings. It is not easy to know whether any given behaviour is defensive or not. A person may be critical of others because they feel bad about themselves (defensive) or because they are giving justifiable feedback to someone to help them improve (non-defensive). The key indicators of defensive behaviour are:

1 The behaviour is inappropriate to the situation

2 The behaviour is overused

3 The person would feel particularly uncomfortable if they did not use this behaviour

4 The feelings associated with the behaviour are excessively prolonged, e.g. feeling guilty long after the event

For example, if a person likes to take charge of events and be in control, but finds it extremely difficult and uncomfortable not being in charge or following others, then this is likely to be a defensive behaviour. The challenge for any individual is to become aware of their defensive behaviours, because the purpose of a defence is to distort a person's self perception and reduce awareness of their painful feelings. One way to identify defences is to review the EIP scales in relation to the four defensive indicators above.

4.3.3 The Attitude Matrix descriptions

People inevitably spend time in each of the four positions. Under sufficient stress they will fall out of the Ideal position into one of the other three positions. How easily they do this depends on how far they are normally from the top right corner. The four Core Attitudes within the matrix are summarised below.

The Attitude Matrix

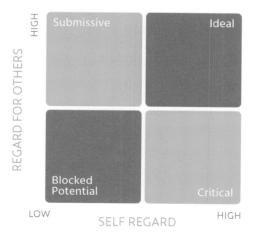

Figure 4.1

Ideal

The top right quadrant is labelled Ideal and is the most positive position. Scoring highly on both Attitude scales is a strong basis for developing personal and interpersonal effectiveness. It indicates a generally positive perception of self and of others which helps in coping effectively with life's demands, being open to self-development and behaving with Emotional Intelligence as measured by the other 14 EIP scales.

Blocked Potential

The bottom left quadrant is labelled Blocked Potential and is the least emotionally intelligent position. If both Attitude scale scores are low in relation to the comparison group, it indicates that currently, or during times of stress, an individual may have a more negative perception of themselves and of others. They may therefore find it more difficult to cope with life's demands and possibly become critical of themselves and of others. They may be feeling stuck and unsure of how to change their feelings, behaviour, and circumstances, tending to see more problems than solutions.

Critical

The bottom right quadrant is labelled Critical. If the Self Regard score is higher than the Regard for Others score it suggests that under stress, they may tend to become critical and blaming of others. The Critical position links to several aspects of Emotional Intelligence such as being less aware of others, less flexible towards others, Mistrusting, Aggressive, and Over Independent. Note that the Critical position is also a mask for low Self Regard, as blaming others can be a coping strategy to distract a person from considering the negative feelings they have about themselves.

Submissive

The top left quadrant is labelled Submissive. If the Regard for Others score is higher than the Self Regard score, it suggests that under stress an individual may tend to become self-blaming and negative towards themselves. This may manifest in aspects of Emotional Intelligence such as being less confident (low Personal Power), less focused on what they want (low Goal Directedness), Dependent, Over Trusting of others, and backing down in conflict (Passive).

4.4   The Feeling Matrix descriptions

The second matrix (Figure 4.2) explores the balance between the Feeling scales of Self Awareness and Awareness of Others, and may also be referred to as the Engagement Matrix. These dimensions form the middle layer of the EIP framework. The emotionally intelligent position is to be fully aware and Present, towards the top right corner. The least effective position is to be Less Aware, towards the bottom left corner.

The Feeling Matrix

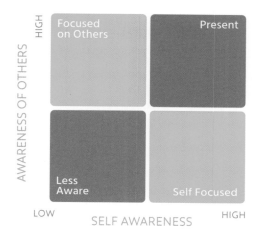

Figure 4.2

Present

The top right quadrant of the Feeling Matrix is labelled Present and is the most positive position. When an individual is Present, they are in touch with their feelings and the feelings of others. They are aware of their surroundings and the people around them. High Self Awareness and Awareness of Others (when combined with high Self Regard) may reflect a sense of feeling alive and energised by life, so may result in being active and experiencing life to the full, such as through learning, self-development, and connecting with people.

Less Aware

The bottom left quadrant is labelled Less Aware and is the area requiring most development. People who score low on both Self Awareness and Awareness of Others may not be closely in touch with their own feelings or the feelings of others. If a person does not notice their own feelings, then they have little internal feedback on what they personally want and about how to manage their own behaviour. Equally, if they do not notice others, then they may have difficulty understanding people, building friendships, and socialising. In the long run, they may feel their lives are not fulfilled and feel out of touch with themselves and people around them.

Self Focused

The bottom right quadrant (high Self Awareness and low Awareness of Others) is labelled Self Focused. This is essentially when a person focuses more on themselves than on others and becomes self-absorbed. One of the best ways to improve self-esteem is to connect with people, attend to others' needs, and not to ruminate on one's own feelings.

Self Focused can indicate being more self-contained and not being drawn to or interested in other people. This may be fine if a person chooses to live a solitary existence, but not so good if, like most people, they operate in a social context both in and out of work.

Focused on Others

The top left quadrant (low Self Awareness and high Awareness of Others) is labelled Focused on Others. There can be a tendency for some people to be more attentive to the feelings of others than to what matters to themselves. In the short-term this may be positive for others; however, if people do not look after their own needs and become exhausted or unwell, it can become increasingly difficult for them to help other people. Furthermore, Self Awareness is an important element for developing Awareness of Others, as empathy towards others is experienced as a feeling the individual has within their own body.

4.5   The Behaviour Matrix descriptions

The third matrix (Figure 4.3) shows the balance between the Behaviour scales of Self Management and Relationship Management, and may also be referred to as the Performance Matrix. These two parts form the top layer of the EIP framework and are about how people apply themselves to be both personally and interpersonally effective. The emotionally intelligent position is to be Effective (high on both scales); the least desirable position is to be Self Limiting (low on both scales).

Unlike the Attitude and Feeling matrices, which represent a single EIP scale along each axis, the Behaviour Matrix represents a cluster of EIP scales along each axis. Self Management includes most of the linear scales and one multi-scale. Relationship Management includes most of the multi-scales and one linear scale, as shown below:

Self Management

— Emotional Resilience

— Personal Power

— Goal Directedness

— Flexibility

— Authenticity

— Balanced Outlook (multi-scale)

Relationship Management

— Trust

— Emotional Expression and Control

— Conflict Handling

— Interdependence

— Connecting with Others (linear scale)

The Behaviour Matrix

Figure 4.3

Effective

The top right quadrant of the Behaviour Matrix, labelled Effective, is the most positive position, where both Behaviour scale scores (Self Management and Relationship Management) are high in relation to the comparison group. It suggests that a person is operating effectively and is capable of balanced leadership, building strong relationships, and achieving their goals, whether that is on their own or through working with others. They are likely to be self-motivated, productive, and they can make things happen and remain focused. They are also probably good at understanding others, building rapport, and getting the best from others, and as a result may do well in roles requiring cooperation and group interaction.

Self Limiting

The lower left quadrant is labelled Self Limiting and is the area requiring most development. Scoring low on both dimensions presents a fairly negative picture of how a person's Emotional Intelligence manifests in practice. With a Self Limiting profile, an individual may still hold positive attitudes and be aware of feelings but fail to put this into action in their life. If so, they may need to find ways of being more proactive or learn some key life skills to start employing their hidden potential.

Self Driven

The bottom right quadrant is labelled Self Driven. If Self Management is higher than Relationship Management, a person may be more productive and effective at managing their own behaviour and achieving their own goals than doing this through others. Perhaps they like to do things to their own high standards and may find building relationships, influencing, and working with others more difficult and less motivating. They could improve this by becoming more proactive in their Relationship Management, such as making time for others, acting assertively, being spontaneous, building trust, and sharing their feelings with others.

Facilitative

The top left quadrant is labelled Facilitative. When Relationship Management is higher than Self Management this suggests that an individual may enjoy group interaction and joint endeavours, be effective at engaging others, and at building cooperative relationships. However, they may find it more difficult managing their own behaviour to motivate themselves and achieve their personal goals. Becoming more comfortable with spending time alone, and reflecting on their personal goals and how they are performing, might prove useful to someone with a Facilitative profile.

Although the EIP matrices may seem categorical in their interpretation, there are two important considerations users should take into account. First, which of the four quadrants a person's score relates to indicates their typical default position, particularly when under stress. This does not mean they are permanently in this position, as people will spend time in each of the four quadrants. It is the role of the coach to explore how much time they spend in each position, what causes them to fall out of the ideal top right quadrant, and how they manage to get themselves back there. Second, where an individual is positioned within a quadrant is also important. For instance, a person who is positioned in the top right corner of the Blocked Potential quadrant is also bordering on the bottom edge of the Ideal quadrant. This is reflected by a more precise narrative description in the EIP Report.

This chapter has provided an explanation and interpretation of the EIP framework and an organising structure for understanding Emotional Intelligence. The next chapter goes into greater detail by examining and interpreting the 16 EIP scales.

SUMMARY POINTS
FROM CHAPTER FOUR

The different elements of Emotional Intelligence (the theory and the 16 EIP scales) are integrated and organised by the EIP framework.

The cornerstone to EI and the EIP framework is Self Regard. Ultimately, all the EIP scales are there to develop Self Regard and unconditional self-acceptance.

The EIP framework separates EI into two streams: Personal Intelligence and Interpersonal Intelligence. Both elements are made up of three levels:

— Attitude (Self Regard and Regard for Others)

— Feeling (Self Awareness and Awareness of Others)

— Behaviour (Self Management and Relationship Management)

Each level of the EIP framework (Attitude, Feeling, and Behaviour) is paired into a 2x2 matrix resulting in four positions or quadrants. The quadrants provide an ideal platform for coaching, by asking the client the following questions:

— "What percentage of time do you spend in each of the four positions?"

— "What causes you to fall out of the green position?"

— "How do you get back into the green position?"

The Attitude Matrix explores the deepest level of the EIP framework, which describes the relationship between the Core Attitudes of Self Regard and Regard for Others (the first two EIP scales). Based on TA theory, this determines four Life Positions:

— Ideal

— Blocked Potential

— Critical

— Submissive

Any time a person falls outside of the Ideal position they are entering a defensive position which may be reflected by low scores on any of the other EIP scales. Defences are formed as attitudes, experienced as feelings, and expressed as rigid and inappropriate behaviours.

The Feeling Matrix combines the middle level of the EIP framework; Self Awareness and Awareness of Others. The four positions of the Feeling Matrix are:

— Present

— Less Aware

— Self Focused

— Focused on Others

The Behaviour Matrix combines the top level of the EIP framework: Self Management and Relationship Management. The four positions of the Behaviour Matrix are:

— Effective

— Self Limiting

— Self Driven

— Facilitative

Under sufficient stress, people tend to move away from the green position and towards the red or amber positions. How long they spend in these zones before returning to the green position depends largely on their level of Emotional Intelligence.

CHAPTER FIVE
INTERPRETING THE EIP SCALES

INTRODUCTION

This chapter looks at the meaning of the EIP scales and the relationships between them. Interpreting the complete EIP and its 16 scales is a skill that can be continually developed, and there are a number of levels of expertise. To help the user acquire the knowledge and skills of interpretation, the following eight levels are recommended.

Eight Levels of Interpretation for the EIP scales

1   Understand the 16 EIP scale definitions (Chapter Three; Table 3.2).

2   Understand the meaning of low, average, and high scores for each scale (Chapter Five).

3   Examine the relationship between pairs of scales (Chapter Five).

4   Consider the relationship between groups of scales (Chapter Five; 5.5).

5   Look for overall scale patterns and relationships using the EIP framework and matrices (Chapter Four).

6   For the inquisitive user, they may be interested in the statistical relationship between scales (EIP3 Technical Manual).[1]

7   For more advanced interpretation of the scales refer to Appendix One.

8   Over time the user will gain much of their deeper understanding of scales through using the EIP with different clients. (A detailed explanation of how to explore the EIP with clients is given in Chapter Six).

What follows is a description of the first four Levels of Interpretation, starting with an interpretation of the EIP scales for low (Sten 1-3), average (Sten 4-7), and high (Sten 8-10) scores. There is also a description of scale combinations, and how EIP scales may influence and support development of other EIP scales. Looking at the relationship between pairs of scales in this way is a useful starting point for interpreting scale profiles. The final section looks at typical client scenarios and which EIP scales may be of most relevance.

The first set of EIP scales to be examined are the linear scales (scales 1-10) where high scores represent higher EI. There is no negative interpretation given to high scores on linear scales, such as having too much Self Regard (arrogant) or being too flexible (changeable). Instead, the user should look for other scales that may be lacking, such as Regard for Others to balance high Self Regard, and Goal Directedness to balance high Flexibility. The second set of scales to be discussed (scales 11-15) are the multi-scales.

An example of a multi-scale is Balanced Outlook where people can be too high (Over Optimistic) or too low (Pessimistic) with the ideal being in the middle (Realistically Optimistic). Multi-scale patterns are explained in Chapter Six; 6.3.1. Each of the EIP scales will now be discussed in turn from 1-16 within their sections on the EIP framework.

5.1 The Attitude scales

The Attitude scales of Self Regard and Regard for Others form the foundation of the EIP framework and therefore strongly influence all aspects of Emotional Intelligence.

Scale 1: Self Regard

Self Regard is the degree to which an individual accepts and values themselves.

LOW SCORE	AVERAGE SCORE	HIGH SCORE
Has a tendency to discount positive feedback and put themselves down	Accepting of possible development areas without being too self-critical	Accepts weaknesses without being self-critical
Self-confidence is easily knocked by feelings of self-doubt and insecurity	Is generally self-confident with a reasonable sense of well-being	Has a strong sense of inner confidence and well-being
Has a possible need to continually prove themselves	May give insufficient praise and recognition to themselves	Willing to stretch personal comfort zones
May display defensive or rigid behaviour	May be self-doubting when under pressure	Stays calm and centred, keeping challenges in perspective
Has a preoccupation or excessive worry about personal shortcomings	May occasionally worry about personal shortcomings	Has authentic and non-defensive behaviour

How Self Regard influences other scales:

Self Regard is the primary attitude underpinning EI, representing and influencing all of the EIP scales.

Regard for Others: There are several links between Self Regard and Regard for Others as they form the Attitude Matrix described in Chapter Four; 4.3. For example, a low Regard for Others and high Self Regard may indicate being more critical and blaming of others (masking low Self Regard).

Self Awareness: People with a high Self Regard are more likely to accept and pay attention to all of their feelings (including painful feelings) and therefore be more self-aware.

Emotional Resilience: There is a high correlation between Self Regard and Emotional Resilience; an individual who feels OK about themselves is more likely to cope well with life's problems.

Goal Directedness: People with high Self Regard are likely to pay attention to their own needs, wants, and goals.

Flexibility: A high Self Regard helps an individual move outside of their comfort zones and therefore to be flexible in their learning, behaviour, and in how they respond to change.

Personal Power: Having high Self Regard tends to create greater self-confidence and belief in one's capability (Personal Power).

Connecting with Others: Being open with others risks making oneself vulnerable which requires a degree of self-belief.

Authenticity: A high level of Self Regard may help a person be true to themselves (Authenticity), even if this risks the disapproval of others.

Balanced Outlook: People with high Self Regard are more likely to have an optimistic outlook on things.

Emotional Expression and Control: People are less likely to bottle-up their feelings or have emotional outbursts if they have high Self Regard.

Conflict Handling: High Self Regard will help an individual stand up for themselves and assert their wishes.

Scales that influence Self Regard:

Regard for Others

Emotional Resilience

Personal Power

Conflict Handling

Scale 2: Regard for Others

Regard for Others is the degree to which a person accepts and values others (as distinct from liking or approving of what they do).

LOW SCORE	AVERAGE SCORE	HIGH SCORE
Is less tolerant of and less inclined to listen to others' opinions	Listens to people's concerns and responds to their needs	Takes time to support and develop people
Is less likely to adapt and respond to other people's needs	Is supportive and helpful when choosing to engage with others	Listens well, pays attention, and responds to people's needs
Has a tendency to tell others rather than ask questions of them	Occasionally uses praise and personal encouragement to motivate others	Often uses praise and personal encouragement to motivate people
Can be judgmental, critical, and unsympathetic towards people	May sometimes be critical and unsympathetic towards people	Shows empathy, care, and understanding towards others
May frequently doubt other's competence or feel impatient towards people	May tend to be more task than people focused	Values people and builds strong relationships

How Regard for Others influences other scales:

Regard for Others is the core attitude underpinning the interpersonal aspects of EI.

Awareness of Others: A person is more inclined to listen to others, understand their feelings, and be aware of others if they have high Regard for Others. They may also be less inclined to judge others and are more open to seeing their point of view.

Flexibility: A high Regard for Others helps an individual be amenable and flexible towards the needs of others.

Connecting with Others: People with high Regard for Others are more inclined to see the good in others rather than being critical, which typically helps them build closer connections and relationships.

Trust and **Interdependence:** People with high Regard for Others are more inclined to trust and collaborate with others, although they should be cautious not to become Dependent on or Over Trusting of others.

Conflict Handling: Having high Regard for Others means a person is more likely to understand the needs of others and take their opinions into account.

Scales that influence Regard for Others:

Self Regard

Awareness of Others

Conflict Handling

Interdependence

5.2   The Feeling scales

The Feeling scales of Self Awareness and Awareness of Others form the middle layer of the EIP framework and therefore strongly influence the upper level scales of Self Management and Relationship Management.

Scale 3: Self Awareness

Self Awareness is the degree to which a person is in touch with their physiology, feelings, and intuitions.

LOW SCORE	AVERAGE SCORE	HIGH SCORE
Is less aware of how emotions affect their behaviour	Tends to understand their own emotional responses to different stressors	Correctly interprets different emotions and how they impact on their behaviour
May find it difficult to describe their different emotions	Has an adequate vocabulary for communicating different emotions	Has a wide vocabulary when communicating different emotions
Rarely uses or trusts their intuition	Could develop better use of intuition to support their decision making	Appropriately balances logic and intuition when making decisions
Tends to ignore, hide, or not notice their emotions	May sometimes ignore or compartmentalise emotions	Notices emotions early, such as signs of stress
Lacks awareness of what they like, dislike, want, and need	Displays reasonable awareness of own values and needs	Displays accurate awareness of own values, likes, wants, and needs

How Self Awareness influences other scales:

Self Awareness is central to developing EI, as feelings influence behaviour and all of the EIP scales.

Awareness of Others: Awareness of Others is achieved partly through empathy – which is experiencing the feelings of others within oneself (Self Awareness).

Emotional Resilience: Emotional Resilience requires Self Awareness to be bodily aware, notice early signs of anxiety or stress, and learn how to relax.

Goal Directedness: Self Awareness helps a person to know what they like and want and so helps them to clarify their goals. Self Awareness also helps a person notice, and therefore manage, the impulses which can distract them from achieving their goals.

Connecting with Others: A person needs to be in touch with how they are feeling (Self Awareness) in order to be open about their feelings (one part of Connecting with Others).

Trust: Learning who to trust and when to trust someone is influenced by intuition, which requires an awareness of internal 'gut' feelings.

Balanced Outlook: An aspect of Balanced Outlook involves not being carried away by feelings of excitement or being dragged down by negative feelings, both of which require Self Awareness.

Emotional Expression and Control: By being in touch with their feelings (Self Awareness) people are better able to express and control their feelings appropriately.

Reflective Learning: Being aware of one's feelings in the present moment (Self Awareness) is an essential part of Reflective Learning. The more aware a person is of their feelings, the more they have to reflect upon and learn from.

Scales that influence Self Awareness:

Self Regard

Emotional Expression and Control

Reflective Learning

Scale 4: Awareness of Others

Awareness of Others is the degree to which a person is in touch with the feelings of others.

LOW SCORE	AVERAGE SCORE	HIGH SCORE
May have less interest or curiosity in other people	Generally pays attention to and shows interest in others	Shows a keen interest in, and understanding of, other people
Can be unaware of the impact they have on others	Is sometimes unaware of the impact they have on others	Is observant of people's behaviour and knows how to influence them
May find it difficult to empathise with others	Has a reasonable understanding of people's motivations and needs	Pays attention to and show consideration for people's feelings

LOW SCORE	AVERAGE SCORE	HIGH SCORE
May lack tact and sensitivity with people	May occasionally lack tact, interpersonal sensitivity, or empathy	Displays tact, interpersonal sensitivity, and empathy
May form inaccurate assumptions about others	May occasionally form inaccurate assumptions about others	Has a clear understanding of others' motivations and needs

How Awareness of Others influences other scales:

It would be difficult to develop any aspect of Interpersonal intelligence without a reasonably well-developed Awareness of Others. Accurately gauging how others are feeling is a vital attribute for developing the EIP relationship scales.

Regard for Others: Being aware of how other people are feeling (Awareness of Others) helps someone develop their understanding and consideration towards other people (Regard for Others).

Flexibility: Being aware of individual differences (Awareness of Others) helps an individual adapt appropriately to other people.

Connecting with Others: Having Awareness of Others enables closer connections with other people to be built and developed.

Trust: Knowing who to trust, when, and by how much, requires an Awareness of Others' motivations and intentions.

Conflict Handling: Being aware of the feelings of others helps an individual understand the needs of others, how to overcome conflict, and find mutual agreement.

Reflective Learning: Having Awareness of Others helps a person reflect on and improve their relationships.

Scales that influence Awareness of Others:

Regard for Others

Self Awareness

Connecting with Others

Interdependence

Reflective Learning

5.3 Behaviour: The Self Management scales

Self Management is about how effectively people manage themselves to achieve their desired outcomes. There are six Self Management scales, ordered according to their correlation with Self Regard (the foundation of EI), with Emotional Resilience being the first scale.

Scale 5: Emotional Resilience

Emotional Resilience is the degree to which an individual is able to pick themselves up and bounce back when things go badly for them.

LOW SCORE	AVERAGE SCORE	HIGH SCORE
Has a tendency to exaggerate problems	May sometimes exaggerate problems	Effectively manages feelings and behaviour in times of stress
Becomes easily despondent or takes things to heart	Usually views mistakes as learning opportunities	Takes a balanced view about what can be controlled, and keeps problems in perspective
Takes a long time to bounce back from disappointments	Can take a short while to bounce back from disappointments	Sees mistakes as learning opportunities and bounces back quickly from disappointments
Has a tendency to ruminate on issues or be unforgiving	May become despondent with repeated setbacks	Has a robust capacity to cope with setbacks
Has strong negative feelings such as anxiety and stress	Is generally positive about coping with situations	Remains calm in a crisis and thinks through problems rationally

How Emotional Resilience influences other scales:

If people do not cope well with pressure, stress, and disappointment this is likely to interfere with their capacity to think clearly, solve problems, and therefore develop the other EIP scales.

Self Regard: Emotional Resilience is closely correlated with, and helps maintain, Self Regard. This is opposed to ruminating over problems and bringing oneself down.

Personal Power: People are more likely to believe that they can determine their future (Personal Power) if they feel able to cope with the challenges they may face (Emotional Resilience).

Goal Directedness: High Emotional Resilience helps a person to keep their focus and to not be easily distracted from their goals when times get tough.

Flexibility: Under stress people naturally become more rigid and inflexible. Being able to manage stress effectively (Emotional Resilience) helps us to remain flexible in choosing how to behave when under pressure.

Emotional Expression and Control: Emotional Resilience helps people to manage the expression of their feelings during times of stress.

Balanced Outlook: People are more likely to retain a positive outlook on the future (Balanced Outlook) if they feel able to cope with challenges that lay ahead for them (Emotional Resilience).

Scales that influence Emotional Resilience:

Self Regard

Self Awareness

Flexibility

Connecting with Others

Balanced Outlook

Reflective Learning

Scale 6: Personal Power

Personal Power is the degree to which a person believes that they are in charge of and take sole responsibility for their outcomes.

LOW SCORE	AVERAGE SCORE	HIGH SCORE
Is less likely to seek out opportunities for control and greater responsibility	May seek out some opportunities for wider responsibility	Has the confidence to take the initiative
Has some dependency on others to make decisions or take action	May lack the confidence to exert influence in difficult situations	Identifies clear options and acts decisively
Feels disempowered and frustrated by perceived constraints	Can feel disempowered and frustrated by perceived constraints	Feels empowered and self-determined
May blame others and not accept accountability for their own actions	Takes reasonable control and accountability for their own decisions and actions	Takes responsibility for their own actions and the outcomes

LOW SCORE	AVERAGE SCORE	HIGH SCORE
May see themselves as a victim of circumstance or fate	Usually self-assured and knows how to get the desired result	Has a strong sense of control and influence over circumstances

How Personal Power influences other scales:

Many of the EIP scales are more easily developed if someone has confidence in their own abilities and takes responsibility for their personal development.

Self Regard: Personal Power is associated with high self-confidence, which is a useful lever for increasing Self Regard.

Goal Directedness: Someone with Personal Power is more likely to have the confidence to set and work towards achieving their goals.

Balanced Outlook: Being self-responsible (Personal Power) can lead a person to being more optimistic than pessimistic about their capacity to create a positive future.

Interdependence: Personal Power helps an individual to be more self-determined rather than Dependent on others.

Conflict Handling: Someone with Personal Power is more likely to act assertively by taking action.

Scales that influence Personal Power:

Self Regard

Emotional Resilience

Authenticity

Balanced Outlook

Conflict Handling

Interdependence

Scale 7: Goal Directedness

Goal Directedness is the degree to which a person's behaviour is aligned to their long-term goals.

LOW SCORE	AVERAGE SCORE	HIGH SCORE
May be unclear of what they want in life and their personal goals	Is clear on most personal wants and goals	Is clear on their personal needs, wants and goals

LOW SCORE	AVERAGE SCORE	HIGH SCORE
May be unsure about how to achieve personal goals	Has some idea about how to achieve their personal goals	Has a clear focus on how to achieve their personal goals
Can be impulsive, easily distracted, and lacks sustained concentration	Can sometimes be distracted, impulsive, or lacking in concentration	Can maintain focus and not be easily distracted
Often struggles to set specific goals and targets	May lose sight of broader aims or purpose when under pressure	Understands what motivates them
Dislikes long-term thinking and future planning	Engages in some long-term thinking and future planning	Fully engages in long-term thinking and future planning

How Goal Directedness influences other scales:

Being goal directed provides focus and clarity; it helps a person know what they want to achieve and to set objectives in developing any of the EIP scales.

Self Regard: One of the factors that contributes to a person's Self Regard and happiness is knowing how to get what they want, which is a part of Goal Directedness.

Flexibility: Flexibility is best balanced with Goal Directedness. Flexibility without Goal Directedness can lead to constant change, inconsistency, and little long-term purpose.

Authenticity: High Goal Directedness helps a person to be more consistent, reliable, and dependable in their behaviour, which are all aspects of Authenticity.

Emotional Expression and Control: Focusing on what a person wants to achieve (Goal Directedness) can help them to develop emotional control and reduce impulsive behaviour.

Conflict Handling: If a person knows what they want to achieve (Goal Directedness), they are more likely to be clear and assertive in asking for what they want.

Scales that influence Goal Directedness:

Self Awareness

Emotional Resilience

Personal Power

Flexibility

Authenticity

Balanced Outlook

Interdependence

Reflective Learning

Scale 8: Flexibility

Flexibility is the degree to which a person feels free to adapt their thinking and their behaviour to changing situations.

LOW SCORE	AVERAGE SCORE	HIGH SCORE
May be slower to change or adapt personal ways of working	Usually willing to explore options and experiment	Able to adapt quickly and change to different ways of working
Stays within own comfort zone or avoids new ways of doing things	Able to change or adapt personal ways of working when required	Willing to move outside of comfort zones and try new ways of doing things
Is slow to innovate or embrace new ideas	May be slower to innovate or embrace new ideas	Open to new ideas and learning experiences
Sticks to old habits rather than flexing to situational requirements	Sometimes sticks to own preferences rather than adapting to situational requirements	Willing to explore options and experiment
Less willing to adapt to and accommodate the needs of others	May be less flexible and more rigid when under pressure	Willing to adapt and accommodate the needs of others

How Flexibility influences other scales:

Flexibility supports self-development as people are willing to move outside of their comfort zones and learn more rapidly. It also supports Relationship Management as people are more willing to adapt to others and flex to their styles.

Emotional Resilience: Being flexible by trying different strategies for coping with problems can help in coping with adversity and improving Emotional Resilience.

Goal Directedness: Goal Directedness is best balanced with Flexibility. Goal Directedness without Flexibility may lead to rigid, driven, and uncompromising behaviour.

Conflict Handling: Adapting to others (Flexibility) helps people achieve acceptable compromise and reduce unproductive levels of conflict.

Interdependence: Being flexible towards others enables someone to be more accommodating and collaborative.

Scales that influence Flexibility:

Self Regard

Regard for Others

Awareness of Others

Emotional Resilience

Goal Directedness

Authenticity

Interdependence

Scale 9: Connecting with Others

Connecting with Others is the extent and ease with which an individual makes significant connections with other people.

LOW SCORE	AVERAGE SCORE	HIGH SCORE
May lack social confidence in some situations	Is fairly confident and comfortable engaging with people	Is confident and comfortable engaging with people
Could invest more time in building relationships	Invests some time in building relationships	Invests time and energy in building and maintaining relationships
Can appear guarded, closed, or slightly detached	Generally prepared to acknowledge and express feelings to others	Open with people, shares feelings, and expresses vulnerabilities
May focus more on tasks than on people	At times may appear guarded, closed, or slightly detached	Listens to people and shows appreciation
Takes time to form connections and engage with people	May form close trusting relationships with only a select few individuals	Quickly forms close connections and trusting relationships

How Connecting with Others influences other scales:

Connecting with Others is fundamental to building and maintaining relationships and therefore has an influence on all of the interpersonal scales.

Awareness of Others: Connecting with people helps a person to become more aware of others' needs, wants, and feelings.

Emotional Resilience: An important aspect of coping with adversity (Emotional Resilience) is having trusted friends and colleagues to talk to and connect with.

Authenticity: Connecting with others makes it easier for people to get to know them – an important part of Authenticity.

Trust: Making connections with people is a vital ingredient towards building Trust.

Emotional Expression and Control: People generally find it easier to express their feelings having built closer connections with others.

Scales that influence Connecting with Others:

Self Regard

Regard for Others

Self Awareness

Awareness of Others

Emotional Expression and Control

Trust

Interdependence

Scale 10: Authenticity

Authenticity is the degree to which an individual invites the trust of others by being principled, reliable, consistent, and known.

LOW SCORE	AVERAGE SCORE	HIGH SCORE
Can be potentially closed, difficult to get to know, or hard to read	Is generally open and straightforward with people	Is genuine, straightforward, and easy to get to know
May lack clear principles and values or fail to live by them	Is likely to have reasonable integrity with some guiding values and principles	Is clear about their principles and values, and acts in accordance with them
Can be undependable or inconsistent	Is usually reliable and can be depended upon	Is dependable, consistent, and reliable
Can often change direction in an attempt to meet others' expectations	May change direction in an attempt to meet others expectations	Displays integrity and behaves the same when on their own as when observed by others

LOW SCORE	AVERAGE SCORE	HIGH SCORE
May break promises or agree to things that they do not deliver	May sometimes over-commit on what they can deliver	Will only commit to what they can deliver

How Authenticity influences other scales:

Being authentic means that a person is likely to be consistent which supports the relationship scales. They are also less likely to swing from one extreme to the other on the multi-scales.

Self Regard: Having integrity and being true to oneself helps to build someone's sense of self-worth and Self Regard.

Emotional Resilience: Having principles helps a person cope with setbacks and difficulties in life.

Personal Power and **Goal Directedness:** Having inner guiding principles (Authenticity) means that someone is more likely to be internally driven (Personal Power) and therefore less easily distracted from achieving their goals (Goal Directedness).

Flexibility: Having principles should not be confused with rigidity. Authenticity is about doing what one believes to be right, which may mean moving outside of one's comfort zones (Flexibility).

Emotional Expression and Control: Authenticity is about being sincere, which includes expressing and sharing one's feelings.

Interdependence: Authentic individuals are more likely to be true to themselves than need to be liked or Dependent on others.

Scales that influence Authenticity include:

Self Regard

Goal Directedness

Connecting with Others

Emotional Expression and Control

Conflict Handling

5.4 Behaviour: The Relationship Management scales

Relationship Management is about how people manage their relationships to be inter-personally effective. These scales are scored differently from the linear scales as the most emotionally intelligent score is in the middle range. A high score represents 'too much' and a low score represents 'too little' on this scale. Low, average, and high scores therefore have specific labels, each with its own separate sub-scale.

Scale 11: Trust

Trust is the tendency for a person to place the right amount of Trust in others. The key is not to be Over Trusting or be Mistrusting, but to get the right balance to be Carefully Trusting.

MISTRUSTING	CAREFULLY TRUSTING	OVER TRUSTING
Is reluctant to delegate and may take too much on themselves	Delegates responsibility appropriately	Places trust in others' abilities too easily
Questions other people's motives	Has realistic expectations of others' abilities	May be taken advantage of or be let down by others
Keeps people at a distance to avoid becoming vulnerable	Accepting of others and gives them the benefit of the doubt where appropriate	Assumes the best in others and may ignore or not notice their faults
May micro-manage people's work	Monitors people's progress in a supportive manner	Doesn't monitor or check up on people
Often lacks confidence in other people's abilities	Their trust in others is based on evidence as well as intuition	Dislikes questioning others or being seen as Mistrusting

How Trust influences other scales:

Being Carefully Trusting is a prerequisite for developing most other EIP Interpersonal scales and is developed largely through being authentic and consistent with people (Authenticity), and having Regard for Others.

Connecting with Others: A lack of Trust can often get in the way of people being willing to open up and therefore hinders connecting with others.

Balanced Outlook: Knowing when to Trust others helps to avoid being let down by them and feeling disappointed (Pessimistic).

Conflict Handling: Trusting others appropriately may help in negotiations (Conflict Handling), such as knowing when to trust a person and when to be more cautious.

Interdependence: Carefully Trusting others may lead to greater collaboration, while Over Trusting can lead to being over Dependent, and Mistrusting can lead to being Over Independent.

Scales that influence Trust:

Regard for Others

Self Awareness

Awareness of Others

Connecting with Others

Authenticity

Balanced Outlook

Interdependence

Scale 12: Balanced Outlook

Balanced Outlook is the degree to which an individual balances optimism with realism.

PESSIMISTIC	REALISTICALLY OPTIMISTIC	OVER OPTIMISTIC
Expects the worst and avoids taking risks	Demonstrates cautious judgment and sound decision making	Over-optimism may lead to disappointment
May over-generalise or exaggerate difficulties	Keeps problems and difficulties in perspective	May overlook, dismiss, or ignore problems
Focuses on identifying problems rather than solutions	Identifies opportunities and finds solutions to problems	Often displays a tendency to take risks
Has a tendency to use critical, negative, or discouraging language	Accurately assesses if ideas will work in practice	May have a tendency to make overly optimistic assumptions
May express less enthusiasm and encouragement to others	Inspires confidence in others	Can be over-enthusiastic about possibilities

How Balanced Outlook influences other scales:

Having a Realistically Optimistic outlook creates a generally more positive orientation in how the individual manages their own behaviour and their relationships across all aspects of EI. Avoiding over optimism helps prevent disappointment and feelings of pessimism.

Emotional Resilience: Holding a positive outlook helps a person to cope with life's challenges.

Personal Power: Having positive expectations of the future gives someone self-belief and confidence.

Goal Directedness: Having ambitions supports a person in setting achievable development goals.

Trust: Being realistic can help a person avoid Over Trusting others.

Reflective Learning: Being realistic (about both strengths and weaknesses) enables an individual to learn from past experience.

Scales that influence Balanced Outlook:

Self Regard

Self Awareness

Emotional Resilience

Personal Power

Trust

Scale 13: Emotional Expression and Control

Emotional Expression and Control is the degree to which an individual achieves appropriate balance in the expression and control of their emotions.

UNDER CONTROLLED	FREE AND IN CHARGE	OVER CONTROLLED
May bottle-up feelings until they burst out (Under Controlled)	Can control their feelings when necessary to do so	May bottle-up feelings (Over Controlled) until they burst out
Can over-react, causing conflict with others	Motivates others through enthusiasm and appreciation	May feel self-conscious and lack social confidence
Has strong emotions that may interfere with their capacity to think clearly and act appropriately	Is comfortable expressing their full range of feelings	May feel uncomfortable sharing feelings
Can become overwhelmed by strong emotions	Displays emotional maturity and does not over-react	Can be overly task focused, logical, or business-like
May be easily provoked, upset, or become angry quickly	Is even-tempered and emotionally balanced	May find it difficult to show passion and enthusiasm

How Emotional Expression and Control influences other scales:

Emotional expression is mostly determined by what is going on internally for a person (their thoughts and feelings). However, it manifests externally, influencing many aspects of their relationships.

Self Awareness: Verbalising feelings can help a person to become more aware of and understand their feelings and emotions.

Connecting with Others: Being able to express oneself and one's emotions helps in building connections with people.

Authenticity: By managing and controlling the expression of their emotions appropriately, others feel that they are more consistent and predictable.

Conflict Handling: Expressing oneself in an appropriate manner helps a person to be Assertive rather than Aggressive or Passive.

Interdependence: People who do not express their feelings may become isolated from others (Over Independent).

Scales that influence Emotional Expression and Control:

Self Awareness

Goal Directedness

Connecting with Others

Authenticity

Conflict Handling

Reflective Learning

Scale 14: Conflict Handling

Conflict Handling is how well conflict is handled; how Assertive a person is.

PASSIVE	ASSERTIVE	AGGRESSIVE
Is less inclined to assert their wishes or opinions	Is comfortable asserting their wishes and opinions	Has a tendency to dominate others or take control
Avoids or finds giving performance feedback uncomfortable	Is happy to both give and receive feedback	Is less inclined to listen or take the needs of others into consideration
Overly accommodating or backs down easily	Can be firm while remaining respectful	Tackles difficult conversations in a confrontational or hostile manner

PASSIVE	ASSERTIVE	AGGRESSIVE
May become frustrated and eventually lose their temper	Challenges others without being aggressive	Loses their temper with people
Avoids conflict and finds disagreement uncomfortable	Comfortable negotiating and willing to compromise	May be seen as 'bossy' or uncompromising

How Conflict Handling influences other scales:

Conflict Handling is a good scale for illustrating some of the main aspects of EI such as having Regard for Others and managing one's emotions. When people are Aggressive or Passive it can have negative consequences on their relationships and in getting their needs met.

Self Regard and **Regard for Others:** Assertive behaviour is a good demonstration of balancing one's own interests with the interests of others.

Personal Power: By being Assertive, someone is better at influencing others to achieve what they set out to do.

Authenticity: Being consistent and calm in how conflict is managed, rather than Aggressive or Passive, gains the trust of others.

Emotional Expression and Control: Effective conflict handling skills supports a person in managing how they express their emotions.

Interdependence: Minimising Aggressive behaviour helps to create more harmonious and productive relationships with others.

Scales that influence Conflict Handling:

Self Regard

Regard for Others

Awareness of Others

Goal Directedness

Flexibility

Trust

Emotional Expression and Control

Interdependence

Reflective Learning

Scale 15: Interdependence

Interdependence is how well an individual manages to balance taking themselves and others into account.

DEPENDENT	INTERDEPENDENT	OVER INDEPENDENT
Often dislikes working on their own	Works effectively on their own or as part of a team	May take on too much responsibility by not including others
Can be easily influenced by other's opinions	Values others' skills and contributions	Others may want more communication from them
Can find it difficult or uncomfortable to make decisions on their own	Is comfortable either making their own decisions or relying on others	Prefers to make their own decisions and be self-reliant
May seek regular reassurance, guidance, or approval from others	Can take on responsibility and act decisively when required	Is more of an individualist than a team player
Less inclined to stretch comfort zones or take risks without support	Consults others and seeks advice when necessary	May fail to consult others or seek their advice

How Interdependence influences other scales:

Collaboration and teamwork are important elements in building relationships, and it is equally important to be able to work independently when required.

Regard for Others: Including others in one's decision making and actions (Interdependence) demonstrates Regard for Others.

Awareness of Others: Collaborating with others helps in building understanding of others and knowing what matters to them (Awareness of Others).

Personal Power: Being willing to make independent decisions and not being over Dependent on others, demonstrates and builds Personal Power.

Goal Directedness: Being able to work and act independently when required helps someone remain focused and not be distracted from their goals.

Flexibility: Being able to adapt between working with others and working alone shows Flexibility.

Connecting with Others: Collaboration and teamwork are important elements for building and maintaining connections with others.

Trust: Working with others or in a team is likely to build Trust.

Conflict Handling: Not being over Dependent on others helps build assertiveness.

Scales that influence Interdependence:

Regard for Others

Personal Power

Flexibility

Trust

Conflict Handling

Scale 16: Reflective Learning

Reflective Learning is the degree to which Emotional Intelligence is enhanced by someone thinking about what they and others feel, think, and do, noticing the outcomes these produce, and altering their future patterns accordingly.

LOW SCORE	AVERAGE SCORE	HIGH SCORE
May not know what to develop or how	Has some awareness of their strengths and development needs	Clearly understands their strengths and development needs
May prefer to stay as they are rather than risk change	Is open to developing or broadening their skill set	Seeks opportunities to develop and broaden their skill set
May actively dislike or avoid self-reflection	Sometimes reflects and learns from past experience	Engages in regular self-reflection
May not seek or listen to constructive feedback	Is receptive to some constructive feedback	Seeks and is receptive to feedback from others
May have little interest in self-development	Recognises the benefits of personal development	Plans and acts upon their self-development needs

How Reflective Learning influences other scales:

Reflective Learning is a scale specifically for developing EI and all of the EIP scales. Practising Reflective Learning is therefore an essential part of personal and interpersonal development.

Emotional Resilience: Reflective Learning helps an individual learn from experience and therefore how to cope with similar adversity in the future.

Goal Directedness: Incorporating past experience when deciding on future actions is fundamental to a person knowing what they want (Goal Directedness).

Authenticity: In order to be authentic, a person must review whether they are acting in accordance with their values and guiding principles (Reflective Learning and Conflict Handling).

Emotional Expression and Control and **Conflict Handling:** Reflecting on past situations helps a person to recognise whether their behaviour has been proportionate and led to constructive outcomes or not.

Scales that influence Reflective Learning:

Self Awareness

Awareness of Others

Balanced Outlook

5.5 Interpreting scale patterns

The scale descriptions given so far in this chapter explain the relationship between pairs of scales which is a useful starting point for interpretation. However, when interpreting a complete profile, it may be necessary to consider the relationship between several scales together. With 16 EIP scales there are too many combinations to provide an interpretation of all permutations. One way to look at scale patterns is by using the EIP framework and the matrix boxes, as described in Chapter Four.

Another method for interpreting several scales together is to consider the profile in relation to a specific matter or issue that the individual wishes to address. This makes the search for patterns more manageable and relevant to the individual's needs. The ten scenarios which follow explain those scales which are possible causes and also those scales which support the individual's development.

Scenario 1

An individual is having difficulty standing up to their manager.

Possible causes may include:

Conflict Handling: The most relevant scale may be Conflict Handling and checking whether they are too Passive and lack assertiveness.

Self Regard: Underlying this may be a low Self Regard and high Regard for Others (Submissive position on the Attitude Matrix).

Goal Directedness: They may not have specific goals or have expressed their intentions clearly to their manager.

Over Controlled: Perhaps they have difficulty expressing themselves or bottle-up their feelings.

Scales that may support their development:

Emotional Expression and Control: Rehearsing how to express themselves will help to raise their assertiveness.

Awareness of Others: Are they aware of what their manager is thinking and feeling about them and what their manager wants from them?

Trust and Authenticity: Have they gained the Trust of their manager by delivering on their promises?

Connecting with Others: Have they invested time in building a personal connection with their manager?

Scenario 2

An individual is not coping with the pressure of their work.

Possible causes may include:

Emotional Resilience: The immediate scale to consider here is Emotional Resilience as they would probably benefit from developing their coping skills.

Self Regard: Underlying this may be a low Self Regard, indicating a longer-term and more pervasive issue affecting their wider self-esteem.

Balanced Outlook: Also consider their Balanced Outlook, to see if they tend to assume the worst and exaggerate or generalise problems.

Scales that may support their development:

Conflict Handling and **Trust:** If they are not managing their workload they may consider developing their assertiveness by learning to push back and delegate work to others (Trust), or to ask others for support.

Goal Directedness: They could develop their Goal Directedness so as to prioritise what is most important.

Connecting with Others and **Interdependence:** If they need more support from others then they could develop their Connecting with Others and their Interdependence.

Personal Power: A common cause of dissatisfaction and stress is not feeling in control. Helping them to recognise that they have choices and to use their strengths will empower them.

Self Awareness: Help them to notice the signs of stress early such as mild anxiety, or feelings of uncertainty, so that they can deal with them sooner before they become less manageable.

Scenario 3

A newly appointed leader is failing to motivate their team.

Possible causes may include:

Interdependence: Are they working closely enough with their team?

Connecting with Others: Are they building close working relationships with individuals?

Trust: Consider their leadership style. Do they micro-manage (Mistrusting) or leave people with little direction on what to do (Over Trusting)?

Scales that may support their development:

Personal Power and **Goal Directedness:** Do they display confidence, conviction and clear leadership to others?

Authenticity: As a leader are they seen as consistent, fair, and dependable by their team?

Regard for Others: Do they believe in, appreciate, and value their team members as individuals?

Scenario 4

An individual upsets their colleagues and is resistant to change.

Possible causes may include:

Regard for Others: It depends on how they have upset their colleagues; are they a bully or arrogant (high Self Regard and low Regard for Others)? Or do they just not seem to care?

Awareness of Others: Are they insensitive to others?

Connecting with Others and **Interdependence:** Do they lack interpersonal skills?

Under Controlled and **Aggressive:** Do they suffer from sudden emotional outbursts or anger?

Goal Directedness and **Flexibility:** Upsetting colleagues combined with their resistance to change may indicate that they are highly driven but inflexible (high Goal Directedness and low Flexibility).

Scales that may support their development:

Awareness of Others: They may benefit from becoming more aware of how their own behaviour impacts on others.

Reflective Learning: Taking time to reflect on their actions and considering how they could behave differently will support their development.

Scenario 5

A middle-aged individual is feeling demotivated and unfulfilled by their work.

Possible causes may include:

Self Regard and **Self Awareness:** People who have invested greatly in their family and their work but haven't paid sufficient attention to what they also want for themselves may experience a lack of personal fulfilment.

Goal Directedness: Maybe they get too easily distracted from achieving their own goals.

Pessimistic: Perhaps they have lost their sense of optimism and excitement about the future.

Authenticity: Are they in a role which is incongruent with what they value in life?

Scales that may support their development:

Reflective Learning: Help them to reflect on their past, present, and future.

Self Awareness: Identify what makes them feel happy, motivated, and excited.

Flexibility: Encourage them to look at their options and be creative.

Goal Directedness and **Balanced Outlook:** Help them to set realistic goals and objectives for their future.

Personal Power, Emotional Resilience, and **Connecting with Others:** They may need to build their confidence, draw upon their strengths, and get support from others, to make what may be quite significant life changes.

Scenario 6

An individual who is highly productive lets themselves and others down by being unreliable and inconsistent at work.

Possible causes may include:

Goal Directedness: It is not unusual for a person's strength to also be their 'Achilles heel'. If someone is drawn to pursue ideas and possibilities, they may focus less on details and completion. They may also be easily distracted and have poor impulse control.

Authenticity: They may want to please others so make promises they are unable to keep. They may also be unpredictable and inconsistent.

Over Optimistic: They may be unreliable due to having unrealistic expectations that don't get achieved.

Scales that may support their development:

Self Awareness: The key is not to curb their creativity but to help them to become more structured, realistic, and focused. This may come from improving their Self Awareness and the other scales listed previously.

Flexibility: Ironically, they may also need to develop their capacity to change. Being constantly unreliable and inconsistent is a rigid habit that can indicate low Flexibility.

Scenario 7

An individual has difficulty managing their emotions and has occasional aggressive outbursts, being prone to 'emotional flooding'.

Possible causes may include:

Emotional Expression and Control and **Conflict Handling:** One reason people have aggressive outbursts is because they ignore or try to repress their feelings. This is indicated in the EIP by the 'rebound' profiles, such as being high on both Passive and Aggressive or being high on both emotionally Over Controlled and emotionally Under Controlled.

Regard for Others: Aggressive behaviour may also suggest an underlying low Regard for Others which may by association, also be masking low Self Regard.

Emotional Resilience: Being emotionally Under Controlled may also be the result of high anxiety and a fear of not being able to cope (low Emotional Resilience).

Scales that may support their development:

Self Awareness: They may benefit from learning to notice feelings sooner before they grow, by developing their Self Awareness.

Emotional Expression and Control and **Assertiveness:** By letting their emotions out sooner and being less passive they may avoid rebounding and aggressive outbursts.

Scenario 8

An individual has experienced a sudden drop in performance and is feeling despondent.

Possible causes may include:

Self Regard: Where there is a sudden change in a person's behaviour, it is useful to find out how they were previous to this and what has happened to cause their drop in performance. It may be reflected in a perceived low Self Regard.

Balanced Outlook: They may have created a 'negative loop' whereby a drop in performance creates despondency (pessimism) and despondency creates a drop in performance.

Personal Power: Performance is often related to feelings of control and competence. Look for any aspect in their life that may have lowered their feelings of Personal Power such as negative feedback, less autonomy, or increased stress at work.

Emotional Resilience: Focus on their inner resources and minimise a downward decline to increase their Emotional Resilience.

Self Awareness: Help them understand what really motivates them to provide a more positive focus.

Goal Directedness: Focus on solutions to improve their performance and feelings of optimism.

Personal Power: Recognise their strengths and what they can do to increase their feelings of control.

Connecting with Others and **Interdependence:** Encourage them to ask for help or assistance from others to make them feel more supported and less alone.

Scenario 9

An individual was surprised to receive negative 360 feedback from their colleagues about being difficult to get along with.

Awareness of Others: If the feedback is surprising to the individual it may indicate a low Awareness of Others. This may suggest that they do not listen sufficiently to others or notice their own impact on others.

Regard for Others: Being difficult to get along with could be due to a host of different reasons, such as not showing others sufficient respect or care.

Flexibility: They may be too rigid and uncompromising.

Trust: Any of the previous behaviours can erode Trust.

Conflict Handling: Low Trust can lead to conflict or to guarded behaviours.

Interdependence: Conflict and mistrust will interfere with effective teamwork.

Self Regard: Negative 360 feedback can be damaging to a person's self-esteem. It is important they get specific feedback so that they can verify its accuracy and also decide if it is something they wish to address.

Reflective Learning: Being aware of this feedback can help them to improve their relationships by reflecting on past events.

Connecting with Others: They could invest time in repairing and maintaining their relationships, and in developing new connections.

Scenario 10

An individual scores highly on most aspects of the EIP and gets consistently positive feedback from others. They are unsure what they can do to develop further.

Possible causes may include:

Self Awareness and **Reflective Learning:** If a client is unsure as to what they can develop, they may benefit from heightening their Self Awareness and spending more time reflecting on their experiences.

Balanced Outlook: They may also be Over Optimistic and not notice potential problems or miss opportunities for self-development.

Self Regard and **Regard for Others:** Check their attitude is not coming from the Critical position, "I am OK, others are Not OK", which may suggest they have an inaccurate self-perception.

Scales that may support their development:

Flexibility: Even when all scores are high there will still be room for further improvement. If they scored a 'nine', ask them to imagine what a 'ten' would look like. If they responded 'agree' to any positive items, ask them why they didn't respond with 'strongly agree'. Notice if they spend time justifying themselves; this may indicate they are less open to exploring how they can change (Flexibility).

Goal Directedness: Personal development does not have to be about dealing with problems and weaknesses. A person may also be looking for continuous improvement, aspiration, fine tuning, enhancement, future goals, and going from 'good to great'.

This chapter has given an interpretation of the EIP scales and some of the most common relationships between them. The next two chapters look at how to apply this learning through using the EIP for development and assessment.

SUMMARY POINTS
FROM CHAPTER FIVE

Of the 16 EIP scales, 11 are linear, where high scores represent high EI, and five are multi-scales, where individuals may score 'too high' as well as 'too low'.

The 16 EIP scales are inter-correlated as they all stem from the same single construct (Self Regard). The relationship between the scales is described in this chapter.

Interpretation of scale scores given in the EIP reports should be treated as potential hypotheses that need to be explored with the client. Interpreting combinations of scales is a skill that requires knowledge of the scales and subjective interpretation acquired through experience.

Eight skill Levels of Interpretation are recommended. Over time the user can develop their skills and move up through the eight levels. Learning to interpret the meaning of the EIP scales begins with understanding the scale definitions.

It is advisable and easier to start by combining single scales before combining multiple scales. One way to look for themes between scales is to cluster them within the six parts of the EIP framework, as described in Chapter Four. The user will develop deeper skills of interpretation through practical experience of coaching clients with the EIP (see Chapter Six).

When interpreting the whole profile it is easier and more relevant to address a specific question or objective that the client has, such as "How could I be a more effective team leader?" Then examine and interpret the profile from this perspective. Several example scenarios are given in this chapter.

SECTION THREE
APPLYING THE EMOTIONAL INTELLIGENCE PROFILE

The first two sections of this book have been largely theoretical and knowledge based, explaining the underpinning principles of EI, how this led to the development of the EIP, and an interpretation of the EIP scales and framework. With an understanding of EI theory and knowledge of the EIP product, Section Three explains how to apply this for both assessment and development in the workplace.

The EIP may be used for several different applications including: team working, talent management, leadership development, careers guidance, culture change, conflict resolution, personal counselling, group work, selection assessment, and 360 feedback. The most frequent applications of the tool are in coaching for professional development, and to support selection and the job interview. These will be the contexts for describing how to apply the EIP in this section.

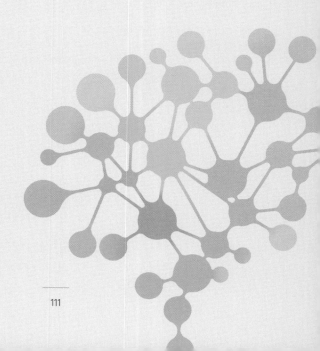

CHAPTER SIX
COACHING WITH THE EIP

INTRODUCTION

This chapter offers advice and best practice on how to administer, interpret, explore, and coach clients using the EIP. A six-step process is recommended when using the EIP for coaching (Section 6.4), and some key coaching skills of particular relevance to coaching with EI are explained (Section 6.7).

6.1 How to prepare for coaching with the EIP

Before deciding to use the EIP, the coach needs to consider the purpose, benefits, and implications of doing so. Typically, the EIP is used to support an individual's professional development, often as part of a coaching programme or group development event. The coach may initially consider how the EIP will fit within the entire process, such as:

— What is the specific purpose for using the tool?

— Is the EIP the only source of feedback or will it include other data such as 360 feedback?

— How much time is available for exploring the results? (Between one and two hours is usual practice).

— Which version of the EIP Report will be used?

— Who will have access to the results?

— When and how will the report be shown to the client (coachee)?

— How will the client be supported after the EIP exploration session?

It is the first question in particular that needs to be agreed with the client. Ideally the coach will find out before using the EIP what the client wants to achieve from the coaching programme and what their specific goals for development are. Without a clear agenda, using the tool can be likened to a 'fishing expedition', i.e. seeing what turns up, rather than giving the client what they want or adding value. Establishing the client's objectives prior to the exploration session enables the time available to be focused and productive.

6.2   Administration of the EIP

A question often asked by clients before completing the EIP is: "Should I be thinking specifically about work?" Our advice on this is whatever comes to mind for the client on each question is what matters, whether this is work or non-work related. As the EIP is designed to measure the 'whole person', changing any aspects of a person's EI (as defined by the EIP scales) will change them in all aspects of their life. Learning to be a better IT programmer, for example, will do just that, but developing an individual's Emotional Resilience will help them cope better with setbacks whatever the context, be they personal or professional.

To prepare people for completing the EIP, it is important to help them access an appropriate mindset. If the client is feeling highly anxious about something that happened that day, this may influence their responses and how they presently perceive themselves. For the purpose of self-development, it is useful for them to consider other aspects of their life. Ask the client to recall four events, one positive and one negative from both their work and their non-work life, then to reflect on what happened and how they were feeling at that time. This activity helps the client to take a broader perspective on themselves when responding to the EIP questions.

It is recommended that the individual undertakes the EIP questionnaire in a quiet place without distractions and that they allow themselves at least thirty minutes to complete the 158 questions in a single sitting. If, however, they need to complete the questionnaire in more than one sitting, any completed questions will be saved, and they can log on to finish the questions at a later date.

6.3   Interpretation of the EIP Report

Once the client has completed the EIP questionnaire, the administrator can instantly generate the selected report. The most comprehensive of the EIP reports is the Executive Report. Before sharing their report with them, the coach may choose to spend time examining the report and form hypotheses about the results in relation to the client's objectives. If their objective is to deal more effectively with conflict, the coach may pay particular attention to the Conflict Handling scale. The purpose of forming hypotheses is to be able to discuss and check this out with the client.

The cover page of the Executive Report includes the client's name, the date of completion, and the selected comparison group. The first page has an introduction and list of contents followed by an explanation of Emotional Intelligence and the EIP framework. It is important to explain the EIP framework to the client in a way that they can relate to, such as linking it to their work competencies. The profile pages list the client's scores on each of the 16 EIP scales. These are ordered according to the EIP framework shown in Chapter Three, Table 3.2.

The first profile page lists the linear scales (1-10) where high scores represent high EI. It is important to remember that, as with all psychometric measures, the EIP is open to error. As a rule of thumb, it is standard practice to accept one Sten either side of their score to account for potential error in self-reporting. To mitigate against this, the coach should seek to validate the client's scores during the exploration session by:

— Gauging the client's level of self-awareness

— Seeing if the scores match their expectations

— Exploring if the scores help explain their circumstances

— Discussing the accuracy of their answers to specific questions

— Corroborating scores with other available evidence

Looking at the large amount of data contained in a profile can initially be quite overwhelming, so the five-step approach described below is recommended:

1 **Look for key features:** Are there any scales that stand out as being particularly high or low, and are there clear strengths and development areas?

2 **Look for themes across scales:** It may help at this stage to look at the EIP framework scores. Are they stronger on Self Management or Relationship Management scales? Are there differences between the three levels of Attitude, Feeling, and Behaviour?

3 **Look for overall patterns between scales:** For example, high scores on Emotional Resilience, Goal Directedness, and Personal Power may suggest the client is quite strong-minded and confident.

4 **Examine specific scales of interest:** Read the more detailed scale interpretation, and examine their answers to specific questions given in the Executive Report.

5 **Keep in mind the client's objectives:** It is far easier to interpret a profile in relation to a specific question or issue that the client wants to address. (For examples see Chapter Five; 5.5.)

The key here is to be open and creative when considering possible interpretations. The coach is not expected to have all of the 'answers' before the coaching session; being over-prepared can be a barrier to fully listening to the client. Remember, this stage is only about forming hypotheses in preparation for the coaching session. The coach should be willing to abandon or form new interpretations during the coaching session depending on what transpires from their exploration.

6.3.1 Multi-scale scoring

The second page of the profile lists the Relationship Management scales or the multi-scales. On these scales, more is not necessarily better as it is possible to have 'too much' as well as 'too little' on a scale. For instance, Conflict Handling is about getting the correct middle balance of being Assertive, i.e. not being Passive (too little) and not being Aggressive (too much). The multi-scales measure all three levels separately: the 'too much' and 'too little' scales are shown in red because high scores on these scales are not desirable; and the middle scale is shown in green because high scores on this scale are desirable.

Having an EI measure with three sub-scales is unique. Typically, other measures have a single scale with opposite ends, such as Passive at one end, Aggressive at the other, and Assertive in the middle. Difficulties can arise in using this single scale approach if people score in the middle. Consider someone who is usually Passive until they can no longer contain their frustration and then they become Aggressive. On a single scale, the two extremes (Passive and Aggressive) would balance each other out and the score would appear in the middle of the scale as Assertive. Since people's behaviour and emotions are variable, it is necessary to have scales that measure this variation. In this example, where a person rebounds from being Passive to Aggressive, it would show on the EIP as being high on both the red sub-scales and low on the green sub-scale. Due to its shape, this is called the 'tuning fork' or 'rebound profile', as shown in Figure 6.1. A rebound profile can occur on all of the multi-scales, for example: Over Trusting someone (too high) can lead to being let down and becoming Mistrusting (too low); being Over Optimistic (too high) may lead to disappointment and then feeling Pessimistic (too low). A rebound may be likened to a see-saw where a person may bounce from one extreme to the other.

Example of a 'rebound/tuning fork' profile

Figure 6.1

Passive   9

Assertive   2

Aggressive   7

Clients often comment that the multi-scales are very insightful as they show patterns of their emotions and behaviour that have been missed by previous conventional measures. There are also other multi-scale patterns to look out for, such as the 'rifle' profile where a person scores highly on the 'too little' scale, average on the middle scale and low on the 'too much' scale (see Figure 6.2). For the Trust scale this would indicate that they are typically Mistrusting and rarely Over Trusting. The reason for this may not be that they want to be Mistrusting, but that they fear being Over Trusting, such as a police officer who doesn't want to be naïve so errs on the side of suspicion. The opposite pattern to this is the 'step' profile: scoring high on Over Trusting and low on Mistrusting (see Figure 6.3). One possible reason might be they fear being Mistrusting and consequently fall into being Over Trusting, such as a manager who doesn't want to appear Mistrusting of their team. The ideal profile would be to score high in the middle (Carefully Trusting) and low on the extremes (see Figure 6.4).

Example of a 'rifle' profile

Mistrusting
Carefully Trusting
Over Trusting

Figure 6.2

Example of a 'step' profile

Mistrusting
Carefully Trusting
Over Trusting

Figure 6.3

Example of an 'ideal' profile

Mistrusting
Carefully Trusting
Over Trusting

Figure 6.4

Two other possible multi-scale profiles are to have all low scores or all high scores. A person scoring low on all three sub-scales may not have related well to the questions or they may be feeling 'flat' and disengaged. Alternatively, scoring high on all three multi-scales may suggest they are quite changeable and possibly inconsistent in their behaviour, something that could be verified by a low score on Authenticity (scale 10).

The previous descriptions account for most of the 27 possible permutations of high, average, and low multi-scale score combinations. The multi-scales are scored from 1-10, which for three sub-scales gives 1000 possible permutations of scores for each multi-scale. To help with the interpretation of this, the reports include a narrative description, reduced to one of 48 permutations. However, any computerised interpretation is objective and purely based on the limited information collected from the questionnaire. In addition to this a coach needs to use their subjective skills by being aware of, listening to, and exploring alternative interpretations with their client. (More details on the scoring of EIP scales is given in Chapter Three; 3.3.2.)

The next large section of the profile is the Narrative which provides an interpretation of each scale score for the reader, plus a short summary and development points. It is important to remember that these interpretations are hypotheses only for the reader to consider, and that the development points are suggestions that should act as a starting point. The Narrative is also based on the individual's scale scores and is only as relevant as their scores are accurate.

6.3.2 The Item Analysis

As well as the multi-scales, another original feature of the EIP is the Item Analysis section that lists the client's answers and scores to each question. This can be found at the back of the EIP Executive Report. One reason the items are listed in this report is that they are intended to be provocative discussion points about the scale construct. Listing the items is very valuable for personal development; it enables detailed discussion about the scales and the opportunity to explore the meaning of the client's answers, helping them to see exactly why they scored as they did. Ultimately the results of any self-report questionnaire only measure what the person meant by their responses to the questions, which can only be discussed if the respondent has access to their answers. The client is the expert on themselves, and is therefore best placed to interpret their own scores and answers, guided and supported by the coach. All too often ownership is taken away from the client and the coach is seen as the expert with the answers. This is comparable to the traditional medical model where the doctor diagnoses and prescribes, effectively disempowering the patient. Having the items available to the client gives them ownership of their report, allows them to understand and give their own interpretation of their responses, and so encourages greater self-responsibility for their development. In this way, the coach models emotionally intelligent Interdependence (scale 15).

6.3.3 The EIP framework and matrices

A Summary Profile appears at the back of the Executive Report but also exists as a separate report in itself (the Development Summary Report). It shows the EIP framework which is colour coded as red, amber, or green to give a quick visual representation of the scores in each of the six parts of the framework. The six parts are made up of three separate sections or pairs that represent each level of the EIP framework: Attitude, Feeling, and Behaviour.

Each of these levels are also shown as a 2x2 matrix with a blue ball indicating where the person scored in comparison to the norm group selected. These matrices are explained in detail in Chapter Four and provide the coach with a useful additional perspective. Important questions for the coach to ask their client are:

— "What percentage of time do you spend in each of the four quadrants?"

— "What causes you to fall out of the Ideal (top right) quadrant into each of the other three?"

— "How do you move back to the Ideal quadrant once you have dropped out of it?"

— "What feelings (and what behaviours) are associated with being in each quadrant for you?"

The final page of the Summary Profile includes three development points, based on the individual's three lowest scale scores, and three strengths based on their three highest scale scores. This page may be used separately as a brief summary and is also available as a separate profile called the Snapshot Report. This report is ideal to use when working with groups or if there is limited time for individual coaching.

6.4   Exploring the EIP with a client

Having prepared an analysis and interpretation of the EIP, the coach is ready to begin the coaching session. There are several different ways in which to reveal the EIP scores and results to the client, each having their own merits and drawbacks. One method is to give the report to the client and allow them time to read it for a while. The report can be quite provocative and sometimes gets a strong reaction. A benefit of this is that it can provoke discussion and the individual inevitably has questions to direct the process. The potential downsides are: the client may misunderstand the information, they may only focus on the highest and lowest scores, or they could be swamped by too much information. An experienced coach however, can answer questions confidently and reassure the client.

A more structured approach is to address scale sections in turn: the Attitude scales, followed by the Awareness scales, then the Self Management scales, and finally the Relationship Management scales. This allows the coach to gradually build the client's understanding of each section and is less likely to overwhelm the client. This process works particularly well when working with groups. It may involve covering a section such as Self Management in one day, and having the group complete a range of activities specifically for developing these scales.

A third approach to presenting the profile asks the client firstly to self-rate against each of the scales before providing them with feedback on how they scored on the EIP. This provides an interesting comparison between their general self-perception and their actual EIP scores. The Exploration Guide produced by JCA Global is specifically designed for this purpose, taking the client through stages of activity, to make the process more experiential than intellectual.

A fourth approach, if the client is less interested in reviewing single scales, is to look at the big picture. This can be done by exploring the EIP framework in the Summary Profile section. Each coach will find a way that works best for them, and their approach can be adapted to suit their client, which may be any variation of the above. Whichever approach is taken, there are six recommended steps that apply to them all, these are described in Section 6.4.1 which follows.

6.4.1 Six steps of exploration

The feedback process is referred to as an 'exploration' rather than 'feedback' as this more clearly reflects the nature of the process which is a joint exploratory discussion. This process has been split into six steps and provides the coach with a useful structure for exploration. In practice these steps may be adapted or taken in a different order. There is much to be said for going with the flow and energy of the client.

Step One — Agree the purpose and contract

It is important early on to agree a contract with the client, including: What does the client wants from the process? Who will see their information? What is the role of the coach? And how long will the process take? From the outset the skilled coach will approach the coaching session with an emotionally intelligent mindset of high Self Regard and high Regard for Others. This is another reason why the process is described as an exploration rather than feedback. Some traditional ways of using personality questionnaires have been from a more judgmental position, where the coach is seen as the expert, giving feedback and interpreting the client's results for them. The exploration process assumes that the individual is the expert on themselves and the coach invites the client to explain and interpret their results. When using the EIP, it is helpful if the client can see what answers they gave to each question and what scales each question relates to. Only the individual knows why they answered the question as they did and what they meant by this. The role of the coach is to ask the questions that will help the individual make sense of the information in relation to their own life.

Step Two — Build rapport and gather information

Building a good rapport early on is essential as this will help define the level and quality of communication the coach has with the client. As the discussion progresses, a skilled coach will gradually help their client to reflect more deeply, starting with their behaviour, then their thoughts, their feelings, and finally their deeper attitudes. It is often easier for the client to start by talking about their present situation on a topic they can easily relate to and feel comfortable sharing. For example, "What you are doing currently in your job?", and then to track backwards, "How did you come to be doing that?" The conversation can then drift into discussing their behaviours: "What did you enjoy doing and how did you do that?" As the client becomes more relaxed and in touch with their thoughts and feelings, the coach can go deeper and ask them to share their feelings, attitudes, and motivation: "How were you feeling at that moment?"; "What was going through your mind?"; and "Why was that important to you?"

While building rapport, the coach can observe and notice the client's behaviour and interactions with them. It may be useful to feed this back to them: "I notice your whole body became tense when you were describing this." However, be careful not to make them feel uncomfortable or self-conscious. Building rapport also allows background information to be gathered on the client that will help to understand their circumstances and place their objectives for the session in context: "Tell me more about why you find it difficult managing your new team?" This may be drawn upon and referred to when exploring their EIP scores: "Do you see a link between your low score on Connecting with Others and the issue you described earlier with your team?" A word of warning: building rapport can easily move into Step Four (exploration) in which case it may be appropriate to suggest a pause to introduce the EIP (Step Three) before exploring the EIP scales with the client.

Step Three — Explain the EIP Report

It is important to give the client an understanding of Emotional Intelligence early on in the process. As with most things, this is best explained simply without going into too much detail: "Have you come across the term Emotional Intelligence before?" and "What does it mean to you?" Refer them to the EIP framework: "This is JCA Global's model of EI which looks at how you manage your own behaviour (the left column) and your relationships (the right column). You will see that it is separated into three levels, the deepest level which is your attitude towards yourself and others, the middle level which is your own self-awareness and your awareness of others' feelings, and the top level which is related to your behaviour and what you actually do. Self Management includes things like coping with setbacks, motivating yourself, and adapting to change. Relationship Management looks at areas such as trusting people, managing conflict and working as part of a team." It can be useful at this stage to refer to examples from the client's organisational competencies if you have access to them, so they can see the clear relevance of EI to their work: "Relationship Management relates to your work competencies such as team working, communicating effectively, and influencing others."

The client may wish to discuss some aspects of the EIP framework further, such as how the arrows connect to the different aspects of EI. Again, be prepared with a practical example, and point to the relevant boxes: "Regard for Others (bottom right) underpins all of the Interpersonal scales. For example, if you have a negative and critical attitude towards others, then you may be less open to hearing what they have to say, so are less aware of others (middle right). This may be because you have already formed your opinion of them, which may make it more difficult for you to trust and get along with people, which will therefore lower your Relationship Management (top right)."

Before moving on to explore the results, it is important to emphasise and reiterate throughout that all aspects of EI are changeable and can be developed. Emphasise too that EI is not one thing: people are likely to be stronger in some areas than in others. Also, explain that the EIP is a self-report questionnaire; it is only one source of feedback and therefore open to error.

At this point the coach may choose to explain how the EIP is scored using the norm comparison group and Stens (alternatively they may wait until discussing the first scale). Sten scores may broadly be divided as follows: 1-2 (well below average), 3-4 (below average), 5-6 (average), 7-8 (above average), 9-10 (well above average), with 'average' referring to the mid-point of the norm group being applied. An example would be: "We have compared your answers to the answers from a large sample of senior managers. How your answers compare is represented on a scale from one to ten. Overall you rated yourself slightly lower (a Sten score of four) than the comparison group rated themselves on this scale." It is important to rehearse this explanation as it can easily become confusing and cause the client to lose confidence in the process or their coach. It is also helpful to have a reasonable understanding of how Sten scores are calculated should clients wish to know these details (see Chapter Three; 3.3.2).

The coach may continue their explanation: "If you scored lower than the comparison group there are three possible reasons. One, you are lower than other senior managers in this scale, two, that you under-rated yourself in this area, or three, that most senior managers tend to over-rate themselves in this area. This is what we will now explore."

Another area that requires explanation is the Relationship Management scales or multi-scales, as these are less familiar to people than linear scales: "It is possible to have too much as well as too little on these scales. For example, with Trust, people can be Mistrusting and Over Trusting, but the ideal is to be in the middle – Carefully Trusting. This is why we measure this scale in three parts. The ideal is to score high on the green bars and low on the red bars. The overall score is summarised by the blue bar on top. A high blue score indicates you may have the right balance of Trust. Think of the ideal like a see-saw – you want to keep it in balance and avoid swinging from one extreme to the other."

Step Four — Explore the EIP Report with the client

Many of the coaching skills required for exploring the EIP are covered later in this chapter. However, a few essential aspects include:

— Be client led and ask questions, such as: "Which scales are of interest to you?"; "What does this mean to you?"; "How is this scale relevant?"; "What would you like to explore next?"

— Relate scales and results to the client's circumstances

— Look for scale patterns and themes to draw out key points

— Test out hypotheses: "Could this mean that you ...?"

— Validate the accuracy of their scores through discussion

— Avoid getting too focused on the scores or data and bring the conversation back to the client

— Keep focused on their objectives and keep it relevant

— Allow time for reflection. Silence is often processing time, so don't be afraid of it

— Include activities within the process such as drawing a 'life-line' of key events

— Open up exploration at this stage rather than seeking solutions

— Allow them to interpret their results; remember it is an exploration, not feedback

— Draw upon all relevant aspects of the report, such as the Item Analysis, the Attitude Matrix and Narrative interpretations

The exploration phase is about opening up the discussion to consider all the information, discuss hypotheses and explore possibilities. The aim is to draw out meaning from the EIP in terms of scale patterns and insights that relate to the client's life. This may also involve exploring themes in more depth such as the client's thoughts, feelings and attitudes. For example, a client may identify a pattern of being emotionally closed and inhibited, reflected in scale 13 (Over Controlled), which may make it more difficult for them to connect with others (scale 9) and people may find them more difficult to read (Authenticity; scale 10). Further discussion may reveal that they are inhibited because they feel anxious around people they do not know well, that they think people are not interested in them, or they may think, "It is better to be quiet than to risk making a fool of myself."

Overall, it is important to explore the client's circumstances in sufficient breadth and depth before progressing to Step Five of setting goals and turning 'exploration' into 'action'.

Step Five — Set personal development goals

Personal development coaching is about making changes that helps the individual improve and develop in what they do. Some coaches place little emphasis on setting goals, assuming it to be an automatic consequence of the exploration phase. Unfortunately, unless the client leaves the coaching session with a clear commitment for action, it is likely they will return to their day-to-day habits and put the coaching session to the back of their mind.

Step Five moves the client from the Feeling (Awareness) part of the EIP framework into the Behaviour (Management) part. EI is sometimes criticised for being too 'soft' when, in fact, EI is really about doing the 'hard stuff' as it involves making difficult changes. There are perhaps two main reasons why people do not carry out their development goals: the first is that they do not truly want the chosen goals for themselves; and the second is that the goals are too large or unsustainable. Once back in their routine habits of daily life, a person's motivation to carry out their development actions can soon wane. As such, it is essential to set objectives that are focused, practical, and easily achieved. The development goals must also be something the person is motivated to do for themselves.

Following the exploration phase, it is a good idea to invite the client to write down all of their thoughts and reflections from the exploration in enough detail to act as a reminder should they come to revisit them in the future. They can then identify from this what they want to develop. The next step is to prepare the client with an action plan that they will implement after completion of the coaching session to facilitate their personal development. The following activity has been found to work very well for this:

The 21-day Habit Change exercise

A Select one aspect or scale from the EIP that interests you right now.
Example: "Conflict Handling – being too Passive".

B Describe a behaviour you wish to change.
"Agreeing to do things for people that I don't have time for and don't want to do".

C Describe what the pay-offs and drawbacks of this behaviour are.
Pay-offs – "People seem to like me, and I avoid conflict."
Drawbacks – "I am overworked; I sometimes let people down and then I feel bad about myself."

D Describe a behaviour you would like to do instead?
"To be more assertive and say 'no' to people when I feel it's appropriate."

E What would be the pay-offs and drawbacks of this?
Pay-offs – "I would get more work done and I would get more respect from people."
Drawbacks – "People may not like me and I may be seen as aggressive or unco-operative."

F Write down one specific action you can take by completing the following phrase:
"Every day for the next 21 days I will …"
"Say to people 'Can you give me a moment to think about that?', when they ask me to do something."

There are several aspects to this exercise that can help make it successful. It is important to ask the client to select something that interests them right now, because this is something they will have energy for. Also start with a broad area, such as Conflict Handling which means the specific behaviour they choose to change relates to and affects the whole aspect of Conflict Handling. Asking about the client's 'pay-offs' and 'drawbacks' helps to check how much they want to make the change and explores any other barriers to them making this change. It may be necessary at this stage to change a deeper blocker first. For example, if someone wants to be more Assertive but doesn't feel they have the confidence (Personal Power) to do this, then building their confidence could become their first goal.

The client's commitment should be short and easy for them to implement. The reason for a 21-day commitment is that habits are created mostly through repetition; research has shown that it takes 21 days to start forming habits[1] and up to 66 days for these to become embedded as new neural networks.[2] It also helps if the client is encouraged to declare their commitment (tell people about it) as other people may support them and create more of an incentive for them to follow it through. Finally, it helps to find a person who will act as a 'buddy' and check that they are doing their commitment on a daily basis. The buddy's role is mainly to get the client 'back on the wagon' if they should lapse. Giving up after a setback is one of the most common reasons for people not making an initial change into an enduring habit. The very action of the client successfully making one single change will provide considerable reinforcement to them that they have the capacity to change, and by adopting this attitude (EI Attitude 7; Change is possible) they will find it easier to make changes in the future.

Another benefit of the behavioural habit change technique is that it also helps change the client's underlying attitude. It has already been explained how attitude change leads to behaviour change (see Chapter One; 1.5) but the reverse can also be true, through a concept originally defined by Festinger as cognitive dissonance.[3] Behaving in a way that contradicts a person's attitude creates a state of anxiety (dissonance) compelling them to either change their behaviour to be consistent with their attitude or change their attitude to be consistent with their new behaviour. This explains why it can be quite uncomfortable to change a behavioural habit and why doing so requires prolonged repetition. Continually reinforcing a specific behaviour that is incongruent with their attitudes creates doubt and uncertainty in the emotional (limbic) brain, opening up their attitudes to question from the higher thinking brain so that new attitudes may be formed. (Refer to Chapter Eight; 8.3 for suggestions on how to change attitudes.)

Step Six — Close the session

Having advised the client of the timeframe at the start of the session, it is helpful to let them know when they are approaching the end. Allow them time to wind down gradually, rather than having a sudden finish. Check if there is anything they would like to pick up on or ask. If there is a lot to discuss, plan how this could be carried forward in a follow up meeting. Ask them how, in summary, they feel about the process. Confirm the agreed actions they are going to take between now and the next meeting and how these relate to their objectives. Then confirm arrangements for the next meeting and how they can contact you, their coach, if they have any concerns or questions. Remind them of what happens to the results and about confidentiality. Finally, close with a positive and encouraging comment, such as, "I think you made some excellent progress today in identifying your priorities and setting yourself a clear objective."

The six steps of exploration

Prepare	Produce the correct report
	Examine the data and generate hypotheses
	Review the development suggestions in the EIP
1 **Agree the contract**	Make introductions
	Confirm the time frame
	Agree the process
	Check what the client wants to achieve from the session
	Explain this is a two-way process, an exploration not feedback
	Confirm aspects of confidentiality
2 **Build rapport**	Discuss their circumstances and relevant context
	Start with easy opening questions (about their situation and their work)
	Listen and be aware of their body language
	Use appropriate follow-on questions (about their thoughts, feelings, and attitudes)
	Review their objectives
3 **Explain the EIP**	Explain why the EIP is being used, and the purpose of the report selected
	Explain Emotional Intelligence (the EIP framework)
	Describe the exploration process
	Explain scoring, measurement error, multi-scales, and norms
	Explain that EI is developable
4 **Explore the EIP**	Explore the client's interpretations and reactions
	Provide guidance on interpretation
	Challenge and explore
	Clearly explain the scale meanings
	Refer to specific items
	Work at a client-led pace and structure
	Look for themes and patterns within the report scores

5	Set goals	Allow time for reflection (have them record this)
		Agree specific goals
		Create a personal development plan
		Identify one area where they will take action
6	Close	Summarise outcomes
		Discuss any final questions
		Agree the next steps
		Confirm confidentiality
		Confirm contact details and the coach's availability
		Leave them with a positive message

6.4.2 Discussing the relative difference in high and low scores

Unlike personality measures, the EIP is evaluative, presenting the client with scores that represent higher (better) or lower (less effective) levels of EI. Although having a 'score' may be a helpful benchmark for individuals, scores should only be used as indicators to provoke useful conversation for the benefit of the client. It is essential that the coach and client both remember that EI is changeable and the scores represent a person's self-perception only.

The EIP is a normative-based instrument as people are generally interested in how they compare with others. It is important to reassure the individual early on about norm-based scores, for example: "People often become concerned by low scores, but remember that they reflect your own answers to the questionnaire (which you can review on the Item Analysis section of the report). Also the group that you have been compared against is already at a high level (managers/leaders), so a scale score of five may become a seven and could actually be quite high if you had been compared to the general population."

An alternative to using the scores normatively is to compare the relative scores between scales, as done in the Snapshot Report. It can be more relevant and useful to compare the relative higher and lower scores for someone, regardless of how they compare to the norm group. A person may score low on all scales compared to the norm group, but relative to themselves, some of the scales will be higher than other scales. If the purpose of the EIP is for personal development and identifying key areas to work on, then the most relevant benchmark for any individual is themselves.

Another reason for recommending a 'self' comparison is that people have their own perception and benchmark for each question they answer. If a person has particularly high standards for themselves and tends to mix with people who do the same, then they are likely to be tougher on themselves in responding to the questionnaire. This is something the coach should consider when discussing the client's scores: does the client over-rate or under-rate themselves? One factor that determines whether people rate themselves more positively or negatively is their level or stage of personal development.[4]

Stage One	Unconscious incompetence (the client is unaware of what they do not know)
Stage Two	Conscious incompetence (the client becomes aware of what they do not know)
Stage Three	Conscious competence (the client has learned something new)
Stage Four	Unconscious competence (the new learning has become automatic and habitual)

People who are at Stage One are more likely to over-rate themselves. They may lack Self Awareness and self-knowledge, and possibly come from a Critical life position (I'm OK, You are Not OK), tending to blame others rather than accept self-responsibility.

Getting people to Stage Two can require considerable input from the coach through different means such as 360 feedback and is often met with resistance from the client. As the client moves through the stages, they typically take on more responsibility for their own development and the coach has less input. Sometimes people who have completed the EIP questionnaire rate themselves lower the second time around because, through their coaching, they have become more aware of what they want to develop in themselves. One reason for asking people to practise self-reflection before completing the EIP is to move their level of awareness from Stage One up to Stage Two. This is particularly important for people who do not engage in much self-reflection (scale 16). These people are more likely to over-rate themselves on the EIP and may not develop greatly until they are compelled to do so. Stage Two may be accompanied by a reduction in self-confidence as the individual drops some of their defences which may have served to protect them from uncomfortable feelings. This drop in confidence is only temporary, as in Stage Three the individual will develop more effective, non-defensive behaviours to replace them.

Once the client implements their learning and makes changes (competence Stages Three and Four) then they will usually start to rate themselves higher again on the EIP, as there is now a sense that they are achieving the development goals they set for themselves. In other words, a person scoring low may be at the start of their current development journey (conscious incompetence) and a person scoring high may be at the end of that phase in their development journey (unconscious competence). People may move up as well as down on their EIP scores as they progress through Stages One to Four and repeat this each time they move on to a higher level of awareness in their personal development.

In practice, the stages continue indefinitely as Stage Four is followed immediately by Stage One, but at a higher level. This may be explained to the client as follows: "Personal development is an ongoing journey where ever-increasing levels may be attained. Some highly emotionally intelligent people score themselves quite low on the EIP questionnaire because they set themselves a high standard they wish to achieve. Equally, scoring high doesn't mean a person has nothing more to develop, just that they have neared the end of this phase in their journey and will soon be ready for the next phase. The next phase will begin when they become aware of other things that they want to develop and consequently their scores may drop again on the scales. Therefore, the real benchmark for personal development is oneself. Think of scale scores as an 'emotional barometer', scores may move up and down depending on where a person is on their journey of personal development."

Overall, it is important that the coach considers the client's level of personal development (Stages One to Four) and encourages them to look at their relative scores in addition to their normative scores.

6.4.3 Handling client resistance

The EIP scale scores, interpretation, and implications can be challenging for a client to understand and explain, and may sometimes elicit some resistance. There are several ways the coach can make the EIP results more manageable and less threatening.

— **Has rapport been established?** Without this it is very difficult to have an open and non-defensive conversation. Equally, the coach needs to be non-defensive and model EI behaviour and attitudes.

— **Have the objectives and purpose been agreed?** Be sure the client wants to explore the report and that their general questions or concerns have been discussed. It may be that they are very cynical towards psychometric testing. For instance, they may have had a negative experience of receiving test feedback or were not selected for a job that applied psychometric assessment of some kind.

— **Do they understand the limitations of the questionnaire?** The EIP is a self-report questionnaire and is based on their self-perception only. As with all forms of measurement, there is room for error. If they want to understand a score, refer them to their Item Analysis; they can then judge for themselves what they meant by their answers.

— **Do they understand how the EIP is scored?** Remind them that the EIP is norm referenced and tell them which norm group was used in generating their report.

— **Discuss their implicit benchmark.** When answering the EIP questions some people have a high internal benchmark, particularly if they have low Self Regard, a 'Be Perfect' driver, or if they have engaged in a significant amount of personal development. As such, it is often more useful to consider their relative higher and lower scores rather than to look at how they compared to a norm group.

— **Help them learn how to use the reports.** Explain that the EIP results should not be considered in isolation but in combination with all other forms of feedback they have had. Encourage them to look at strengths as well as development areas.

— **Explain that the development of EI is a continuous journey.** As self-awareness increases so too does the client's recognition of their strengths and development areas.

People's reactions to the EIP Report can be informative to the coach. Some people will score high but be self-critical and disappointed in themselves. Others will score low and be curious, positive, and engaged in their learning. The scores are there to create the conversation and to raise awareness, they are not what define a person or their performance.

6.5   Applying the EIP in groups

The EIP is mainly applied through one-to-one coaching. Alternatively, it may be used as part of a group workshop for EI development. An advantage of using the EIP within a group is that individuals can practise developing their EI in pairs or small groups and they can co-coach and support one another while in a safe learning environment. Facilitating a group EI workshop is outside the realms of this book and requires expertise in group facilitation. However, below is some general guidance on delivering the EIP within a group setting.

At the outset, before releasing the EIP results, it is important to create an open atmosphere within the group where individuals are willing to communicate honestly and take responsibility for their own development. As with individual feedback, the facilitator should give a general explanation of EI, describe how the scales are scored and how to interpret the report. To make group feedback manageable and to structure the workshop process, it is recommended to explore the EIP scales by sections based on the EIP framework (Awareness scales, Self Management scales, Relationship Management scales, and Attitude scales). For each section, provide practical and relevant activities to help individuals process the information and set appropriate actions for their development. It is generally recommended to explore the Attitude scales later in the process as these are deeper constructs and easier to put into context having explored the other scales. It is advisable to offer individuals the opportunity for a one-to-one conversation about their profile with the facilitator, such as at the end of the workshop or by including a second facilitator. In general, to explore the EIP Executive Reports in a group setting (of up to ten people), run appropriate activities, and identify development actions, would take a minimum of two days.

A lighter option to using the full Executive Report with a group is to use the Snapshot Report. This report identifies someone's highest and lowest three EIP scales but does not include Sten scores, making it ideal to use as a group introduction to EI.

6.6 Applying the EIP with other products

The EIP is not a panacea but a tool and model that supports personal development. EI is one part in the process of personal development and is sandwiched between personality and behavioural competence. As described in Chapter One, EI is what turns personality and potential into effective performance.

It therefore makes sense to measure both the input to EI (personality) and the output from EI (behavioural competence). The JCA Global Hub provides an integrated platform for measuring all three areas via diagnostic questionnaires:

— **Personality Type Profile:**[5] Helps the individual understand their personality and potential. An indicator of 16 personality types derived from Jungian type theory.[6]

— **Emotional Intelligence Profile (EIP):** Enables the individual to understand how well they manage their personality and potential, and what to do to improve this. Links between personality type and the EIP may be found in reference seven.[7]

— **Behaviours 360:** Shows how effectively the individual is performing in the workplace (as measured by the organisation's behavioural competencies).

The key ingredient for turning personality into effective behaviour is Emotional Intelligence. Consider the metaphor of a jet engine (Emotional Intelligence) that sucks in air (personality) turning this into power and performance (effective behaviour). This can be presented by the formula:

PERSONALITY + EI = PERFORMANCE

In summary, the suite of tools measures how effectively a person manages their personality to sustain effective behaviour and performance in the workplace. Where possible, it is recommended that the coach uses a combination of these three questionnaires to help their client obtain maximum benefit from their coaching. The coach may first choose to explore the feedback from the Behaviours 360 Questionnaire (behavioural competencies), as this will help the client set their objectives, define what is going well and what they would like to improve. The Personality Type Profile may then be used to help the client understand how their typical style and characteristics influence their behaviour and performance in the workplace. At this stage the client may be seeking more insight into why they behave in this way (their feelings, thoughts, and attitudes that drive their behaviour) and what they can do to develop this, as measured by the EIP.

It is not unusual for clients to complete the Behaviours 360 Questionnaire again at a later date, to measure what impact the coaching has had on their behaviour and performance. It is also recommended that they repeat the EIP at a later date as this will identify how their EI has developed and which aspects of EI may be helping or hindering their development. It is less common practice to repeat the Personality Type Profile, as personality type is unlikely to change over time.

6.6.1 Exploring the Emotional Intelligence Profile 360 (EIP360)

One further product that is often used in combination with the EIP is the EIP360. This is shorter than the EIP and has fewer items, measuring only the six parts of the EIP framework rather than the 16 EIP scales. It would be unreasonable to expect other people to complete the whole EIP questionnaire on someone else, partly because of the time required to complete it and also because of the detailed knowledge of the other person necessary for answering some of the items. By using the EIP360 in combination with the EIP, the client can make a direct comparison between their self-perception and others' perceptions of them on the EIP framework, which can be extremely valuable in supporting their ongoing development.

The EIP360 can be used separately or in addition to the EIP and is especially useful for raising someone's self-awareness. If a person lacks self-awareness, then their self-reported answers to the EIP may be less accurate. Also, feedback from others is particularly important on scales such as Authenticity (the degree to which you tend to be reliable, consistent, and known to others) which may be more accurately measured by others rather than by the individual themselves. Using 360 feedback therefore provides an additional source of evidence to confirm or challenge one's self-perception.

All feedback can be useful in providing different perspectives. There is sometimes a danger of assuming psychometric questionnaire data is more valid than other sources of feedback. Psychometric measures add particular value in that they provide objectivity, but each approach is of value for different reasons. Applying several types of feedback is recommended for coaching, as this helps to identify themes, challenge assumptions, and avoid over-reliance on one set of data. Alternative sources of feedback may include:

— Asking people for immediate feedback
— Completing standardised questionnaires
— Visualisation or guided imagery activities
— Role-play scenarios
— A person's general self-perception
— Observing and noticing one's behaviour and feelings
— Noticing other people's reactions to oneself

— Reflecting on one's experiences

— Assessment style activities

The EIP360 is designed to gather information quickly from several respondents. This is both quantitative (from the scales) and qualitative (from people's comments). Most approaches to 360s place emphasis on keeping results anonymous to encourage people to give their honest opinions. Unfortunately, this also leads to the recipient spending time trying to work out who said what about them. The ideal goal of 360 feedback is to achieve a level of openness where individuals or groups can sit face to face and share their thoughts, feelings, wants, and concerns with each other in a compassionate and non-defensive manner. However, a challenge may occur with 360 feedback when the feedback does not match one's own self-perception. There are several possible reasons for this, either due to the individual (self) or their raters (others).

Why 360 scores don't match self-perceptions

SELF	OTHERS
The individual over-rates themselves	The questionnaire is inaccurate
The individual under-rates themselves	The rater has a personal agenda
The individual does not know themselves well	Others over-rate the individual or idolise them
The individual is closed and difficult to read	Others under-rate the individual or do not like them
The individual presents a false image of themselves	Others do not know the individual very well

Table 6.1

If the client disagrees with the feedback or does not recognise it, they may be asked to consider the possibility that 1% of the feedback may be true, as a way of encouraging them to consider it rather than discount it entirely. Although feedback from others can be uncomfortable, exploring the 360 profiles follows the same principles as the EIP.

— Before sharing the 360 data with the client, check the results for any potentially difficult feedback (such as where they were rated lower by others than they rate themselves, or for any harsh and negative comments).

— If using the EIP and the EIP360 together, look at whether the results are consistent or different.

— Decide on what order the feedback will be given. Providing 360 feedback first usually helps the client identify their development goals, while the EIP helps them understand how to develop them.

— When examining the results, look first at the overall scale difference between the client's responses and the rater's responses, and where the client rated themselves higher or lower than others did.

— Then consider differences between groups of raters: line manager, peers, and their direct reports. The EIP360 Report also highlights items with the greatest difference including where they rated themselves higher than others rated them (blind spots), and where they rated themselves lower than others rated them (hidden potential).

Typically, individuals have a tendency to focus on negative feedback, but it is important to encourage them to balance this with positive feedback and their 'hidden potential'. The 360 Report also shows the exact rating given by each rater on each item should they choose to explore the spread of responses. For example, do all raters score them the same, or is there wide variation? If there is a wide range of ratings, then it could be that the individual gives a different impression to different people and is inconsistent. Alternatively, if the scores tend to cluster, this may suggest consistency and stability across different situations and colleagues. For many people, the most valuable part of the 360 Report are the qualitative comments, which provides a personal insight in narrative form from the raters as to why they gave the scores they did on the scales.

In summary, exploring the EIP360 is a similar process to using the EIP in helping the client to understand the scale meanings, look for patterns in the data, identify practical development actions, and focus on specific strengths that they can exploit.

6.7 Effective coaching skills when using the EIP

Following the recommended steps when using the EIP will help structure the coaching session. Success also depends upon the skills of the coach and the commitment of the client to make these changes for themselves. There are four key ingredients to make coaching with the EIP successful. These are written in ascending order of importance, as each element is dependent upon the next one if it is to achieve the ultimate outcome of helping the client develop their EI.

1   **Application of the EIP Report:** The EIP Report and results should be seen as only the start of the process, to provoke thinking and discussion rather than an end in itself.

2   **Knowledge of the coach:** The EIP results are only useful if the coach is fluent in EI knowledge. The effective coach has a sound understanding of the theory behind the EIP results, the EIP framework, the EIP scales, and how to develop EI.

3   **Skills of the coach:** Behind an in-depth knowledge of the EIP sits the skills of the coach in building rapport, engaging the client, asking helpful questions, challenging appropriately, and creating solutions.

4   **Client commitment to developing their EI:** All the above are resources to facilitate change in the client. Change in the client may be defined in terms of how the client feels and acts as a consequence of the coaching process. It is ultimately the client's responsibility to commit to making any changes happen within their lives.

So far, this chapter has examined the first two of these points, enabling the coach to explore and interpret the EIP with their client. The rest of this chapter provides a concise overview of some essential coaching skills required when working with a client using the EIP (point three). This is followed in Chapter Eight by a discussion on how to develop EI in oneself and others (point four).

Be an emotionally intelligent coach: Before helping others to develop their EI, it is of vital importance that the coach has engaged in and developed their own EI to a high standard. All scales on the EIP are important to being an effective and emotionally intelligent coach. In particular, having an attitude of high Self Regard and Regard for Others underpins and filters through to all other scales.

Relevance of the EIP scales to coaching

SCALE	RELEVANCE TO BEING A COACH
1 Self Regard	Having self-belief as a coach and not being defensive
2 Regard for Others	Have compassion for and a desire to help the client develop
3 Self Awareness	Self-monitor feelings so as to manage one's behaviour with the client
4 Awareness of Others	Notice and pay attention to the client's needs and feelings
5 Emotional Resilience	Persevere when facing setbacks with the client
6 Personal Power	Have and demonstrate confidence in the coaching process
7 Goal Directedness	Keep the coaching and the client focused on their objectives
8 Flexibility	Adapt to the needs of the client and be willing to try different approaches
9 Connecting with Others	Build rapport and engage with the client

Table 6.2

SCALE	RELEVANCE TO BEING A COACH
10 Authenticity	Be able to separate oneself from the client's issues and have a set of inner guiding principles
11 Trust	Build a trusting relationship with the client, but also be open to challenging them appropriately
12 Balanced Outlook	Focus on positive outcomes and do not be drawn into negative thinking
13 Emotional Expression and Control	Demonstrate interest and compassion without being overly drawn into the client's emotions
14 Conflict Handling	Question, challenge, and debate with clients in a calm and respectful manner
15 Interdependence	Work in partnership with the client while retaining an appropriate degree of separation
16 Reflective Learning	Continually develop as a coach and do not to become complacent

It is also important for the coach to develop their self-knowledge, so they become aware of their own needs and do not use the coaching session as a means of getting their own needs met for say, attention or status. For example, a coach with the 'rescuer' defence may invent or exaggerate client problems, want to be seen as providing the 'cure' and create client dependence on them. Taken to an extreme they could fall into the realm of becoming manipulators, or self-appointed 'gurus'.

Be a self-aware coach: Exploration of the EIP is a two-way process between the coach and the client. The dynamics of this interaction depends upon both personalities and, despite following a well-prepared approach, some pairings will work more smoothly than others. It is important for the coach to be aware of their own preferences and habits and the type of clients they find more difficult to work with. Do they feel intimidated by certain people? Do they prefer coaching people of a certain age or gender? The coach should recognise how they respond to these clients: Do they become too self-conscious and stop attending to what the client is saying? Do they try to rush the process? Do they try to assert too much control or avoid challenging the client? As a general rule it is recommended that the coach has experienced personal development at least to the level at which they are coaching their client. The coach should be experienced and comfortable in discussing their own feelings, if they are to ask clients to do the same; and as they are helping the client to change their habits then they should have practised habit change themselves. This does not mean that the coach needs to be an expert in everything they are coaching, such as being an effective leader, but having relevant experience is valuable and adds credibility.

Prepare fully: A primary skill for effective coaching is to prepare before meeting the client. This helps the coach organise their time, anticipate any challenges, and keep focused on the client rather than thinking about what they will be doing next. This is particularly important for the less experienced coach or if they have had less practise with the EIP. Preparation may include aspects such as:

— Reviewing the client's profile

— Preparing some questions to ask

— Having a clear structure to follow

— Having a range of activities that they are confident at using and know tend to work well

— Having a range of useful references for the client's development

— Also refer to Section 6.1 on How to prepare ...

A caveat to good preparation is not to fall into the trap of becoming over-rehearsed or so familiar with a routine that the coach stops paying attention to the person in front of them and their specific needs. The coach must be sure to work within the client's frame of reference, rather than expecting them to fit within their expectations, theories, or the EIP framework.

Build rapport: There are various factors that makes the coaching experience more natural, relaxed, and productive. One of these is building rapport with the client. Rapport exists between two people when they are both synchronised in their communication and there is a natural ebb and flow in conversation. This is usually recognisable in that both people automatically adopt similar behaviours, such as posture, breathing, and tone of voice. It is possible to induce rapport more quickly by adopting similar actions to the other person, known as 'matching and mirroring'. A natural benefit in gaining rapport is that it lowers people's arousal level, as the emotional brain can anticipate a person's actions and does not perceive them as a threat. Once in rapport, people are reluctant to break it and a skilled coach uses this to lead the client into a positive emotional state. The coach may prepare themselves before meeting with the client so as to feel relaxed and unhurried. This shows in their posture, voice, and breathing, which is automatically detected by the client. The coach can also observe the client's emotional state when they meet; if the client is anxious it may help for the coach to slow down and relax gradually, so as to allow the client to naturally relax with them.

Create an atmosphere for change: The rapport created by the coach will determine the atmosphere (the emotional state) of the coaching session. This can take a little while to instil, but once the client feels relaxed and has a positive and open mindset, then personal change tends to happen far more rapidly. An important element in creating an atmosphere for change is for the client to slow down and relax. This helps them to engage with their feelings and reduce the amount of mental distraction (self-talk). Simple ways to do this are:

— To agree from the outset the timings and process
— Turn off mobile phones
— Use a quiet and comfortable room with natural light and comfortable chairs
— Talk in a calm way and don't appear rushed
— Ideally be away from their office

Also, don't seek out solutions too soon as this tends to restrict how deeply the coach listens to their client and gets to understand their circumstances and underlying needs.

Listen at a deeper level: An essential element to coaching is effective listening, which may seem obvious but is difficult to do well. Most conversations between people involve a small amount of listening before the other person gives their opinion or shares something about themselves. A deeper level of listening involves the coach focusing their full attention on the talker, reflecting back what the person has said (possibly in a more positive way), asking for more information, clarifying questions, probing about their feelings, or simply allowing for silences. The challenge for the coach is to suspend any tendency to interpret and find immediate solutions, which would reduce their capacity for open and non-judgmental listening. Keeping an open mind and tolerating ambiguity allows for deeper intuitive insights to emerge, to hear patterns in what the client is saying, to understand their feelings better, and to notice subtleties such as what the client is not saying that may be important. By focusing attention on the client and their concerns, the unconscious brain sooner or later supplies the answers. Suspending judgment or at least being aware of inner self-talk is an advanced skill that requires continued practice by the coach.

Listen for underlying needs: Clients often present innumerable issues and problems which seem too many or insurmountable and it is all too easy to be drawn into a long discussion attempting to 'solve' each problem in turn. This approach is often futile, as each time a solution is presented, the client searches for reasons why they are right and entrenches their own negative thoughts. Rather than seeking to resolve each issue, the coach can listen to the client without forming judgments or answers. The longer the coach suspends their judgment, the more their intuition will identify common underlying patterns across the client's related issues. Beneath many apparent problems are basic human emotional needs that are not being met, such as the need for connection, autonomy, control, attention, meaning, and challenge (these are described further in

Chapter Eight; Table 8.2). Reflecting back the underlying need to the client, for example: "It sounds like you are presently experiencing a lack of control in your life", can help the client focus, simplify and get to the core essence of their issues.

Look for simple solutions first: It may be tempting for the coach to show off their psychological expertise to a client and demonstrate great insight and wisdom. However, complex problems do not necessarily require complex solutions. Sometimes they are best solved with simple practical approaches; small changes are easier to implement and can have a domino effect on other related problems. For example, a person may be suffering from low self-esteem due to a difficulty in forming relationships because they have never learned the basics of how to make small talk. Teaching them some simple ground rules of communication, such as remembering a person's name, to ask people open questions, and to listen to their response, could be far more effective than lengthy discussions about their childhood. On this point, it is important too that the coach is not drawn into areas beyond their level of expertise.

Notice the client's behaviour during coaching: Identifying areas for the client's development often becomes evident through observing the client's behaviour, language, and how they interact during coaching. For example: a client who has received feedback for being unreliable at work turns up late for the coaching session; a client who is not connecting with their team does not express their feelings during coaching; a client who at work has few clear personal goals constantly digresses in conversation during coaching; or a client who as a leader is struggling to gain the trust of colleagues uses critical and blaming language when discussing others. It is extremely powerful to make the client aware of this in a tactful and helpful manner: "I notice you used the word 'incompetent' several times to describe your colleague. How do you feel towards them?" This also provides clues as to the client's underpinning attitudes.

Be skilful in the use of language: Words are tools of the trade for a coach. Used knowingly, they can help the client access and use different parts of their brain. Asking the client, "What do you think?" prompts their left analytical brain, an important resource for problem solving. Asking them to use feeling words gets them to pay attention to their body and to self-observe. Using more abstract language tends to activate their imagination and the right brain, which processes information metaphorically. This can be a highly effective way of influencing the unconscious and deeper emotional parts of the brain that form a person's attitudes and drive much of their behaviour. The following suggestive statements engage the client's imagination to initiate positive and proactive thinking, feeling, and behaviour: "Can you imagine how it would be for you to feel more confident?"; "If you didn't have this concern how would your life be then?"; "I am wondering whether you will use this approach often or just occasionally?"; and "How do you feel now you are starting to relax?"

Avoid colluding with the client: As a coach there is a natural tendency to want to agree with and maintain harmony with the client. The job of the coach is not to be their friend but to help them move forward. This often requires pushing them outside of their comfort zone. The client is likely to want to spend their coaching time doing what they feel most comfortable doing, which is often the thing they least need to develop. If the client enjoys exploring their feelings deeply, then they may benefit more from taking action; if the client likes goal setting then they may benefit more from stepping back; if they are highly analytical and cognitive then they may learn more from noticing their feelings. Notice what the client prefers to discuss: do they focus mostly on the past and avoid discussing the future; or are they mostly looking ahead without learning from past experience?

The tendency to collude may come from the coach having similar preferences to the client, such as both preferring to explore ideas and not being very realistic, or both getting stuck on details and not considering the wider picture. It is entirely possible to have what feels like a very enjoyable dialogue because the coach and client both enjoy discussing the same thing, yet the client gains very little personal development.

Notice the client's resistance: Managing one's own behaviour as a coach is one side of the coin; the other side is getting the client to take responsibility for their own development. Clients may intentionally or unconsciously attempt to sabotage the coaching process and their own chances of success. This may be in practical ways, such as not completing the questionnaire, turning up late or being interrupted during coaching. If so, consider whether this is an aspect for the client's personal development. For example, does the client often let people down? Do they like to assert control? Are they very disorganised? Do they avoid feedback and self-reflection? Also be observant of any behaviours that distract from their personal development, such as:

— They may choose to debate the technical aspects of the questionnaire or the definition of the items. Giving them confidence in the tool is important but remind them that the purpose of coaching is to focus on them and avoid being drawn into long technical discussions. Refer them instead to the EIP Technical Manual[8] that they may read after the session.

— A client may be over-enthusiastic and keen to embrace everything the coach says; be careful not to be drawn into becoming their 'guru' or encouraging over dependence on you. If they do seem to be overly dependent, then reflect this observation back to them.

— Some clients are more difficult to open up and expect the coach to be the expert and do all the talking. This may be driven by a suspicion or fear of the process. It may be necessary to go back to rapport building and an explanation of the EIP. Also check if they have any concerns and re-contract the process if needed.

— Listen to the client's language for signs of not taking responsibility and reflect this back to them. Do they detach by saying "you" instead of "I" when talking about themselves? Do they focus externally and blame others, rather than looking at what they can do about it? Do they say things like "It's just the way I am", "I can't help it", or do they use vague or non-committal language such as "I will try", or "I suppose so"?

Tactfully push clients: Sometimes clients find it extremely difficult to identify anything that they want to change or develop as they rate themselves very highly on nearly all of the scales. This may be because they lack awareness, or they feel resistant to showing a weakness (a Be Strong or Be Perfect defence). Ask their permission to challenge them: "May I suggest something here?" (which they may like) and put these hypotheses to them. An alternative strategy for challenging them is to emphasise how highly they rated themselves but discuss how there is always room for improvement, as opposed to there being a 'weakness', and ask them how they could make even better use of their strengths and move from 'good' to 'great'. The important thing is for the client to experience the benefit of active self-development. If they are constantly making excuses or justifying themselves then push them to consider the possibility of some improvement; "If there was room for a 1% improvement, what would it be?" Look more carefully at the Item Analysis section – it is unlikely they 'Strongly agree' with every positive item and 'Strongly disagree' with every negative item. Also look at the scale scores, if they scored 'nine', ask them what a score of 'ten' would look like for them. Remind them that having a high score indicates they are near the end of this phase in their development journey, and are now ready for the next phase, and to set their benchmarks even higher.

Focus on solutions: The EIP is designed to identify what blocks a person from reaching their natural potential, which starts from the assumption that 'people have a natural propensity towards growth and health' (EI Attitude 8). From this premise, it is important that the coach focuses the client on what they can do to develop their EI, and does not get drawn into the unhealthy trap of continually discussing (and therefore unconsciously reinforcing) the client's issues, problems, weaknesses, difficulties, and challenges, etc. The coach may start by finding out what the client's inner resources are and how it is they have managed to cope so well despite these challenges. Ask questions that elicit their strengths and focus on solutions, such as: "Which scales are your relative strengths?"; "What would make this a worthwhile session for you?"; "How have you coped with these problems?"; "How did you manage before this happened?"; "Talk me through this step by step"; "Describe to me the future you want to create"; "How will you know when you have it?" Using 'how' rather than 'why' questions tends to be more constructive, asking about the future rather than the past is more progressive, and talking about 'what is' rather than 'what is not' is more positive.

Psychology often encourages people to unpick problems and understand the reasons 'why'. Intellectually this may be interesting but understanding the causes does not necessarily enable people to change. Knowing what works and putting this into practice does however, make a difference. For example, keeping a solutions diary instead of a problems diary, doing something different instead of repeating the same mistake, and taking action instead of putting up with things, will lead to more successful outcomes.

Set realistic expectations: An important skill for being an effective coach is to set the correct level of expectation: too much and the individual may fail and become disheartened; too little and they may become bored and underperform. There is an optimal level of expectation and motivation described by Csikszentihalyi as 'flow'.[9] This is when a person feels 'at one' with their experience, being challenged but not stressed in working towards their goal, allowing them to meet or slightly exceed their expectations (releasing the feel-good neurochemical dopamine). One of the reasons people fail to move towards their goals is because they are waiting to feel motivated or inspired before taking action. This is a common misconception, as motivation comes from taking action. The first small step can be difficult, but it creates energy and motivation which in turn makes the next step easier to take and so the cycle continues of action-motivation-action.

Help the client integrate change: Life is a continuous process of change. Part of being emotionally intelligent is learning to integrate changes into one's life to create balance. It is like 'riding a bicycle', where a person must keep moving to stay balanced. Along the journey there will be rocky terrain and sometimes the person may fall off or need to carry extra things in their basket. Whatever happens, the journey is always changing, and the person must learn how to adapt, incorporate, and integrate the changes in themselves and their environment. A useful model to help with change is described by Prochaska and DiClemente's Stages of Change.[10] Working through this with the client and the related EIP scales provides a useful structure (Table 6.3).

Stages of Change and the EIP scales

Table 6.3

STAGE OF CHANGE	RELATED EIP SCALES	EXAMPLE
Pre-contemplation (Not Ready)	Self Awareness Awareness of Others	Receiving negative 360 feedback and noticing how they feel about this
Contemplation (Weighing up options)	Reflective Learning	Reflecting on why they got this feedback: is it true? Do they want to change?
Preparation (Planning)	Flexibility Goal Directedness	Choosing to do something about this such as discussing it with their line manager
Action (Implementing the plan)	Emotional Resilience Personal Power	Practise and try out the agreed actions

STAGE OF CHANGE	RELATED EIP SCALES	EXAMPLE
Maintenance (Keeping it going)	Connecting with Others Authenticity	Complete a 21-day Habit Change and get support from others

A particularly important aspect of change is how individuals cope with stress, respond to adversities, and recover from setbacks, i.e. their resilience. The four-stage process which follows (Table 6.4) is adapted from the Challenge Model of Resilience by O'Leary.[11] The EIP scales have been mapped onto these four stages to create the Thrive Model of Resilience and an EIP Resilience Report. Note that all of the EIP scales could have an influence at each stage in the process, but the mapping shows which scales are likely to be most important at each stage. These four stages are cyclical, so that learning from adversity (Thrive) will build greater capacity to respond appropriately to future setbacks (Survive).

Stages of resilience and the EIP scales

STAGE OF RESILIENCE	RELATED EIP SCALES	INTERPRETATION
Survive How we initially respond to adversity	Self Regard Regard for Others Emotional Expression and Control Conflict Handling	People differ in their resistance to stress. Our capacity to remain calm, think clearly, and act appropriately under adversity is largely determined by our self-esteem and capacity to manage emotions
Adapt How we adjust to change and adversity	Self Awareness Awareness of Others Flexibility Interdependence	Adapting to adversity requires paying attention to our feelings, reactions and behaviour, moving outside of our comfort zones, adapting to the situation, and drawing upon the support of others
Recover How we bounce back from adversity	Emotional Resilience Personal Power Goal Directedness Balanced Outlook	Recovering from setbacks requires taking responsibility for ourselves and not being a victim, actively finding solutions to problems, setting clear objectives, and having the self-belief, drive, and determination to make this happen

Table 6.4

STAGE OF RESILIENCE	RELATED EIP SCALES	INTERPRETATION	
Thrive How we grow and become more resilient following adversity	Connecting with Others Authenticity Trust Reflective Learning	To Thrive after adversity requires the ability to reflect and learn from past experiences, build trusting and supportive relationships, and behave consistently with our values and principles in life	

This chapter has provided an explanation on how to apply the EIP, the process for exploring the EIP reports, and the skills for coaching with the EIP. The next chapter will focus more specifically on using the EIP in assessment and selection.

SUMMARY POINTS
FROM CHAPTER SIX

Before using the EIP, the coach needs to acquire the relevant knowledge and skills to administer, interpret, and explore all parts of the EIP reports.

The coaching process is an exploration rather than feedback. Emphasis is placed on the client being the expert on themselves, rather than the coach.

A six-step process for exploring the EIP with the client is recommended. This includes agreeing the purpose, building rapport, explaining the EIP, exploring the EIP results, setting development goals, and closing the session.

Coaching with the EIP requires some core skills including the ability to build rapport, the skills to listen at a deeper level, the experience to create an atmosphere of change, and the techniques to focus the client on solutions and taking action.

The skilled EIP coach has also developed their own EI. They should be sufficiently self-aware to notice their own resistance and defences as a coach, as well as those of their client.

Although the EIP uses normative scoring, for development purposes it can be just as useful and relevant to consider the client's relative balance of scores, such as where they score higher or lower relative to their own scales scores.

The EIP may be used in combination with other tools. Combining the EIP with the Personality Type Profile and Behaviours 360 provides a comprehensive assessment of the individual to support their personal and professional development.

There is also a 360 degree version of the EIP. When used in combination with the EIP, the client can make a direct comparison between their self-perception and others' perceptions of them.

The EIP can also be applied within a group setting. It is recommended that group exploration is broken down into chunks based on the six parts of the EIP framework.

CHAPTER SEVEN
USING THE EIP FOR ASSESSMENT

INTRODUCTION

The EIP was originally created as a development tool. However, since its launch there has been strong demand from clients to create a version of the EIP that may also be used for assessment purposes such as candidate selection, internal promotion, talent identification, and changing job roles. One benefit of using the EIP for assessment is that it focuses specifically on the emotional aspects of performance so it is more targeted than a generic personality measure. This is particularly useful when assessing for roles that involve high emotional labour*, emotional resilience, and interpersonal effectiveness such as in leadership, customer service, or sales. EIP may also add significant value in sectors that are typically lower on interpersonal EI, such as STEM roles (Science, Technology, Engineering, Maths/finance) where EI can also add considerable value.[1,2,3] In 2016, JCA Global embarked on an extensive revision of the questionnaire that allowed the EIP to be used for both development and assessment purposes, i.e. across the employee life cycle at work. The revised version, referred to on promotional material as EIP3, retains the same theoretical model and scale constructs as the original EIP, but with significant updates to the questionnaire items and a new set of assessment and development reports.

Much of what was written in Chapter Six, on how to use the EIP for development, also applies to using the EIP for assessment. For assessment, the main purpose of the reports is to provide information for the assessor to support selection and promotion decisions, while for development it is to coach and support the respondent. It is with this purpose in mind that the four stages of using the EIP for assessment are now described: preparation, administration, interpretation, and interview.

* Emotional labour: the process by which workers are expected to manage their feelings and their expression to fulfil the emotional requirements of a job.[4]

7.1 Preparation

Before deciding to use the EIP or any other form of assessment, it is important to establish what attributes are necessary and desirable to perform effectively in the job role or tasks being assessed. This is best achieved by producing a clear description of the job requirements (a job description) and conducting a job analysis to identify what differentiates higher performance from lower performance in the role. This may be done systematically using formalised techniques such as critical incident analysis, repertory grids, and visionary interviews. Alternatively, it can be done less formally by asking current job holders and line managers to select the competencies and qualities they think are important for the role.

Having identified the qualities that define effective performance for a specific job role, the assessor can then describe these qualities in the form of a person specification. It is from this specification that the assessor will then decide on the most appropriate blend of assessment methods to be used. One of the most comprehensive assessment solutions is known as an 'assessment centre' where multiple approaches are employed, such as self-report questionnaires, ability tests, interviews, group activities, and presentations.[5] Measuring each attribute more than once and using different methods of assessment can help in reducing errors during the process and can increase the accuracy of measurement resulting in more valid assessment decisions. This is one reason why it is recommended that the EIP is not used in isolation, but combined with other forms of assessment including an assessment interview.

There may be several stages to an assessment process, such as initial applications, an online applicant sift, first stage interviews, and a final assessment event. Building and conducting a complete assessment approach requires specialist expertise and knowledge, such as the Test User Occupational Psychology qualifications from the British Psychological Society.[6] As the EIP is intended to be used as part of the interview, it is more likely to be employed at the later stages of selection to assess the final set of applicants rather than during the earlier stages. Note that the EIP should always be accompanied by a feedback interview, and scores from the EIP should never be used in isolation. Deciding to include the EIP as part of the assessment process is dependent on several factors.

Reasons to use the EIP in assessment may include:

— To measure individual EI within a recognised set of scale constructs

— To provide structure, standardisation, and objectivity to the EI assessment interview

— To efficiently gather information on an individual's EI (using an online self-report format)

— To identify individual growth potential and to assess a candidate's EI training needs

— To relate the EIP scale scores to performance-based work competencies

— To relate the EIP scale scores to potential derailers of leadership performance

Reasons not to use the EIP for assessment may include:

— If assessors are not trained in the EIP or in interviewing skills

— If there is no clear job description or person specification

— If EI attributes are not relevant to the job

— If there is no additional form of assessment, such as an interview, to corroborate results with

— If scores are being used purely as a 'pass-fail' cut-off score

— If there are significant practical limitations, such as insufficient interview time or online inaccessibility

— If there are other ethical barriers in play, such as adverse impact[*] or language barriers

Essentially, it is the responsibility of the qualified EIP user to be confident that the EIP is being used ethically and appropriately by their clients or within their organisation. The qualified EIP user may not be the person managing the wider assessment process, but they are responsible for how the EIP is being administered, interpreted, and applied. These and other considerations are now discussed.

To generate the online EIP Report, the administrator will select the relevant report(s) and the appropriate norm comparison group. Several norm groups are available; it is generally advised to choose a norm group that most closely represents the job level and job sector being assessed. Latest details on the norm groups are available in the EIP3 Technical Manual.[7]

[*] Adverse impact means there is potential for discrimination against a minority demographic group in the selection process.[8]

7.2   Administration

Administering the EIP for assessment is much the same process as administration for development. In both cases, individuals complete the same online questionnaire with the same standardised administration instructions. Candidates are advised to complete the questions in one sitting, in a quiet setting, and not dwell too long on responses. In practice, no single question will do justice to a person's EI, and thinking too long on any item can lead to more questions than answers! The questionnaire is designed to be answered by giving a first natural response, but at the same time not rushing through without allowing time to understand and consider the questions. It is the combination of many questions that make up any single scale score. As a guide, it should take between 20 to 40 minutes to complete the 158 items in the EIP questionnaire, plus five minutes for the initial demographic questions and reading the instructions.

It is more reassuring for candidates (and helps gain their cooperation) if, before receiving their online request to complete the questionnaire, they are given a wider briefing as to why they have been asked to complete the EIP, and how it forms part of the overall assessment process. This may include advising them on the following points:

— The EIP is one part of the assessment process which may also include other questionnaires, tests, or other forms of assessment. Explain that selection decisions are based on all the available evidence of which the EIP is one source of information.

— The EIP is not an ability test, i.e. it is not an actual 'test', as there are no objectively right or wrong answers and there is no set time limit.

— The EIP questionnaire measures aspects of personal and interpersonal behaviour that have been identified as being relevant to the job. Candidates do not necessarily need to know about the concept or label of 'Emotional Intelligence', although it may be of interest to let them know that this is what the questionnaire measures.

— The results of the questionnaire will be discussed with them in a separate meeting, to give them an opportunity to ask any questions and clarify the meaning of their results.

— The questionnaire data is confidential; it will only be used for the purposes of this specific assessment, and it will not be kept on record for future use (unless agreed otherwise with the candidate, such as for their own personal development).

One of the main reasons for informing candidates of these points is that it encourages a more honest and open response to the EIP items. More often than not, administration is conducted remotely in unsupervised conditions. The administrator should still seek to reassure candidates, answer their questions, gain their commitment to the process, and provide contact details should they have any questions or require technical support.

When providing candidates with information about the EIP assessment, it is also important to find out if the candidate has any special requirements. For example, candidates with impairments or disabilities may need adjustments to be made to the administration process. Employers have a duty to make reasonable adjustments for candidates, and often these are straightforward, such as creating larger font sizes and different coloured screens, or verbalising material through a reader.

The EIP is completed online and therefore requires candidates to have a suitable internet browser with an up to date version (all major browsers are supported). Candidates need to be able to view the instructions and questions on-screen and use an input device (typically a mouse or keyboard) to choose their responses. Standard accessibility tools on the candidate's computer can be used when completing the EIP (e.g. Windows contains several features to optimise the visual display, read on-screen text, or use alternative input devices). Unlike ability tests, questionnaires such as the EIP do not have any time limit so candidates can take as much time as they need to complete the questionnaire.

If the candidate informs you that they may require adjustments to the administration process, then this should be discussed with them to identify exactly what is required. Each individual is unique and it is important to understand their particular needs to provide them with a suitable administration experience. If required, there are also several advisory organisations who may be able to provide guidance and support depending on the nature of the candidate's impairment or disability.

7.3   Interpretation

How to interpret the EIP scales is fully explained in Chapter Five. The focus here is on how interpretation of the assessment reports differs from the development reports. There are two types of report that the EIP user may generate for use in assessment:

1   **The Expert Report**, which includes the EIP scale profile and is intended for qualified EIP users only. This is supported by a Participant Feedback Report that may be given to the candidate.

2   **The Interview Guide**, which is intended for managers who may not be trained in the EIP but will be interviewing job candidates. This is supported by the Candidate Feedback Report which may be given to the candidate.

As with the developmental reports, the EIP assessor will prepare by reviewing the candidate's EIP scores, interpreting scale combinations, and making their hypotheses. This may be done with direct reference to the job specification to help ascertain areas of strength and possible concerns in relation to the requirements of the role. From their interpretation of the EIP, they will formulate hypotheses on what aspects they want to explore and questions the assessor will ask during the interview to elicit essential information from the candidate. When using EIP for assessment as opposed to development, there is a different emphasis on how scores are interpreted. The assessor will interpret scores in relation to the comparison norm group and if appropriate make comparisons between candidates; for development the coach may place greater emphasis on the relative balance between the individual's scale scores, rather than how they compare to the norm group or with other individuals.

7.3.1 The Expert Report

The Expert Report is intended for use by the qualified EIP user and therefore includes all 16 EIP scale scores with a short narrative interpretation on each. Unlike the Executive Report (used in development), the Expert Report does not include the matrices or the Item Analysis. The matrices are useful models for coaching and exploring an individual's deeper patterns, but this depth of analysis is less relevant to assessment. The Item Analysis is useful for discussing an individual's EIP scale scores, but this level of discussion in an interview is also less appropriate for assessment. One further difference is the replacement of development points with interviewer prompts which are more relevant to assessment.

The main addition to the Expert Report is the inclusion of nine 'Defensive Habits' (see Table 7.1). These are derived from the EIP red scales (i.e. the 'too much' and 'too little' multi-scales), and from other closely correlated EIP linear scales. The rationale here is that defensive behaviours are often indicated by overuse (too much) and under use (too little) of specific behaviours.[9] For example, an individual who has a fear of being rejected by others may defend themselves against these painful feelings by seeking constant attention (too much) or by avoiding others entirely (too little). This over-compensating or avoidant behaviour is often referred to in workplace literature as 'derailment'.[10]

If other related linear scales also point in the same negative direction as the red multi-scale, then this reinforces the likelihood that the individual may present a Defensive Habit. A Defensive Habit is characterised by rigid and inflexible behaviour, often triggered when an individual feels under pressure or stressed. The benefit or 'pay-off' from a Defensive Habit is in helping the individual to feel less anxious in the shorter term while they behave like this. The downside within recruitment is that defensive behaviours are maladaptive and unhelpful, subsequently undermining relationships and impairing performance (see Table 7.1).

The reason the defences are called 'habits' is because they are often acquired at a young age as a coping mechanism, which over time becomes ingrained, automated, and habitual. Although they are mainly described by their behaviours, Defensive Habits also include associated attitudes, thoughts, and feelings. The nine Defensive Habits separate into two conceptually and statistically distinct factors that may be classified by the Core Attitudes of low Self Regard (I am Not OK) and low Regard for Others (You are Not OK). Further explanation of how defences may manifest from these Core Attitudes is provided in Chapter Four; 4.3.2.

The nine Defensive Habits and the EIP scales from which they were derived are listed in Table 7.2. Proportionally, the red multi-scale is given 50% weighting and the other 50% is shared equally between the linear scales. Therefore, each Defensive Habit is largely represented by a single red multi-scale. The only red multi-scale not included as a Defensive Habit is Over Trusting, which statistically correlates positively rather than negatively with the linear scales. The nine Defensive Habits are ordered by the degree to which they are correlated with each other, i.e. neighbouring defences are more closely correlated. More detailed interpretation of the nine Defensive Habits and their links to the EIP scales is provided in the Expert Report.

Defensive Habits, Attitudes and Behaviours

DEFENSIVE HABIT (MULTI-SCALE)	DEFENSIVE ATTITUDE (PAY-OFF)	DEFENSIVE BEHAVIOURS
Domineering (Aggressive)	I can protect myself from feeling vulnerable by taking control and having authority	Confrontational, antagonistic, uncompromising, forceful, argumentative, and competitive
Detached (Over Controlled)	I can protect myself from being hurt by others by remaining emotionally detached	Cold, distant, emotionally inhibited, closed, unexpressive, and lacks spontaneity
Guarded (Mistrusting)	I can protect myself from being let down by people by not trusting others	Cautious, mistrusting, sceptical, cynical, critical, and questioning
Avoidant (Over Independent)	I can protect myself from feeling excluded by relying upon nobody but myself	Self-sufficient, independent, inflexible, stubborn, autonomous, and non-conforming
Despondent (Pessimistic)	I can protect myself from disappointment by assuming the worst	Pessimistic, negative, self-critical, discouraging, defeatist, and unenthusiastic
Reactive (Under Controlled)	I can protect myself from feeling ignored by demanding attention from others	Emotionally reactive, anxious, unpredictable, disruptive, volatile, and impulsive
Compliant (Passive)	I can protect myself from disapproval and rejection by being highly conforming	Passive, deferential, unassertive, modest, over-burdened, and overly accommodating
Reliant (Dependent)	I can protect myself from being blamed or shamed by seeking constant reassurance	Lacks confidence and initiative, over-dependent, seeks approval, follower, and procrastinator
Idealistic (Over Optimistic)	I can protect myself from the harsh realities of life by pretending everything is positive	Over-optimistic, impractical, unrealistic, unreliable, and lacks focus

Table 7.1

Defensive Habits and their contributing EIP scales

DEFENSIVE ATTITUDE	DEFENSIVE HABIT	CONTRIBUTING MULTI-SCALE	CONTRIBUTING LINEAR SCALES (LOW SCORES)
YOU ARE NOT OK (Low Regard for Others)	Domineering	Aggressive	Regard for Others Awareness of Others
	Detached	Over Controlled	Self Awareness Connecting with Others
	Guarded	Mistrusting	Regard for Others Connecting with Others
	Avoidant	Over Independent	Regard for Others Flexibility Connecting with Others
I AM NOT OK (Low Self Regard)	Despondent	Pessimistic	Self Regard Personal Power Emotional Resilience
	Reactive	Under Controlled	Self Regard Emotional Resilience Authenticity
	Compliant	Passive	Self Regard Personal Power Authenticity
	Reliant	Dependent	Self Regard Goal Directedness Authenticity
	Idealistic	Over Optimistic	Goal Directedness Authenticity

Table 7.2

Another benefit of the Defensive Habits is that they provide an interpretation of typical EIP scale combinations, helping the user to recognise important patterns and relationships between scales. When all of the relevant EIP scales for a Defensive Habit are pointing in a negative direction, this gives greater confidence in interpreting this set of scale scores as a defence. However, the user should be mindful that with more scales there are more permutations and complexities in interpretation, particularly when EIP scale scores do not point in the same direction. The more experienced user may choose to explore such anomalies with the candidate.

Defensive Habits are scored by levels of risk on a 1-5 banding:

Band 1 (Sten 1-2) = very low risk

Band 2 (Sten 3-4) = low risk

Band 3 (Sten 5-6) = some risk

Band 4 (Sten 7-8) = risk

Band 5 (Sten 9-10) = high risk

It is important to note that the Defensive Habits should not be interpreted as categorical descriptors, but rather as possible areas that the interviewer should explore using the interview or prompt questions provided. For example, it may be hypothesised that someone with a 'high risk' score of five is more likely to demonstrate the Defensive Habit behaviours more frequently than someone with a 'low risk' score of two. Also remember that Defensive Habits are not personality descriptors, but indicators of how an individual may behave particularly when under pressure and stress.

Another useful way of conceptualising the Defensive Habits is through Karen Horney's model of 'neurotic trends'[11] (which we have termed Defensive Attitudes). This model is also used in other popular measures of leadership derailment.[10] The nine Defensive Habits can be conceptually and statistically grouped into the three clusters in Horney's model as follows:

Three conceptual clusters for the Defensive Habits

DEFENSIVE ATTITUDE (HORNEY'S MODEL)	DESCRIPTION	EIP DEFENSIVE HABIT
Moving towards people	Characterised by someone who "accepts their own helplessness and in spite of their estrangement and fears, tries to win the affection of others and to lean on them"	Compliant Reliant Idealistic
Moving against people	Characterised by someone who "accepts and takes for granted the hostility around them, and determines, consciously or unconsciously, to fight"	Domineering Guarded Reactive
Moving away from people	Characterised by someone who "wants neither to belong nor to fight but keeps apart. They feel they have not much in common with others; people do not understand them anyhow"	Detached Avoidant Despondent

Table 7.3

Horney's model provides a useful illustration of how several Defensive Habits may cluster together, although any interpretation of such combinations should be done cautiously. Remember that Defensive Habits are already extrapolations from a combination of EIP scales, so combining Defensive Habits is an even more complex and tentative level of interpretation. Recognising and interpreting such defensive patterns is a skill that may be acquired through gaining considerable experience of using the EIP.

7.3.2 The Participant Feedback Report

The Expert Report is intended for the assessor only, rather than to be given to the candidate. However, it is good practice to offer some level of feedback to the candidate whether or not they are successful in being selected. Using the Participant Feedback Report provides a quick and simple way of offering something back to the candidate which can aid their future job searches and self-development. Providing this service also leaves a good impression with the candidate and builds the reputation of the organisation as a fair and ethical employer.

The Participant Feedback Report is similar to the Snapshot Report in that it highlights the three EIP scales for which the individual rated themselves highest and the three they rated lowest, i.e. their relative strengths and development areas. The report does not show any scores or a comparison with the norm group. The Participant Feedback Report may be discussed with the candidate during the interview or given to them when they leave.

7.3.3 The Interview Guide

The Interview Guide is designed to give relevant information from the EIP for use in an interview. This is typically for managers who have sufficient skills and experience in conducting job interviews but are not qualified users of the EIP. Managers need adequate training to understand and interpret the Interview Guide, which may be provided by a trained EIP user. It is the responsibility of the EIP qualified user to ensure the competence of managers who use the Interview Guide, and also that the Interview Guide is used appropriately.

The Interview Guide includes a set of EI-related, work-based competencies alongside relevant interview questions that are derived from the EIP scale scores. Ten relevant competencies were selected from the JCA competency library through a process of expert mapping and statistical validation between EIP scales and competencies (see Table 7.4).[7] Competencies describe workplace behaviours that have been shown to correlate with and predict successful job performance. Before using the Interview Guide, it is important for assessors to identify which of the competencies are relevant to the job by comparing them to the person specification and job description. The number of competencies to be discussed with the candidate will determine the amount of time required for the interview.

A key benefit of using competencies is that they simplify the interpretation process for the assessor. Competency scales are easily understood in relation to workplace activities and unlike the EIP are discrete scales that do not need to be interpreted in combination with other scales. The results themselves are presented as 'competency potential' scores. This is to emphasise the fact that the scores are based on self-report information provided by the individual, rather than being an objective assessment of behavioural capability. The competency potential scores, similar to the Defensive Habits, are presented as a banding from one to five (from 'low potential' to 'high potential'). One reason for using these broader bands is to accommodate for a greater margin of error in interpretation. Both the Defensive Habits and competency potential scores are derived from combining several EIP scale scores, increasing the potential error of interpretation, and making the interview an important part of validating the results. The trained EIP user may choose to use the Interview Guide in combination with the Expert Report to gain more insight and confidence in their interpretation.

Contained within the Interview Guide is a three-stage process to ensure appropriate and ethical use within an assessment context:

— **Stage 1** is to select which of the ten competencies are desirable or essential for the job role

— **Stage 2** is to use the information and questions provided to conduct the interview

— **Stage 3** is for the interviewer to rate the candidate against the selected competencies and write down a summary of their interview findings

Encouraging the interviewer to follow these three stages with appropriate training from the qualified EIP user will lead to a more successful outcome.

EI competencies and their contributing EIP scales

FACTOR	COMPETENCY	CONTRIBUTING SCALES (IN ORDER OF WEIGHTING)	DESCRIPTION
Personal Effectiveness	Showing resilience	Emotional Resilience Self Regard Self Awareness	Displays self-confidence; copes effectively with pressure and stress; remains composed under pressure; recovers quickly from setbacks and criticism
	Driving for success	Goal Directedness Personal Power Emotional Resilience	Proactively seeks out opportunities; seizes opportunities; makes things happen; takes calculated risks

Table 7.4

FACTOR	COMPETENCY	CONTRIBUTING SCALES (IN ORDER OF WEIGHTING)	DESCRIPTION
	Acting with initiative	Personal Power Flexibility Self Regard	Sets stretching goals; focuses on the end goal; shows persistence and tenacity to exceed goals; works in an enthusiastic and committed way
	Responding to change	Flexibility Balanced Outlook Emotional Resilience	Embraces variety at work; copes with ambiguity; responds positively to the changing environment; promotes change to others
	Growth potential	Self Awareness Flexibility Reflective Learning Personal Power	Shows learning agility; displays motivation in acquiring new skills and knowledge; shows openness to feedback and self-development
Interpersonal Effectiveness	Valuing people	Regard for Others Trust Awareness of Others	Values the strengths and individual differences of others; listens and pays attention to others on a personal level; shows appreciation; displays trust towards others
	Connecting with people	Connecting with Others Awareness of Others Regard for Others	Relates well to people at all levels; uses diplomacy and tact appropriately; builds constructive and effective relationships with people; shows warmth and enthusiasm when interacting with others
	Influencing people	Conflict Handling Connecting with Others Emotional Expression and Control Personal Power	Persuades others and gains agreement; negotiates with others to ensure a 'win-win' situation; challenges other people's ideas in an appropriate manner; promotes ideas effectively by appealing to emotions

FACTOR	COMPETENCY	CONTRIBUTING SCALES (IN ORDER OF WEIGHTING)	DESCRIPTION
	Inspiring others	Balanced Outlook Connecting with Others Authenticity Emotional Expression and Control	Creates a clear and compelling vision; presents an optimistic and positive view of the future; provides a sense of meaning and purpose to work; inspires others to strive for their best performance
	Coaching and developing others	Awareness of Others Trust Interdependence Conflict Handling	Provides coaching support to others; offers useful ongoing formal and informal feedback; invests time and resources in developing others; builds the confidence of others

7.3.4 The Candidate Feedback Report

As with the Participant Feedback Report, the Candidate Feedback Report is intended as a short report that may be given directly to the candidate. This report highlights two competencies from the Interview Guide for which the individual rated themselves highest, and the two competencies for which the individual rated themselves lowest.

Note that both the Participant and Candidate Feedback Reports are written for the candidate, i.e. "You are ...", while both the Expert Report and Interview Guide are written for the assessor, i.e. "He/she is ...". The Expert Report and Participant Feedback Report refer to 'the participant', as opposed to 'the candidate'. This is because these reports may be used for development purposes also.

7.3.5 Positive self-perception

A perennial concern with self-report measures is they are open to faking, as candidates may be tempted to present what they consider to be a more favourable impression of themselves (social desirability). However, research in this area indicates that social desirability has a limited effect on the psychometric validity of self-report questionnaires like the EIP.[12,13] Therefore it should not be a significant concern in the assessment process, but the assessor should still be mindful of this. To some extent, being able to manage oneself to give a positive impression is a valuable attribute; however, the assessor will want to identify how the candidate typically behaves, as well as how they may perform at their best or at their worst.

As described earlier, gaining cooperation of the candidate during the administration process is one way of promoting openness. It is also worth checking the individual's responses for potential distortion. If the individual scores very high (Sten 9 and 10) on nearly all positive scales this is statistically unusual, though still possible. Built within the questionnaire is a marker of positive self-perception. A high score on positive self-perception would indicate someone who is likely to be very self-confident in relation to their own capability and may possibly over-rate themselves. A low score would indicate someone who tends to be self-critical and may possibly under-rate themselves. Areas of doubt should be highlighted by the interviewer for more careful exploration with the candidate. The interviewer may, for example, ask the candidate for more detailed examples of when they have demonstrated competence in these areas.

7.4   Interview

In contrast to the coaching exploration session, the purpose of the assessment interview is for the assessor to better understand the candidate, rather than for the candidate to better understand themselves. This clearly changes the dynamic of the relationship, placing the assessor's intentions ahead of the candidates. However, the interview will be far more effective if the assessor can still create an atmosphere of openness and trust with the candidate. This may be achieved by following a similar process to that described for a coaching exploration (see Chapter Six): agree the contract, build rapport, conduct the interview, and draw conclusions.

7.4.1 Agree the contract

First, explain to the candidate how long the interview will take. Normally allow 45 minutes to discuss the Interview Guide, or an hour if using the Expert Report. Explain that they will receive a Feedback Report and thank them for taking the time to complete the questionnaire. Explain how their results are being used and that part of the assessor's job is to summarise what emerges from the interview and to share this with the assessment panel. Confirm confidentiality with the candidate and let them know who will have access to their results. At this stage in the assessment process they may be one of the final candidates, so in this case the emphasis of the interview is likely to be more about 'how' they would do the job rather than 'can' they do the job. Remind them that this is an opportunity for them to tell the assessor about themselves, during which the assessor should make notes for later reference. Finally, confirm with the candidate if there are any further questions regarding the discussion.

7.4.2 Build rapport

The main aim of building rapport is to gain the trust of the candidate and help put them at ease, so that they can think clearly and perform at their best. For example, consider the use of language – using words like 'conversation' or 'discussion' instead of 'interview' and 'assessment' will relax the candidate and improve the dialogue. Pay attention to room layout and body language – being on the opposite side of a desk and looking down at documents and reports will probably appear more intimidating to candidates. Learning how to put candidates at ease with small talk and light questions will encourage them into a more relaxed mindset and create a more favourable atmosphere. The rapport phase may well merge into the interview phase by asking the candidate about their present circumstances, previous experiences, and future aspirations. The key is to get them talking openly and to encourage the flow of conversation.

7.4.3 Conduct the interview

Indicate to the candidate that the 'interview' is about to begin by asking if they are ready to talk through the questionnaire they completed previously. It may be that they have completed several other questionnaires, exercises or tests, so remind them of the relevant questionnaire. Begin by asking how they found answering the questions and whether they have completed something similar before, such as a personality questionnaire. Occasionally this will glean additional insight about the candidate if they are willing to disclose what they recall from them. The Interview Guide includes specific questions to probe around each of the competencies that aid in testing out interpretations by looking for evidence that either confirm or disconfirm these hypotheses. For more essential competencies, or for competencies that appear over-rated (see Positive self-perception, Section 7.3.5), seek more thorough evidence and examples from the candidate. Look to identify both their current capability and potential for growth. A candidate with high potential may be more attractive than one who is currently capable but lacks 'growth potential'.

When using the assessment reports, maintain the flow of the interview by linking the next question to the previous answer: "That's an interesting point you make, how would you apply this to …?", and don't feel the need to rigidly stick to the question script. Above all, listen carefully, pay close attention to the candidate, show interest in what they say, and avoid showing disapproval. Indicate when the interview is getting close to the end and check if there is anything further they wish to clarify before giving them their Candidate or Participant Feedback Report.

7.4.4 Draw conclusions

There are recommended procedures for evaluating information from assessment data that apply when using the EIP.[5] The first stage is to draw out hypotheses from the EIP results and competencies as part of the interpretation phase (Section 7.3). Then, test out these hypotheses during the interview, and record what you hear and observe. Following the interview, review your notes and summarise these against each of the relevant competencies. You can then produce a score against each of the competencies based on an agreed scoring and weighting system, such as the one to five scoring system provided in the Interview Guide. These scores are then integrated with information and data from any other assessment activities completed by candidates. The final stage, often called the 'wash-up', invites you to share your views of the candidate and discuss the overall picture provided from the assessment data, before drawing conclusions and making selection decisions.

The previous description is an overview of a typical interview assessment process, but there are other more sophisticated skills that may be acquired by experienced and trained interviewers. Many of these are similar to the skills of an experienced coach, such as how to build rapport or how to explore the EIP profile as described in the previous chapter. It is recommended that all assessors are given training in interviewing skills prior to using the Interview Guide.

7.5   Wider questions for consideration

This chapter has described how to use the EIP in an assessment context. There are many aspects to using the EIP in assessment not covered here that are described in other chapters, such as the construction of the EIP (Chapter Three), interpretation of the EIP scales (Chapter Five), how the EIP relates to leadership, and evidence that the EIP predicts performance (Chapter Nine). Using the EIP for assessment may raise specific questions that differ to those that arise for development. Some of the more common questions that may be asked by managers, clients, or other stakeholders are answered next.

1   "If EI is developable, is it appropriate to measure it for selection and assessment?"

Measuring a person's EI provides a useful indication as to their current EI strengths and areas for development which is essential in a selection context. EI can be developed, but this takes time and concerted effort. To make EI stick requires embedding EI habits and attitudes. For example, 21 days of focused practice will start the process of changing a specific habit. Results from studies looking at the test-retest reliability of the EIP[7] questionnaire also confirm that under normal conditions, an individual's EIP profile is relatively stable over a period of four months.

2   "Are EIP results influenced by a person's current circumstances?"

Current circumstances may be reflected in a candidate's EIP scores if they are significant emotional events, such as redundancy, divorce, or job promotion. Such critical life events are important considerations when interviewing a candidate as they inevitably affect how the person feels and behaves. More day-to-day changes that have low emotional impact are less likely to show up in their profile. Furthermore, how a person responds to significant life events may also reflect underlying factors that are relevant to the job, such as how they cope with adversity.

3   "Are EIP results influenced by a person's current mood, such as having a bad day at work?"

An individual's self-perception may be influenced by their current emotional state.[14] Respondents are therefore advised not to complete the EIP when they are feeling highly emotional or tired. Before completing the EIP, it is recommended that respondents are asked to reflect on different situations that have been positive and negative, both in and out of work, so as to contemplate their circumstances more broadly.

4   "Can a person still be emotionally intelligent if they get low EIP scores?"

Yes, they can, through conscious and deliberate practice (remember that EI is described as 'the practice of ...' i.e. a verb, or something that person does in the present). However, consciously practising EI requires concerted effort, which is unsustainable if in the long-term it is not embedded as automated habits and attitudes. It is these ingrained habits and attitudes that manifest as typical behaviours, reflecting more stable characteristics that are measured by the EIP behaviour scales.

5   "Do people over-rate themselves in an assessment setting?"

Common to all self-report questionnaires is a greater tendency for people to over-rate themselves in an assessment context. We recommend corroborating EIP results with other forms of evidence including an interview discussion. The EIP provides an indication of 'Positive self-perception' to alert the assessor to this issue (see Section 7.3.5).

6   "Do people with high self-awareness rate themselves lower in EI?"

Sometimes when people become more aware of what they want to change and develop as an individual, they may temporarily rate themselves lower in EI. This tends to happen when they have experienced profound self-insight, such as during development coaching. In assessment contexts this is rarely the case. Our test-retest data shows that EI remains fairly stable unless individuals engage in concerted self-development over a period of time, in which case their EIP scores will usually improve.[7]

7   "How accurate are the EIP results?"

As with all forms of psychometric self-assessment there is a margin of error. For the EIP this is approximated to one Sten score either side of the individual's actual score. This is one reason why the EIP results should be supported by an interview and other assessment data, rather than used in isolation. Evidence for the validity of the EIP is presented in the Technical Manual.[7]

8   "Is it appropriate to measure scales like Self Regard in an assessment?"

All EIP scales may be of relevance to assessment when interpreting a profile. Trained EIP users know not to treat EIP scales in isolation, but instead to look for patterns between several scales to generate hypotheses about a candidate for discussion. Non-trained EIP ·

users will receive a report based on workplace competencies (the Interview Guide) that are derived from a combination of EIP scales, removing the need for specific knowledge of the scales and how they may interact.

9   "How might EIP be used in conjunction with a personality profile?"

The EIP focuses on emotional and social aspects of behaviour. It therefore provides a more nuanced interpretation of the affective/emotional aspects of generic personality. We define EI as 'how effectively an individual manages their personality', so the EIP usually complements most personality measures very well. The user should be trained in both instruments and therefore be able to make connections between the scales on both products. For many popular personality measures, JCA Global has made theoretical and psychometric links between scales. These are available in the EIP3 Technical Manual.[7]

10   "Does the EIP discriminate against any groups with protected minority character-istics?"

Analyses of group differences in EIP scales have been conducted on large samples of respondents. These studies are reported in the EIP3 Technical Manual.[7] The results from these studies indicate that average differences in relation to gender, age, and ethnicity are generally small. The size of these differences is in line with expectations, and even the largest differences observed equate to less than one Sten score difference. Assessors should still be aware of these differences in accordance with good assessment practice, but they do not present any cause for concern.

Chapter Seven has described how to use the EIP assessment reports as part of an interview process in the context of candidate selection. This builds on many of the skills described in the previous chapter on how to use the EIP in coaching.

SUMMARY POINTS
FROM CHAPTER SEVEN

The EIP assessment reports are based on the same EIP scales and theoretical model as the EIP development reports.

There are two assessment reports: an Expert Report for the qualified EIP user (plus a Participant Feedback Report) and an Interview Guide for the assessor (plus a Candidate Feedback Report).

The Expert Report includes 16 EIP scales, plus nine common Defensive Habits. The Interview Guide is based on ten EI-related workplace competencies derived from the EIP scales, and includes interview questions.

The Participant Feedback Report provides individuals with a summary of their top three and bottom three scoring EIP scales. The Candidate Feedback Report provides the candidate with a summary of their higher and lower scoring competencies.

The Defensive Habits section in the Expert Report highlights nine aspects of EI where individuals typically become more defensive and rigid, potentially causing them to derail and perform at their worst. Each Defensive Habit is derived primarily from one red multi-scale plus two or three negatively correlated linear scales.

The EIP assessment reports are intended for use as part of an interview process. They are therefore more likely to be used to assess the final few candidates than for sifting large numbers of candidates. It is recommended that EIP scores are never used in isolation to sift out candidates and should always be accompanied by a feedback interview.

As with any use of the EIP, the user should have the appropriate skills to apply the EIP reports in their relevant context, e.g. coaching skills if used for coaching, and interviewer skills if used for assessment.

When using the EIP for assessment, it is good practice to conduct a thorough job analysis and person specification, to use the EIP in conjunction with an interview, and to corroborate results with other supporting assessment evidence.

CHAPTER EIGHT
HOW TO DEVELOP EMOTIONAL INTELLIGENCE

INTRODUCTION

The very process of a client completing the EIP and reflecting on their responses can help to raise their self-awareness and understanding. By exploring their EIP Report with their coach, they are able to interpret their scale scores, recognise patterns within themselves, and identify what they want to develop and change. The next stage is to make these changes happen through taking action. All too often, people become stuck at the middle Awareness (Feeling) level of the EIP framework and fail to implement change at the Behaviour level. This chapter provides suggestions on how to make this happen, so that good intentions are turned into enduring habits and attitudes. These suggestions are not intended to be step-by-step instructions, but rather a guide for the coach to help draw upon their existing skills and expertise.

The first part of this chapter describes how to develop Emotional Intelligence through the six psychological stages of EI (SAFE-TBO), described in Chapter Two. The second part of this chapter gives more specific suggestions on how to develop EI in each of the 16 EIP scales.

8.1   Processes for developing Emotional Intelligence

Of the many human attributes that differentiate higher performance in the workplace, the majority may be summarised by the acronym KASH: Knowledge, Attitude, Skills, and Habits.[1] When organisations are asked which of these they invest in most for people development, the answer is usually skills and knowledge. However, when asked which of these are more long-term predictors of performance and make a sustained difference, the answer is typically attitudes and habits. These are both the province of Emotional Intelligence, and the answer to sustainable change.[2,3] Skills and knowledge on the other hand, can be developed much more effectively when people hold complimentary attitudes and habits, making change easier and therefore more likely to stick.

Attitudes and habits form part of the psychological process by which people perceive, interpret, and act upon their experiences. Each part of this process falls between the initial stimulus of an event and the resulting outcome of their behaviour, as illustrated by the example in Table 8.1.

Example of the six stages of EI

1	**Stimulus**	A manager calls out to their PA: "Where are those files?"
2	**Attitude**	The PA perceives this as being told they are too slow.
3	**Feeling/Emotion**	The PA feels annoyed and upset.
4	**Thinking**	They think to themselves: "You don't appreciate how hard I work for you."
5	**Behaviour/Habit**	Their automatic response is to shout back: "I can only do one thing at a time!" A few minutes later the PA slams the files down on their manager's desk.
6	**Outcome**	The outcome is that they don't talk and avoid one another for the rest of the day.

Table 8.1

This six-part process (SAFE-TBO) provides a useful structure for understanding the various mechanisms by which coaching interventions can be made. All of these stages are interconnected, so changing one of them is likely to produce a change in the others and ultimately in the final outcome. The development suggestions which follow are based on many years' experience of using the EIP with individuals and groups and have been found to produce effective results for making change stick.

8.2   How to respond to or change the stimulus

The first stage in psychological processing is initiated by a stimulus, whether this is external such as the telephone ringing, or internal such as feeling thirsty. Stimuli may trigger several emotional, cognitive, or behavioural responses in a person, as illustrated in Table 8.1. The emotionally intelligent individual learns to identify their triggers and manage them accordingly.

Change the stimulus: A stimulus can be anything within the environment that triggers a response in someone; by changing the stimulus a person may also change their response. This may be as simple as an individual avoiding people or situations that bring out the worst in them, or choosing to be with people or stay in situations that bring out the best in them. We can also learn how to create the stimulus we want from others. For example, by making an effort to engage with people, others are likely to reciprocate by being more responsive (a new stimulus), which in turn creates a more positive atmosphere. In other words, there is a cyclical effect between stimulus and response, as one will initiate the other.

Create emotional anchors: In the early 20th century, psychologists demonstrated how animal behaviour is largely the result of conditioned responses. For instance, Pavlov[4] demonstrated how, if a dog was repeatedly given food when a bell rang, it would soon start to expect to be fed and salivate at the sound of the bell. This was termed a 'conditioned' response whereby an emotional and behavioural response could be invoked through reward and reinforcement. A similar technique, known as 'anchoring',[5] has been used to help people manage their emotional state. For example, a person may recall happy memories and their associated feelings while clasping their hands together. After sufficient repetition, the action of clasping hands together becomes an anchor for the associated feelings of their happy memories. Rather like the dog's response to the bell, the individual only needs to activate the stimulus (clasping their hands together) to trigger the conditioned response (happy feelings). This principle can be widened to any set of feelings or behaviours and is similar in principle to how habits are formed through reinforcement, which is discussed later in Section 8.6.

Use self-control: At a neurological level it is possible to intervene between the stimulus being fired and the person's response. Libet[6] showed that there is a half second gap between the signal (an 'action potential') and the automatic response. It takes 0.3 seconds before a person becomes aware of the desire to act, giving them 0.2 seconds to intervene and block their automatic response. In other words, by developing good emotional Self Awareness (scale 3) a person can learn to stop their automatic responses, such as: not being distracted from a task; resisting an emotional outburst; and thinking before acting. There is a caveat, however, as each time an individual inhibits an impulse, the next impulse is more difficult to stop. Research done by Baumeister[7] found that people who had to resist the urge to eat chocolate were less able to resist other similar temptations later on. This would suggest that self-control or willpower on their own are limited resources, and therefore only offer a temporary solution. In the longer-term it is more sustainable to change attitudes and habits, as discussed later in this chapter.

Minimise the threat response: The brain's primary purpose is to keep us alive and it does this by scanning the environment (about five times every second) for possible threats. Evidence shows that some of the most powerful threat stimuli are social factors,[8] which have even been found to activate the same pain and pleasure receptors as physical stimuli. (This contrasts with Maslow's classic need theory that suggests social factors are lower down the hierarchy of needs.)[9] People are primarily motivated to maximise certain social rewards and resist any threat of losing them.[10] Consider the three examples below on how the threat response may be raised or lowered in the workplace depending on how these needs are being met (by the stimulus).

— **Security:** The brain is hardwired to anticipate and predict what will happen, so managers who are consistent and reliable (Authenticity; scale 10) (reward stimulus) create a calmer and more productive environment. A manager who is inconsistent and unpredictable on the other hand is more likely to activate the threat response in others, creating anxiety and defensiveness.

— **Control:** Giving individuals choice and control over their work life (reward stimulus) increases their sense of Personal Power (scale 6). Removing autonomy (threat stimulus), however, increases stress and impairs performance. One study in a nursing home found that residents who were given greater choice over small matters, such as where to place a plant and when to have a meal, lived longer and healthier lives.[11]

— **Emotional Connection:** The boss who is open and fair with others (reward stimulus) is likely to foster an environment of Trust (scale 11) and collaboration (Interdependence; scale 15). In contrast, a perceived sense of unfairness and inequality (threat stimulus) creates strong feelings of mistrust, anger, and hostility.

These and other social and emotional needs are explained in Table 8.2. The next few sections in this chapter look at attitudes, thoughts, feelings, and habits, all of which are inter-related and therefore act as stimuli and responses to each other. For instance, a negative attitude may trigger negative feelings, negative feelings may fuel critical thinking, and critical thinking may create defensive behaviours and habits. Learning how to manage these different psychological elements is what constitutes being emotionally intelligent.

8.3   How to develop constructive attitudes

It has long been known that people are drawn to behave in ways that are consistent with their attitudes, otherwise they experience anxiety compelling them to change how they behave (known as cognitive dissonance).[12] Attitudes create people's emotional responses through a pattern matching process in the emotional brain (described in Chapter Two; 2.4), which in turn drives their thinking and behaviour. Therefore, to change behaviour in the long-term, people must also change their attitudes. For example, teaching a person to say "No" assertively will not last for long if underneath they still feel inadequate (their attitude). Or, introducing a set of customer service competencies is unlikely to achieve the desired outcomes if the employees do not want to be of service to others (their attitude).

The first step to changing attitudes is to become aware of them. Attitudes are intended to help simplify life, so that people do not need to consciously process and choose every action they make. Once someone becomes aware of their attitudes, they cease to be unconscious and automatic, and become open to question, deliberation, and change. Many of the methods described in this chapter help challenge, create doubt in, and undermine negative attitudes, whether this is by changing emotional states, adapting thinking, or creating new habits, all of which influence underlying attitudes.

Create doubt in negative attitudes: Changing attitudes does not require deep psycho-logical therapy; a person needs only to create an element of doubt in their attitudes for them to be open to change. This is because attitudes tend to operate categorically, for example: like/dislike, good/bad, right/wrong. Once attitudes become open to question, they cease to be automatic responses. Instead, they are conscious thoughts open to debate, influence, and change. This is particularly useful when people hold deeply ingrained attitudes. For example, "Nobody likes me", "I am bound to fail", or "Nobody can be trusted". The skill of the coach is not to challenge the person's attitude directly, as this often results in the person thinking of reasons why they are right and entrenching their attitude further. But instead, to engage the individual in an exploration of their attitude, to discuss how it helps them and hinders them, and what may be a more useful alternative attitude to hold.

One such approach, called the 'continuum method',[13] is to ask the client to place their attitude on a zero to ten scale with zero being the lowest, "I am a failure", to ten being what they would like to see, "I am a success". Then, ask them to list what they would see in someone scoring a ten, such as, they would have friends, money, and qualifications, etc. Then ask the individual to score where they are on each of these criteria on a zero to ten scale. The likelihood is they will be higher than zero (zero being no friends, no money, and no qualifications). By moving them away from zero, the attitude ceases to be categorical, breaking down their attitude to specific parts so they are less able to generalise, and by using a zero to ten scale the attitude becomes open to debate. Using zero to ten scales with specific outcomes is also a powerful way of setting targets for goals (Goal Directedness; scale 7) and behaviour change (Personal Power; scale 6).

Start with a 'thrive' mindset: In nature the species that lives to pass on its genes is the one that has well-developed survival instincts and can instantly focus attention on any perceived threat. For this reason, people naturally focus their attention more on the negative than on the positive. For example: people are drawn more rapidly to bad news; they have a better memory for negative events than positive events; they do more to avoid loss than to get a comparable gain; and they put more weight on negative information. Kahneman and Tversky,[14] two psychologists who won the Nobel Prize in Economics, found that the psychological impact of loss is two-and-a-half times more powerful than a comparable gain. One reason for this may be that during difficult times the brain switches to a more primitive survival mode – to protect and conserve – even though the best way to survive modern-day difficulties is more often to look for opportunities and be creative; that is, to have a thrive not a survive mindset.

Knowing that people have a natural propensity to focus their attention on the negative is an important consideration when developing EI. Two scales from the EIP that are strong indicators of a positive mindset are: Personal Power (scale 6) which is about feeling responsible for oneself; and Balanced Outlook (scale 12) which is about feeling realistically hopeful. By adopting and habitually practising a positive growth mindset, people can develop these scales and counter the brain's negative default setting.[15,16] This may include activities such as actively choosing to focus on positive memories and expectations, investing time in friendships, recognising that people are doing the best they can, having compassion towards oneself and others, replaying the caring rather than critical messages received in childhood, and enjoying humour and laughter – which have been shown to boost the immune system and be good for people's health.[17]

Apply positive abstract language: When the creators of Neurolinguistic Programming (NLP), Grinder and Bandler,[18] started to model the behaviours of exceptional communicators they observed that one of the key characteristics of influential therapists was the use of positive abstract language. Here are some examples of positive abstract language used in the coaching context: "You will soon be ready to make the changes you wish"; "The next step you make will be significant"; "You can use your inner confidence to grow and develop"; "You can create the future you desire"; "Your experiences and knowledge will guide you through"; and "You have access to your innate capabilities and gifts." Such statements can be very powerful because the human brain can't help but search for meaning (pattern matches) from the positive abstract words. In all of these examples, the individual draws out their own positive meaning which reinforces existing positive attitudes. It is worth noting that negative abstract language can be equally influential. Statements such as: "This is hopeless"; "I have depression"; and "My motivation has gone", are vague generalisations that create a negative mindset and reinforce negative attitudes. When describing negative experiences, it is important to avoid abstract and vague generalisations, instead be specific and use concrete terms.

Use metaphors and stories: Similar to abstract language are metaphors and stories, which engage the brain in a search for meaning. This triggers areas of the brain involved in new learning, linking ideas, imagination, and being creative. Metaphors and stories capture the imagination causing a type of trance state whereby attitudes can be formed and adapted (as described by the REM state in Chapter Two; 2.4). This can be seen in children who quickly start daydreaming when they hear something interesting, as their pattern matching brain makes meaningful sense of it. A skilled coach often leaves the ending of a metaphor open for the listener's imagination to draw their own conclusions. They also make the metaphor analogous to the individual's circumstances, such as stories of overcoming adversity, morality, and perseverance, and may draw parallels with other parts of the person's life, such as their hobbies and sports, and where they have demonstrated being effective. Some common metaphors used to help people in their personal development include: climbing a mountain (putting things into perspective); taking the stabilisers off a bicycle (letting go); learning to drive a car (developing automatic skills through practice); learning to walk or read as a child (the first steps are the most challenging); and going on a journey (life is unpredictable). Such metaphors can become powerful unconscious motivators, influencing a person's attitudes and behaviour.

Disassociate from negative feelings: There are a growing number of therapeutic and developmental interventions that focus directly on changing the emotional response attached to a person's attitude (a pattern match). Some of these include: the Rewind

Technique by The Human Givens Institute;[19] Disassociation, an NLP technique;[20] Thought Field Therapy (TFT), also known as 'tapping' by Callaghan;[21] Eye Movement Desensitisation (EMDR) by Shapiro;[22] and Amygdala Depotentiation by Ron Ruden.[23] These techniques all have one thing in common: they require the individual to re-experience an event that triggers their emotional response while maintaining a more positive or calmer emotional state. This allows a new and more positive emotion to be attached to the underlying attitude. For example: replacing anxiety with feeling confident when making an important sales pitch; replacing anger with calmness when receiving critical feedback; and changing feelings of pessimism to optimism when faced with a setback. Learning these techniques requires specific training which is provided by these institutes. Some other techniques for calming emotions and managing feelings are described in the section that follows.

8.4   How to manage feelings

Feelings are the direct consequence of stimuli pattern matching with an underlying attitude, and are the primary influence on a person's thoughts and behaviours.[24] Feelings are the key mediators between how attitudes determine behaviours, as illustrated by the three levels of the EIP framework (Chapter Four; 4.1). Feelings drive a person's behaviour in the form of motivation, expectations, needs, wants, fears, likes, hopes, and intentions. If a person decides to improve their relationships, develop their confidence, or enhance their performance, it is their feelings that will drive this change, which is why feelings are integral to developing EI.

Notice feelings early: All feelings are useful in that they are the messengers telling a person how they are doing, what needs they have, and the attitudes they hold. If a person does not notice or attend to their feelings, they will manifest in other ways, usually growing in strength until the person is unable to manage them appropriately. An important aspect of EI is learning to notice feelings early, then to accurately label the feelings and understand what they are telling us. The longer someone ignores, represses, and denies their feelings, the more likely it is that they will be unable to manage them later on. For example, if a person notices when they feel a mild sense of frustration, then they can do something to manage this feeling, such as breathe deeply, consider why they feel this way, or take some positive action to address the cause of their frustration. If they do nothing, the feeling may grow until the person feels consumed with anger or despair, by which time they will be less able to process the feelings calmly and rationally and are more likely to over-react.

Pay attention to feelings: There are several stages to becoming aware of our feelings (and the feelings of others) and acting upon them appropriately.

1   We must first notice the feeling (for example, tension in the stomach that may be a sign of anxiety)

2   Then pay attention to this feeling and give it some significance rather than ignore it (Why do we have this feeling?)

3   Then think about what this feeling means (Maybe we feel anxious about delivering an upcoming presentation)

4   Then decide how to act upon it (We could practise delivering our presentation to a colleague)

If people do not pay attention to their initial feelings, as many people don't, they will be unable to move to the next stage of this process. Paying attention to feelings also gives people an insight into their underlying attitudes. For example, if they feel nervous about making a presentation, this may indicate they have doubts about their competence in this area, or they may have a pessimistic outlook, or they could hold a self-critical attitude. Being aware of feelings also gives people access to their intuition. For instance, if they notice feeling uncomfortable about a decision they have made, it may be that they have missed something important, or if they notice feeling uneasy being with a person, it may be that they do not trust them.

Learn relaxation techniques: A key skill in developing EI is learning how to be emotionally and physically relaxed. There are several very effective ways of doing this, many of which involve techniques for breathing, using the imagination, relaxing all parts of the body, and focusing attention on calming thoughts. The sequence usually involves the individual closing their eyes, sitting comfortably, and minimising any external distractions. This is followed by focusing attention on their breathing and taking longer out-breaths than in-breaths, which helps activate the parasympathetic nervous system which in turn relaxes the body. The individual may then start to become aware of their body by relaxing their muscles, moving up from the feet, into the legs, the torso, up to the shoulders, the head, and finally through the arms, hands, and fingers. They may continue to relax by using their imagination to visualise walking in a place that they find calming, such as on a beach, in the countryside, or on a mountain. Repeating this technique reinforces the experience and makes it easier and quicker to reach the same level of relaxation each time they use it. A popular relaxation technique that employs many of the strategies outlined in this chapter is known as Mindfulness, characterised by non-judgment of and openness to current experiences.[25] Recent evidence found an eight-week mindfulness stress reduction programme led to physical changes in the emotional centres of the brain consistent with improved emotional regulation.[26]

Calm down the emotional brain: When a person practises relaxation techniques, they are effectively calming down the limbic system, which is the part of the brain that triggers emotions. Too much emotion can have significantly negative effects on a person's performance, as in the case of an emotional hijack (described in Chapter Two). This is when the brain perceives a dangerous threat even though none may exist, such as: freezing during an important presentation; panicking when late for a meeting; or losing their temper during a discussion. Under such conditions, a person's performance can sink to hopeless incompetence, their IQ drops dramatically, and reasoning and judgment are easily lost. There are several reasons why poor management of strong emotions can impair a person's performance in this way:

1   Strong emotions narrow a person's attention therefore making them less aware and unable to consider all options

2   They make a person more judgmental in their thinking, as emotional brain thinking tends to be more categorical and less refined

3   They block access to a person's rational thinking brain thereby reducing their capacity to think things through. This is an evolutionary fight-flight-freeze response to danger

4   They make a person more certain, decisive, and less flexible, which can be catastrophic if they are also in the grip of the three points above

5   They make someone less self-aware and less aware of others. The individual may not realise how they are behaving and acting, resulting in them pursuing reckless actions and being oblivious to feedback

Furthermore, everyone else around them is aware of and impacted by how they are behaving, which may greatly damage their relationships. However, if people learn how to manage their emotional state effectively by noticing what causes them anxiety, remaining calm in a crisis, being aware of their feelings in the moment, and listening to feedback from others, all of these negative behaviours can be reversed leading to greater awareness, higher intellectual functioning, more flexible behaviours, better decision making, and improved relationships.

Reduce levels of stress: The effects of excessive emotion and stress are cumulative. Feelings of stress and anxiety are triggered almost instantly through the sympathetic nervous system, but it can take the parasympathetic nervous system up to four hours to fully calm down after a stressful event.[27] Over time, if people experience regular stress then this does not allow them sufficient recovery time and they can spend much of their time in a state of heightened arousal with the negative consequences this has on their thinking, behaviour, and physical health. The danger is that this arousal state can become the individual's typical daily experience, where they feel generally anxious, despondent, unhappy, or depressed. People who experience regular stress benefit from slowing down, reflecting on their experiences, and learning how to relax in order to change their patterns of thinking, feeling, and behaviour to cope better with life's daily challenges.

To recover from long-term stress, they may need to re-evaluate what is important to them and how they want to live their lives. EIP scales that can help in this respect are Emotional Resilience (scale 5), Goal Directedness (scale 7), Authenticity (scale 10), and Reflective learning (scale 16). Developing these scales is discussed later in this chapter; 8.9.

Make time for sleep and recuperation: In Chapter Two; 2.4, it was explained that one of the main ways that arousal and anxiety are reduced is through the natural process of dreaming while asleep. This is the REM phase of sleep, whereby unfulfilled emotional expectations are metaphorically acted out and therefore completed during the dreaming stages of sleep.[28] If an individual does not get sufficient REM sleep, they will wake up feeling tired and less able to deal with the challenges of the day ahead. One of the key ways to support sleep is to lower anxiety during the waking day by learning how to relax. A few essential guidelines to aid restful sleep are: avoid caffeine and alcohol before bed; sleep in a dark environment; keep to regular sleeping patterns wherever possible; do some physical activity during the day; avoid watching television in the bedroom; do not sleep-in excessively; and avoid anxiety-provoking thoughts, such as worrying about tomorrow, before bedtime.

Make change experiential: Feelings are the primary drivers of behaviour. To change behaviour, it is necessary to change the feelings behind them. Feelings are created in the limbic brain, which learns mostly through stimulus-response conditioning or experiential (practical and emotional) reinforcement, i.e. repetition. This contrasts with the higher parts of the brain, the neocortex (or thinking brain), which learns more through acquiring knowledge and information, and making connections. For example, people can become very knowledgeable about themselves by reading books, getting feedback, going on courses, or being coached, but behavioural change only happens if it is backed-up by putting this knowledge into actual physical practice. All too often people know what they 'should' do, but they don't do it in practice. What is learned during a coaching session will only lead to behaviour change if the individual implements and practises it after the coaching has taken place, integrating it meaningfully into their lives.

This difference between the emotional and thinking parts of the brain is illustrated by the case of an amnesic patient whose emotional memory remained intact despite having no knowledge recall of past events.[29] On one occasion his doctor placed a tack in his hand which caused the patient some pain when they shook hands. The next time they met, the patient had no recollection of ever having met his doctor but did not want to shake the doctor's hand. Despite the patient having no conscious cognitive explicit memory (in his thinking brain), he still held an unconscious emotional implicit memory that associated shaking hands with the doctor as painful (in his emotional brain). Much of what drives our behaviour does so at an unconscious emotional level.[30]

Provide opportunity for social interaction: One way to make change experiential is for it to be done interactively within a group. People are innately social and are fundamentally drawn to interact, so it would be hard to justify how EI could be developed without involving some interaction. The changes that take place are often far more dramatic and powerful when carried out collectively rather than individually. This is because other people provide a sense of context and reality to a person's experience. It does not discount the benefit of one-to-one coaching, but coaching is often only a prelude to the action of putting EI into practice with others.

Meet the basic emotional needs: All living things have essential needs that must be met in order for them to thrive and flourish. When people do not fulfil their emotional needs in sufficient balance, they become unhappy, angry, unstable, over-emotional, anxious, or greedy. The Human Givens Institute[31] has identified a set of basic emotional needs that should be met in balance if people are to be emotionally and socially healthy. The EIP scales that help to meet these emotional needs are shown in Table 8.2.

The basic human emotional needs

BASIC EMOTIONAL NEED	DESCRIPTION	RELATED EIP SCALES
Security	People need to feel safe and secure, and able to cope with the demands and challenges of life	Self Regard Emotional Resilience Personal Power
Emotional connection	Having the capacity and opportunity to connect openly and intimately with others	Awareness of Others Connecting with Others Emotional Expression and Control
Control	People need a sense of influence and choice over how they live their lives	Personal Power Flexibility Emotional Expression and Control
Community and status	Humans are social beings and need to belong to groups where they feel valued	Regard for Others Connecting with Others Trust Conflict Handling Interdependence
Privacy	Having the opportunity for personal time and space where the individual can reflect and be alone	Self Regard Interdependence Reflective Learning

Table 8.2

BASIC EMOTIONAL NEED	DESCRIPTION	RELATED EIP SCALES
Achievement	The human brain and body are like muscles that have evolved to be at their healthiest when being utilised and stretched	Goal Directedness Personal Power Balanced Outlook
Attention	The degree to which people receive attention and the form of attention they receive throughout their lives strongly influences their self-esteem	Self Regard Connecting with Others
Meaning and purpose to life	Having meaning and purpose to life is an essential element for emotional well-being. It is derived from three criteria: being stretched and personal growth; being needed and serving others; and connecting with something bigger than themselves	Self Awareness Goal Directedness Authenticity

Learn to use the innate resources: People possess a set of innate resources that equip them to meet their basic emotional needs (Table 8.2). The skill of being emotionally intelligent is in learning how to manage these resources so as to achieve one's potential. Some of the key innate resources, examples of their use and misuse, and how they may be developed through the EIP scales, are given in Table 8.3.

The fundamental human resources

Table 8.3

INNATE RESOURCE	EXAMPLE OF EFFECTIVE USE	EXAMPLE OF MISUSE	RELATED EIP SCALES
Imagination	Visualising positive outcomes	Picturing only what could go wrong	Goal Directedness Balanced Outlook
Creativity	Being insightful and finding solutions to complex problems	Being entirely unrealistic and impractical	Self Awareness Flexibility Personal Power
Logic and objectivity	Working through problems step by step	Ignoring feelings, values, and sensitivities	Self Regard Self Awareness Emotional Resilience

INNATE RESOURCE	EXAMPLE OF EFFECTIVE USE	EXAMPLE OF MISUSE	RELATED EIP SCALES
Self-observation	Noticing their feelings and how they affect motivation	Being totally self-absorbed and unaware of others or the environment	Self Awareness Reflective Learning
Sleep and recovery	Being able to rest and recuperate both physically and emotionally	Feeling constantly tired and run-down, unable to be alert and engaged	Self Awareness Emotional Resilience
Empathy	Adapting and responding to others' individual differences	Making assumptions about how others are feeling, letting others' negative feelings bring them down	Awareness of Others Connecting with Others Trust Interdependence
Relaxation	Breathing techniques to help reduce anxiety	Being over relaxed, bored, and demotivated	Self Awareness Emotional Resilience
Self-choice	Developing appropriate impulse control	Lacking spontaneity, fun, and openness	Personal Power Emotional Expression and Control Conflict Handling
Expectation (thinking about the future)	Planning and preparing for a meeting	Focusing only on the future, rather than learning from the past or enjoying the present	Goal Directedness Balanced Outlook
Learning	Modifying behaviour based on previous experience	Constantly reflecting but not putting learning into action	Authenticity Reflective Learning

8.5   How to manage thinking

Most techniques for 'managing thinking' focus on changing and interrupting irrational or generalised thinking patterns. Irrational thinking is largely the result of excessive emotion. If sufficiently strong, emotions such as desire, hate, or fear can prevent the individual from engaging their rational thinking brain. One sign of this is when people use generalised language such as: "can't", "must", "have to", "never", and "always", which may indicate they are locked into their emotional brain leading to exaggerated and inappropriate thinking and behaviour. Calming down the emotional brain from excessive arousal, to enable clearer thinking, is an essential aspect of Emotional Intelligence and was discussed in the previous section on 'How to manage feelings'. This section on 'How to manage thinking' includes a range of cognitive techniques, such as Reframing, which help the individual use their thinking capacities to understand and manage their feelings, so they can be more rational, objective, and self-managed.

Quieten the rational thinking brain: Calming the emotional brain may be complimented by learning how to quieten the rational thinking brain which allows for more insightful, creative, intuitive, connected, and inspired levels of thinking. People tend to do their most insightful thinking when relaxed and not trying to think. One study by Rock showed that only 10% of people did their best thinking at work, and that their most insightful thinking was during non-work activities such as at play, when resting, during physical exercise, in downtime, while reflecting, or when experiencing something new.[10] These activities share a number of features that are often present at times of quality thinking:

1. The person is 'not trying too hard' to solve a problem, which helps them to switch off the noise of distracting thoughts, inner dialogue, self-conscious inhibition, etc.

2. The activity is 'non-demanding' allowing their mind to wander and make insightful connections.

3. They have 'slowed down' their thinking, giving more time for ideas to connect, rather like taking the scenic route instead of the motorway on a car journey.

4. They may be 'doing something different' from their routine. This physically connects different neurons and forms new associations.

5. They are 'focusing internally' which helps reduce external stimulation and gives access to deeper insights. Intuition and insight come from connecting with deeper-level patterns (accumulated wisdom) and the quieter brain signals.

6. They have a 'positive mindset' which prevents their threat response from being alerted (which would block clear thinking) and activates quieter circuitry in the brain.

7. They are in a 'focused state of attention' (a trance or 'flow' state) where their interest and imagination have been captivated, allowing for longer and deeper levels of concentration.

Developing this deeper level of insightful thinking has several benefits:

A   It is often the only way that more complex problems can be solved.

B   It creates new neural networks so the learning acquired is more permanent.

C   The individual is more likely to take ownership and be motivated by learning through self-discovery.

▷ The instant euphoria gained from an insight releases energy, helping the person to take action.

Use positive reframing: Reframing is a technique often used by the coach to reflect what their client expresses but in a more positive way. For example, "I can't do anything right", may be reframed by the coach as "I hear there are some things you are finding quite challenging at the moment." The word "can't" has been replaced by "challenging", the word "anything" by the words "some things", and adding "at the moment" implies that the situation is temporary. More often than not, the client accepts the reframe and their emotional (limbic) brain unconsciously creates new expectations and patterns to match this more positive description. People can also apply this technique to reframing their feelings. For example, feelings of 'anxiety' may be reframed as 'anticipation', and 'boredom' may be reframed as 'relaxation'. Reframing is particularly useful in areas such as sports motivation, mood enhancement, and building self-confidence. However, the skill of the coach is to balance positive reframing without discounting what the client is saying and to fully acknowledge how they are feeling.

Challenge negative thinking: Other methods for changing negative thinking are more direct than reframing and aim to consciously challenge the individual's excessively emotional and categorical thinking by applying a more analytical and rational approach. For example, you can ask someone what advice they would give a friend who was in a similar situation to themselves. People are often very good at giving sound, rational, and sensible advice to others but are less adept at applying it to themselves. This is because people are less emotionally involved with others than they are with themselves and can therefore think through problems more clearly.

Another way in which people can challenge their negative interpretation of events is to think of several alternative explanations. For example, someone may assume their boss didn't reply to their email because "She doesn't respect me." Alternative reasons may include: "She didn't receive it"; "She hasn't had time to reply"; or "She did reply but the email has been lost." Rather than assume the worst, the individual could be encouraged to choose an explanation that is more probable and helps them to feel better. A modification of this method is to ask the coachee to think of the worst possible explanation, then the best possible explanation, and then what is the most realistic and likely explanation. To help the individual think of the most realistic explanation, they could be asked to recall past experiences where they have been in similar situations and to describe what happened. For instance, they may fear that they will freeze at their next presentation, yet their previous presentations have been well received. Or they may expect their colleague to become very upset at their appraisal, yet they have previously handled such difficult conversations very well. To help them challenge their negative thinking further, the coach may draw upon more tangible evidence, such as feedback from others, performance data, or using the continuum method (described previously in Section 8.3). Once the individual recognises that in the past their overly negative assumptions turned out to be false, they may start to appraise situations more realistically and avoid catastrophising events.

There are many other techniques to help individuals challenge their irrational thinking patterns that may be found in approaches such as cognitive-behavioural techniques, rational emotive therapy, solutions focused coaching, and positive thinking.

Unpack the problem: It can sometimes help someone to examine a problem in detail to identify the sequence of events and common errors in their thinking and interpretation. For example, a coachee may wish to discuss a situation they did not handle very well in the past, such as getting into an argument with a colleague. The following questions will help them to examine and learn from the specific event:

— Describe what happened

— What was the initial trigger?

— How were they feeling immediately prior to this event?

— What were they thinking at the time of the event?

— How did they feel during the event?

— Was this a one-off or a common pattern for them?

— What do they think the other person was thinking and feeling?

— What did they do after the event?

— What could they have done differently before, during, and after the event?

It is also important that the individual is feeling calm when discussing the situation. People often try to resolve their problems when feeling anxious or tired, rather than waiting until they are more relaxed and able to think things through more clearly.

Use the language of choice: People's negative thinking is often reflected in their use of words and language. Negative language typically reflects low choice, low control, and rigid behaviour. Positive language typically reflects high choice, self-responsibility, and flexible behaviour. Some examples of how to use high choice words and language are given in Table 8.4.

Examples of using high choice language

SUGGESTION	LOW CHOICE EXAMPLES (NEGATIVE LANGUAGE)	HIGH CHOICE EXAMPLES (POSITIVE LANGUAGE)
Say "I" instead of "You" when referring to oneself	"You feel angry when ..."	"I feel angry when ..."
State if something is an opinion rather than claiming it to be a fact	"That's true" "This is difficult"	"I think that is true" "I find it difficult"
Use self-empowering words rather than disempowering words	"I should" "I will try" "I have to"	"I will do" "I can do" "I shall do"
Be specific rather than generalising	"It is always like this" "I never win" "Nobody likes me"	"On this occasion" "I was unsuccessful this time" "I don't think Jane likes me"
Use committed language rather than too many non-committal or down-playing words	"Interesting" "Possibly" "I suppose"	"I agree/disagree" "I like/dislike it" "In my opinion ..."
Avoid confusing feelings with thinking	"I feel that is correct" "I feel we should do ..." "You are wrong"	"I think this is correct" "I feel angry, happy, upset, etc." "I feel annoyed when you ..."

Table 8.4

8.6   How to create useful habits of behaviour

Habits are automatic responses that may include behaviours, emotions, and thoughts. For example, a person may have a behavioural habit of not listening to people, an emotional habit of becoming upset by confrontation, and a thinking habit of assuming the worst when things go wrong. Emotional and thinking habits have been explained above, and behavioural habits are now discussed.

Replace negative habits: Behavioural habits are usually automatic and unconscious, so the first step to creating a new habit is to become aware of the existing habit. The next step is then to replace the unhelpful habit with a new and positive habit. Consider the following examples: replace 'blaming others' with 'showing appreciation'; 'blaming oneself' with 'self-compassion'; 'demanding constant attention' with 'listening to people'; 'avoiding people' with 'initiating conversation'; 'compulsively working' with 'taking time for relaxation'; 'over-eating' with 'taking exercise'; 'watching too much television' with 'being outdoors'; and 'being tired' with 'setting personal goals'. One of the difficulties in changing a habit is making it stick, as the existing neural pattern must be replaced by a stronger alternative.[32] This may be achieved through repetition, rehearsal, and reinforcement of the new behaviour pattern to avoid reverting back to the old behavioural habit.

Be motivated to change: Making an initial change in behaviour can be relatively easy but maintaining it can be far more difficult to sustain. All too often, when people are under pressure or the initial motivation for change has passed, they revert back to their old behaviours. One reason for this is that the person does not really want to change. At an unconscious level they may even want to hold on to their negative and defensive behaviour because it still provides them with some benefit. For example, an individual who behaves aggressively may benefit by getting people's attention and getting their own way. The solution to this is to make sure that the person really wants to change and that the pay-off for doing so outweighs any sacrifice of giving up the old habit. It is also important to be sure that the new behaviour is something the person wants for themselves rather than to meet other people's expectations, such as those of their partner or their coach. Motivation to change is largely unconscious, so if an individual is relying solely upon conscious willpower to change, it is likely they will end up doing what they subconsciously want to do.

Focus on one specific behaviour: Another reason why people fail to achieve their goals is that they try to change too much in one go, such as an ambitious new year's resolution, which is unlikely to succeed: "I will be nice to everyone from now on"; "I will only eat healthy food"; "I will always remain positive and happy." More specific alternatives to these could be: "I will do one good thing for someone each day"; "I will eat one whole piece of fruit every day"; or "I will make a point to laugh with someone every day." It is tempting during the enthusiasm of a coaching session to set noble and ambitious goals, but after a day or two back in the daily demands of life, the motivation wanes and people slip back into their automatic habits. The technique of habit change involves making sure the habit is focused on something highly specific that can easily be done and repeated over a period of time so that the new habit becomes reinforced and stronger than the old one. Any behaviour change has a wider impact than the specific change itself. For example, getting a client to develop the habit of remembering people's names helps improve their relationships (Connecting with Others; scale 9) which may then raise their self-esteem. Success breeds success. By learning that habit change is possible (EI Attitude 7) and that it works, the individual may continue to practise it more often, and be motivated to change other things in their life.

Practise a different response: Habits are unconscious automatic responses to stimuli that happen on a daily basis. Consider these examples:

— When answering the telephone, the individual expects the worst
— When opening the fridge, they take out a piece of chocolate
— When meeting a friend, they start by talking about themselves
— When in a hurry, they become irritable

To change an automatic response requires two steps: first becoming aware of the habit and second choosing a new behavioural response. For example:

— When answering the telephone, they could stand up and smile
— When opening the fridge, they could take out a piece of fruit
— When meeting a friend, they could ask about them first
— When in a hurry, they could pause to take six slow deep breaths

Repeating these behaviour changes initially takes deliberate, conscious effort. With repetition they become easier and automatic until the newly installed behaviour becomes a habit that is sustained.

Develop healthy lifestyle habits: Much of Emotional Intelligence focuses on developing the psychological skills described in this chapter, but a healthy mind is also dependent upon a healthy body. Physical health has many benefits for stress reduction, emotional resilience, well-being, and work performance.[33] There are three main ways of building and maintaining a healthy body: rest, nutrition, and exercise. Rest, which includes sleep and recuperation, has been discussed in Chapter Two; 2.5, and is crucial for relaxation and physical recovery. People are usually aware of the importance of exercise and healthy eating but struggle to put this into practice. One reason for this is people's preference for quick fix solutions, such as dieting, detox, abstinence, or intense activity, which are usually only temporary solutions. Making modest increments in healthy eating and regular exercise, as part of a daily lifestyle is far more likely to lead to ingrained habits and long-term success. This can be achieved in the same way as developing psychological habits, through regular repetition of specific changes in behaviour.

8.7   How to create positive outcomes

There are two main elements of EI that help a person achieve positive outcomes. First, to identify what it is that they want, which requires Self Awareness (scale 3). Second, to focus on and not be distracted from, achieving it, which requires Goal Directedness (scale 7). A number of useful suggestions for creating positive outcomes are now given.

Have clear intentions: In order to develop EI, it is important for someone to have clear intentions on what it is they want to achieve, as reflected by Goal Directedness. In neurological terms this means creating expectations that orientate them consciously and unconsciously towards the outcome they want to achieve. The brain is a pattern matching organ and is constantly scanning the environment for matches. This is why optimistic people spot opportunities and pessimistic people focus their attention on barriers and problems. Powerful ways of setting positive expectations are through visualisation, guided imagery, and mental rehearsal.

Plan each step: As well as focusing on the outcome, it is important that the coachee plans how they are going to achieve it. Sometimes people know what they want but go about it in the wrong way, such as not building rapport before making a request, or making a decision without consulting those who may be affected by it. When broken down into sequences of action, there are a surprising number of steps that need to be taken that lead to a positive outcome. Boiling a kettle takes about 20 steps; building a trusting relationship with someone takes many more. Often the coachee leaves the coaching session with clear goals and objectives but without a specific plan on how they are going to achieve them. It is important that they think this through, otherwise they may not start the process or may go about things in the wrong way, find that their goals aren't achieved, and decide to give up.

Access the imagination: Guiding someone to use their imagination to set positive expectations and intentions is quite simple but there are several subtleties to it. The first step is to help the individual to relax physiologically, cognitively, and emotionally. This can be done by getting them to focus on their breathing, to relax every part of their body and to imagine being in a peaceful place. Also, speaking to them in a gradually softening voice using vague and abstract positive language helps create positive feelings. Once relaxed, the person can be guided to visualise whatever outcome they wish to achieve, such as giving a confident presentation, succeeding in sport, or feeling calm and relaxed after a stressful day. The more texture included in their image, such as sound, colour, and smell, the stronger and more compelling the image becomes. Having created a personal positive expectation, they are unconsciously drawn to make this happen through their attitudes, thoughts, and feelings. This is why people who anticipate success tend to succeed, and those who expect to fail are more likely to be unsuccessful. Imagination has the capacity to create negative as well as positive expectations, so it is important that people learn how to use and manage their imagination rather than letting their imagination control them.

Role-play and rehearse success: An extension of visualisation is to use role-play and rehearsal. This makes the experience real and at the same time safe and non-threatening. Imagination and role-play act as a 'reality generator' firing off the same neurons as if the action were completed for real. For example, if someone feels anxious about a meeting they could visualise how they would want it to go and then role-play it several times with a trusted colleague. They may build on this by role-playing their anticipated concerns, helping them to relax and feel more in control (Personal Power; scale 6). A step on from imagination and role-play is to practise it in real life, in low risk situations, and to treat it as a learning event (like having learner plates for a new driver). This takes the pressure off the person and allows them to learn from their mistakes without having high expectations.

These suggestions will help someone create positive outcomes which in turn will build confidence and self-esteem. Creating positive outcomes is the final stage in the six-part process for developing EI. The one factor which strongly influences all of these processes is an individual's Self Regard (scale 1), the subject of our next section.

8.8   How to raise Self Regard through effective communication

The ultimate purpose of raising EI is to enhance Self Regard (unconditional self-acceptance), which is the cornerstone of the EIP framework. Self Regard is largely determined by the communication people experience throughout their lives, both towards themselves and from others.

In Transactional Analysis theory (TA), communication is referred to as a 'stroke' or a 'unit of attention'. An important distinguishing feature of a stroke is whether it is conditional (on a person's behaviour) or unconditional (for a person's being) and whether it is positive or negative. Combining these two essential elements of communication produces the Communication Grid (Table 8.5).[34] This may be used to help understand how people communicate so they can influence and build their own and others' Self Regard.

The Communication Grid

	NEGATIVE STROKE	POSITIVE STROKE	
UNCONDITIONAL (FOR BEING)	Put-down	Value	
CONDITIONAL (FOR DOING)	Feedback	Praise	

Table 8.5

Let positive strokes in: One of the most powerful ways to raise someone's Self Regard is by expressing Value towards them (positive unconditional strokes) and by avoiding Put-downs (unconditional negative strokes). Value is often expressed through the small things people do and spontaneous acts of kindness and consideration, such as acknowledging others through a smile, saying "Good morning", or offering them a drink. Equally, a Put-down can be easily transmitted through a scowl, raising the eyebrows, or by the absence of Value (not saying "good morning").

The most frequent kind of communication we receive is not from others but from ourself and our own self-talk. It is our capacity to accept Value and to reject a Put-down from ourselves and from others that largely determine our level of Self Regard from moment to moment and throughout our lives.

Praise people for what they do: A distinction should be made between Self Regard (the feelings people have towards themselves) and self-confidence (what they believe they are capable of), as someone can be confident but still have low Self Regard. For example, an individual may think they are good at using spreadsheets (i.e. they have confidence) but they may not feel good about themselves (Self Regard). Conversely, an individual may think they are hopeless at using spreadsheets (i.e. they lack confidence) but they still feel good about themselves (Self Regard).

Providing someone with Praise for what they do well is likely to raise a person's confidence but does not necessarily increase their Self Regard. Praise is not a substitute for Value, which is essential for meeting many of our basic emotional needs (see Table 8.2). There is even a risk that if someone is only praised when they do something well, such as high performance or making a profit, then they may feel their Value is conditional upon their performance or profit making. This could have the reverse effect of lowering their Self Regard if they feel their Self Regard is conditional ("I am only OK if ... I perform well or make a profit, etc."), rather than unconditional ("I am a valuable and worthwhile human being even if I don't perform well or make profit.") The antidote to this is to combine Praise with expressed Value.

Praise others to reinforce positive behaviour: Apart from raising confidence in others, Praise is also a powerful way to reinforce and encourage desirable behaviours and is generally more effective than negative Feedback at influencing change. If a person is poor at timekeeping and often late, it may be more effective to Praise them on the occasions they are on-time or early than to criticise them when they are late. As a general rule, people want to be praised and are likely to repeat behaviours that elicit positive reward. An important skill in showing appreciation is noticing when people are doing something well, which requires developing Awareness of Others (scale 4). The more we can notice and Praise others, the more habitual this behaviour becomes and the more we start to automatically recognise the positives in ourselves and others.

Express lots of Value: A concern sometimes raised about showing appreciation is that a person can be given too much Praise and may begin to 'over-rate' themselves. There is an element of truth in this. As Praise is conditional, it can become meaningless or unappreciated if not related to something a person has done to 'deserve' it. However, this is not true when expressing Value towards others; a person cannot receive too much Value (so long as it is sincere). It is not possible to feel 'too OK' or to have too much Self Regard. People sometimes mistakenly attribute arrogance to having too much Self

Regard, when in fact it usually indicates a low Regard for Others which is masking low Self Regard.

As a general rule, the recommended ratio of strokes is to give three Values and two Praises for every single Feedback and to never give a Put-down (to oneself or to others). A useful technique to raise Self Regard and Regard for Others is to write down three Values, two Praises, and one Feedback at the end of each day about oneself and others.

Distinguish Feedback from a Put-down: Feedback is essential if people are to learn and develop, as without it they are likely to repeat the same mistakes. Receiving Feedback also shows that the person cares enough about the other person to help them learn and develop. People are different and have different strengths and weaknesses. Some may be faster, slower, more academic, less academic, musical, or less musical etc. The important point is that people grow to learn that they are unconditionally OK, that is, they are still of value regardless of them being slower, faster, taller, shorter, more musical, or less musical, etc. Experiencing negative Feedback and failure (conditional Feedback) does not mean 'they' are a failure (an unconditional Put-down), but that they are a valuable human being who has not yet been successful at a particular task. If children are not exposed to this reality that people are different (EI Attitude 4) and however you and others are, is OK (EI Attitude 1), through life experiences such as competitive activities, then they do not learn to distinguish Feedback from a Put-down. Potentially, this could come to mean that every piece of future Feedback they receive could be experienced as a Put-down (I am Not OK) lowering their Self Regard. One way to prevent someone turning Feedback into a Put-down is to show them Value alongside the Feedback. For example, a parent may explain to their child that they have done something wrong (Feedback) but show them that they are still loved by giving them a hug afterwards (expressed Value). A manager may give Feedback to a colleague that their performance was poor but show them that they are still a valued member of the team, that they think highly of them, and that they will continue to support them.

If someone does not learn to distinguish their behaviour (Conditional self) from their being (Unconditional self), it can become very difficult in later life for them to accept negative Feedback without interpreting it as a Put-down and consequently it affecting their Self Regard. For example, negative Feedback such as, "The calculation you did was incorrect", may be interpreted as "You think I am stupid", and reinforces their feelings that "I think I am stupid" (a Put-down from themselves). This then becomes the message the individual replays to themselves when receiving Feedback in the future. Three effective ways of preventing people from interpreting negative Feedback as Put-downs are described below.

1   **Be aware of others:** First, be aware of others. Notice how they like to be appreciated and what they may not like. Some people experience humour and banter as a

Value, while others will experience it as a Put-down. For someone who in the past has experienced few positive strokes, a lot of sarcasm, or inconsistent messages (such as a Value followed by a Put-down), it is more difficult for them to accept expressed Value. In such cases it may be necessary that the other person gains their trust, demonstrates that they mean what they say (Authenticity; scale 10), consistently gives high quality Feedback to them, and when they do give Praise, does so in a genuine and sincere way.

2   **Have positive intentions towards others:** Second, to stop people turning Feedback into a Put-down, the individual providing the Feedback should check their intentions towards the other person, that they value and respect them. If they hold resentment, hostility, or dislike towards the other person, they need to look for reasons to feel tolerance, compassion, and understanding towards them as a human being. This is about learning to separate out what the person has done (which may be totally unacceptable behaviour) from who they are (having unconditional Regard for Others). If not, the Feedback giver's attitude leaks out unconsciously in their behaviour, tone of voice, and body language, even if they are very skilled at giving Feedback.

People are highly attuned to detecting incongruity between a person's behaviour and their attitude. On the other hand, those people who have high Regard for Others are able to give Feedback to others without them turning it into a Put-down or raising their defences, leaving the other person's Self Regard intact. Even if they lack Feedback skills or are slightly clumsy, the person receiving the Feedback detects that the other person is on their side, cares about them, and has positive intentions towards them.

3   **Combine Feedback with expressed Value:** People in organisations are often taught to 'sandwich' negative Feedback between two pieces of Praise. This tends to fail in practice because people soon begin to anticipate that every positive stroke is going to be followed with a 'but' ("That was good, 'but' you didn't ..."). A more effective option is to sandwich negative Feedback between two Values such as asking, "Do you have time to talk" (Value), then sharing the Feedback, and then thanking them and asking for their reaction and feelings (Value). Many businesses tend to use Praise and reward to motivate people, gain their commitment, and improve their performance. However, evidence suggests that people are far more motivated when they feel valued.[35] Feeling supported during difficult times – not just when things are going well – and feeling that their boss cares about them personally rather than just about their performances fosters loyalty, commitment, and engagement. These are qualities that many organisations find it difficult to harness and promote.

4   **Learn how to receive Feedback and Praise:** Communication is a two-way process and involves being able to receive as well as give Feedback. Some key guidelines to receiving Feedback are outlined as follows:

- Don't accept a Put-down. These toxic, rude or insulting comments usually say more about the attitude of the person giving them. Understand the Feedback being given and who specifically is giving it. Ask for clarification on the Feedback if required. It is only conditional if specific and supported by clear evidence and examples.
- Distinguish opinion from fact, "You have poor communication skills" would be better phrased as, "I think what you said to Bob was unclear because …".
- Accept positive strokes. People often discount a stroke by thinking, "They are just being nice to me", or bounce it back with, "You are looking good too!" By discounting or dismissing a positive stroke the person giving it may feel they have not been heard and interpret this as a Put-down and be less likely to offer positive strokes in the future.
- When receiving Value or Praise yourself, slow down, take a deep breath and allow this feedback to sink in. Say "Thank you" when receiving a positive stroke. This acknowledges the feedback and also gives a positive stroke back to the other person.

The key principle in receiving Feedback is to keep your Self Regard intact and to remember that being an OK human being is unconditional and not, therefore, dependent on what a person does. Using affirmations such as, "Even though I made a mistake or behaved inappropriately I am still a valuable and worthwhile human being", can help to reinforce this attitude.

This concludes the guidance on how to develop Emotional Intelligence through each of the psychological stages of EI. The next section provides more specific suggestions on how to develop EI in each of the 16 EIP scales.

8.9   Specific guidance on how to develop the EIP scales

The following suggestions on how to develop the 16 EIP scales are presented to help the individual with their self-development. These are by no means definitive and the individual may also be directed to other references for developing each scale, as well as being encouraged to be creative in generating their own ideas. It is recommended that exploration and interpretation of the EIP is undertaken before considering what to develop. In addition to the suggestions made below, refer to Chapter Five for suggestions on which other scales influence and support the development of each scale.

1   Self Regard

- **Show yourself compassion:** Once a day take a few minutes to notice your inner critic and challenge it with the question: "Is that really true?" Ask others who know you well for their opinion on what you doubt about yourself. Remember, Emotional Intelligence is not about being perfect but about self-acceptance.

— **Reject any Put-downs that come your way:** A Put-down is when someone (including yourself) criticises something about who you are as a person rather than what you have done. Every time you say something negative about yourself counter it with something positive.

— **Notice what makes you happy:** Each day do one thing that makes you feel happy: listen to your favourite song, laugh with a friend, or do someone a favour. Then remind yourself of this at the end of each day.

2 Regard for Others

— **Make time for people:** Give others your full attention while you are with them; practise asking questions rather than making statements; and seek to understand another person's point of view first.

— **Show your appreciation:** Notice and recognise when others do something well. Also, do the small things that can make a big difference, such as remembering a person's name, a smile, saying "Good morning", or asking them a question.

— **Be sensitive:** When commenting on performance, balance negative feedback with positive feedback and ensure you focus on behaviour while guarding against making it overly personal.

3 Self Awareness

— **Record your emotions:** Keep a log of your emotions during the day and how they affect your behaviour. This provides a first step in learning how to recognise and manage your emotions.

— **Share your feelings with someone you trust:** Talking through your feelings may help you to learn how they affect your behaviour and performance. Also, widen your use of feeling words, for example, 'happy' may include feeling cheerful, satisfied, confident, and proud.

— **Notice your intuition:** Be prepared to listen to and trust your gut reaction. Next time you make a decision, check whether it feels right intuitively to you, as well as if it is logically the right decision.

4 Awareness of Others

— **Listen attentively:** When discussing how a person is feeling about a situation, reflect it back to them, to demonstrate that you have listened and also to check the accuracy of your understanding.

— **Be observant:** During a conversation or in a meeting observe someone's body language and tone of voice; notice how they talk to you; and look for clues in their facial expressions. You may find you begin to unconsciously subtly mirror their body language, which will build rapport with them.

— **Show empathy:** Increase your empathy by imagining yourself in another person's position and openly acknowledging their feelings during the conversation.

5 Emotional Resilience

— **Look after yourself:** If you are feeling the effects of stress on your physical health, particularly if you are living an unhealthy lifestyle, look after yourself physically – exercise and eat healthily. Remember to build in time for renewal, such as go for a walk, meet friends, or read quietly.

— **Keep problems in perspective:** Ask for support from someone you trust. Talk through your concerns to gain a different perspective and establish a rounded view of the issues.

— **Notice what causes you stress:** Note down how you reacted and the events leading up to a stressful situation. You may then start to identify the initial triggers, how to avoid these, or how to prepare to deal with them more effectively in the future.

6 Personal Power

— **Consider your choices:** When there appears to be no choice, stop and challenge yourself to identify at least three options that have desirable outcomes.

— **Draw upon your experience:** Recall times when you felt empowered for taking on responsibility or being at your best, not just organisationally but also socially, physically, and mentally. Remind yourself of these times when faced with challenging situations.

— **Stretch your comfort zones:** Explore opportunities to get involved in slightly more challenging work that stretches you and increases your confidence and capability.

7 Goal Directedness

— **Put strategies in place for success:** For example, plan ahead, set targets, and have clearly defined objectives. Set realistic time frames to help you move towards your goals. Make the goal specific and ensure it is something you are personally motivated to achieve.

— **Use your resources:** Draw upon other personal qualities to develop your Goal Directedness, such as perseverance, focus, self-discipline, inner conviction, and a will to succeed. Even if you feel that these qualities are initially low, using them will increase them.

— **Develop impulse control:** If you set clear goals for yourself but find it difficult to stay on track, identify what distracts you and aim to eliminate these distractions. Also, consider how your future might be affected if you do not achieve what you set out to do.

8 Flexibility

— **Try out something new:** If you find changing your behaviour difficult, start with small changes which hold no risk, for example, move your watch from the wrist you normally keep it on to the other wrist for a few days. Notice your initial reactions and the time it takes for you to feel comfortable.

— **Change a habit:** Identify one habit that you would like to change and consider a more useful, alternative behaviour instead. Then practise the new behaviour once a day for a few weeks until it replaces the old habit (see the 21-day Habit Change exercise, Chapter Six; 6.4.1).

— **Give yourself time to accept change:** If your immediate reaction to change is resistance, check that you are not rejecting change for the wrong reasons, such as a fear of the unknown, feeling outside of your comfort zone, or ingrained habits.

9 Connecting with Others

— **Talk to people:** Make it part of your daily routine to spend time getting to know people. For example, make a deliberate effort to initiate contact with people and communicate with them face to face.

— **Be more open:** Notice what you don't share when talking with people, and risk being more open than you usually are. For example, when appropriate, share something about yourself on a personal level, express your feelings, or share your vulnerabilities in a way that feels safe to you.

— **Invest time in maintaining relationships:** Identify which area of relationships is stronger for you: depth (close relationships) or breadth (many relationships). Experiment in developing the area that is least strong.

10 Authenticity

— **Be reliable and keep your promises:** Ask a range of people who experience you in different settings whether you are consistent and reliable with them in all situations. Ask them what they would like you to do to improve on this even further. For example, only agree to deliver on things that you know are achievable.

— **Write down your top three values:** On a scale of one to ten rate how much you live by your values. Identify examples of when you have done so. What is one small behaviour change you could make that would help you to act in accordance with your values?

— **Let yourself be known:** To be seen as authentic requires that people feel they know you. Let people know what is important to you, what you like and dislike, what your values are, and what you expect from others. Invite them to share this information about themselves too, in order to maintain a balanced interaction.

11 Trust

Mistrusting

— **Be consistent and fair:** Notice which people or situations cause you to become mistrusting. Is there a common theme? How does your mood affect your levels of Trust?

— **Avoid over-reacting:** Check you do not over-generalise about people or situations. For example, if a person doesn't deliver on one task, do you think they will never deliver on any task and become generally mistrusting of them.

— **Give others an opportunity:** Calibrate your expectations of others (and yourself); are they fair and realistic? Allow room for others to learn from their mistakes, as showing confidence in others helps them to build confidence in themselves.

Over Trusting

— **Listen to your intuition:** Before deciding how much Trust to place in someone, identify what is factual, look at past evidence, and listen to your intuition to avoid being over-trusting.

— **Check your assumptions:** If you have doubts about a person's ability to deliver, offer support and ask questions early, rather than risk being let down later. Also, ask others what they want: do they want more input and support from you or do they feel they are being checked up on?

— **Have realistic expectations:** Before assuming that they will be able to deliver, check whether you have provided people with the right information and communicated your expectations accurately and clearly.

12 Balanced Outlook

Pessimistic

— **Use positive language:** There may be times that you use overly negative language when experiencing difficulties, such as, "It's hopeless, pointless, or will never work." Look to balance or moderate your language with positive messages designed to encourage and motivate, such as, "Good idea"; "Nice job"; or "Well done."

— **Make rational decisions:** When making decisions, check your frame of mind/mood. For example, if you feel annoyed, pause and reflect on whether this is skewing your perception or if you are acting impulsively and could be more objective.

— **Avoid being over critical:** If you are skilled at providing critical analysis then consider carefully how you communicate this to others so as not to appear overly negative. Try asking questions, find something positive to say, or offer solutions.

Over Optimistic

— **Check your decisions:** Continue to use your optimism to engage and motivate others. However, be prepared to look for contradictory evidence and challenge your own judgment to ensure the course of action set is still the right one.

— **Ask for others' opinions:** Balance your enthusiasm with finding out the facts and checking details before finalising a decision. Elicit views from others in order to get a balance of perceptions. Use this information to inform your decision.

— **Take a realistic perspective:** Do you tend to rebound from being overly optimistic to feeling quite pessimistic? If so, check your optimism is realistic. Be cautious to balance opportunities with potential pitfalls. If things don't work out, try not to catastrophise but see what you can usefully learn instead.

13 Emotional Expression and Control

Under Controlled

— **Count to six:** If you feel compelled to express a feeling, pause for six seconds, and allow time before you do or say anything. Think about your feelings, your possible reactions and their likely consequences. If you are prone to emotional outbursts, recognise when this has been inappropriate, then once you feel calm, be prepared to make an apology.

— **Pay attention to your feelings:** Identify which situations cause a strong emotional reaction in you. Notice your feelings early. For example, frustration before it becomes anger and then rage; or anticipation before it becomes anxiety and then panic.

— **Practise relaxation:** Consider incorporating more physical activity into your weekly routine in order to provide additional release from stressful situations. Also practise relaxation techniques such as slow breathing, stretching, or quiet reflection.

Over Controlled

— **Show your passion:** Although high levels of emotional expression may not come naturally to you, work is not devoid of feeling. Make a conscious effort to notice and acknowledge the emotions of others. Demonstrate your passion, for example, overtly state your commitment and show encouragement.

— **Learn from others:** When you are around people who express their feelings openly but with calmness and control, take note of the impact they have on others and you. Ask for their advice on the approach they take.

— **Say what you feel:** Find opportunities to safely and gradually express your feelings more often. Start with feelings and situations you find more comfortable. Record the differences this makes to improving your relationships and achieving your goals.

14 Conflict Handling

Passive

— **Prepare what you will say:** If you feel uncomfortable about disagreement or asking people to do something for you, prepare what you are going to say first and keep it short and to the point.

— **Address the issue early:** Most people feel uncomfortable giving feedback, yet often the person receiving it is more able to deal with it than we expect. If you tend to avoid addressing issues, don't make excuses but deal with them early before they become bigger issues.

— **Listen first, then assert your views:** Conflict is resolved when there is mutual respect and neither party feels under pressure. Find a conducive environment and an appropriate time to hear the other person's views and to fully state yours.

Aggressive

— **Learn how to remain calm:** If you feel yourself becoming frustrated or angry, use techniques to calm down, such as breathing deeply, taking a short break, or expressing feelings before they become too strong.

— **Listen first:** Practise listening to others and reflecting back what you have heard, before giving your opinion. If people don't open up to you, encourage them to do so by asking open questions.

— **Respect others:** Take care that your personal ambition and drive does not have a detrimental effect on others, such as being overly competitive, only focusing on tasks and not people, or losing sight of the team objectives.

15 Interdependence

Dependent

— **Provide a solution:** Before asking others for advice or direction, pause to consider what your personal view is and what you would do if you were the sole decision maker. Be prepared to try activities where there is nobody to provide help and which stretch your comfort zones.

— **Take action:** Do you tend to procrastinate, avoid making decisions, or spend too much time deliberating? Work out which decisions are important to spend time on and which ones you need to act upon. Set yourself a deadline for a decision to be made or action taken.

— **Build self-reliance:** If you are very social and feel the need for considerable interaction, practise working independently. Recognise when this is appropriate, such as focusing on a task, concentrating on details, being comfortable alone, or making your own decisions.

Over Independent

— **Share your expertise:** If you have a preference for being 'an expert', endeavour to share your expertise and thinking with others. Involve people early in a project and elicit their ideas before deciding the way forward.

— **Take others with you:** Having your own inner conviction is a good basis for leading others but ensure you convey this to people in a way that they can engage with. Also look for someone to delegate to, and allocate time to develop and coach them on a regular basis.

— **Support teamwork:** Become more interdependent by creating a team environment where communication and openness is encouraged and where sharing ideas and solutions are welcomed without criticism, ridicule, or risk.

16 Reflective Learning

— **Ask for feedback:** Build a clearer picture of your strengths and development areas. Actively seek feedback from your boss and subordinates. If you can, undertake a 360 feedback process and ask people for their views.

— **Record reflections on your day:** Consider what went well and what could have been better. What one thing did you do well and how could you use this strength more often? What one thing did you do less well and how could you develop this aspect?

— **Reflect upon a challenging experience:** Consider what triggered the event? What did you do, think, and feel at that time? Was it a one-off or is this a common theme in your life? How would you prepare and respond differently next time?

This chapter has provided an overview of how to develop EI and the EIP scales in particular. Further advice on how to develop each scale is given within the EIP reports. The next chapter discusses how EI and the EIP can be applied in the business context in relation to individual leadership, team working, and creating an emotionally intelligent organisation.

SUMMARY POINTS
FROM CHAPTER EIGHT

There are several psychological stages to the process of being emotionally intelligent (SAFE-TBO). This chapter has described how each of these stages provides the opportunity to develop EI. Key suggestions are summarised here.

Some of the most powerful emotional triggers come from a person's social needs, such as for safety, status, consistency, and fairness. Learning to identify and meet these emotional needs can help prevent defensive and rigid behaviours.

Attitudes tend to be evaluative and categorical; creating an element of doubt in someone's underpinning attitudes leaves them open to questions and provides the opportunity for change.

People often know what they 'should' do, but do not behave in this way in practice. Making sustained changes in behaviour requires learning through emotional and experiential activity, and integrating it into our ways of being and doing.

Emotions provide people with feedback about themselves and others. If ignored, negative feelings will increase, such as frustration growing into anger, or anxiety, which can manifest as ill-health and defensive behaviours. By noticing feelings early, people can learn to listen to their body's feedback and respond to their feelings appropriately.

Most irrational or unhelpful thinking is the result of excessive emotion. Too much emotion restricts a person's capacity to think clearly and choose how they behave. Learning how to reduce levels of arousal, by relaxing and managing day-to-day stress, is a vital part of developing EI.

Calming the emotional brain can be complimented by learning how to quieten the rational thinking brain. Together, they allow for more insightful, creative, intuitive, and inspired levels of thinking.

The main reasons people do not achieve their personal development goals are: they don't want them enough, the goals are too large, or they don't know how to achieve them. When changing a habit, it is important that the new behaviour is very specific, achievable, and of clear benefit to the individual.

Imagination is a very powerful human tool for creating a person's own 'virtual reality'. If used effectively, it can help people to reduce their anxiety, create positive feelings, prepare for difficult situations, increase their confidence, and lead to positive outcomes. However, if not managed well, a person's imagination can be equally destructive as it is creative.

Self Regard is the essence of EI and is largely determined by the communication we experience throughout our life. To raise Self Regard we must learn how to accept Praise and reject Put-downs, both from ourselves and from others.

CHAPTER NINE
APPLYING EMOTIONAL INTELLIGENCE AND THE EIP IN ORGANISATIONS

INTRODUCTION

So far, the focus of Section Three has been on the assessment and development of the individual. This final chapter examines EI and the EIP from a business context, answering questions like: What evidence is there that EI improves performance? How does EI relate to leadership? What is an emotionally intelligent team? And, what makes an emotionally intelligent organisation? The three main themes to this chapter are the individual (leadership), teams (relationships), and the organisation (climate).

9.1   The business case for Emotional Intelligence

There are three key criteria that may be considered the 'holy grail' for any construct of personal or professional development such as EI.

1   **It can be developed:**[1,2] It is a quality that a person can change, improve, and sustain, rather than it being fixed.

2   **It is measurable:** Improvement of this attribute can be quantified.

3   **It relates to performance:** It is a desirable quality that can make a positive difference to a person's effectiveness.

Throughout this book the case has been made for the first two criteria: Emotional Intelligence is developable and measurable. The third criteria, that EI (and the EIP) predicts performance and has a bottom line impact on output and productivity in work, will now be explored.

There is clearly something missing for employees in today's workplaces. Research by Gallup[3] found an astonishing 71% of employees were not engaged in their work; Zenger and Folkman[4] found that 46% of employees report low job satisfaction and commitment; and a survey by Freedman[5] reported that 97% of employees said they could be more productive, 49% of whom said they thought that they could be 50% more productive! There is considerable opportunity for increased productivity in the workplace, so how much difference can EI make?

Daniel Goleman[6] in his book 'Emotional Intelligence: why it can matter more than IQ', argues that IQ contributes to about 20% of life success, while the remaining 80% is, to a large extent, influenced by EI. The evidence he presents is mostly anecdotal, yet his explanations have caught the interest of executives the world over. Perhaps this represented a tide of opinion from business leaders who are intuitively aware that the key differentiator of high performers is more emotional and relational than cognitive. This has been supported by several studies, such as the Forum on Manufacturing and Services[7] which revealed that 70% of customers are lost because of EI-related reasons. A global leadership research company that followed 20,000 new hires over three years found 23% failed because of poor understanding and management of emotions.[8] The Denning Centre for Quality Management[9] found that 50% of time in business is wasted due to a lack of trust, and a study by the Royal Navy[10] showed that EI was a better predictor of overall and leadership performance than IQ and managerial competencies. In a leadership survey on 775 senior managers, 89% reported that EI was 'highly important' or 'essential' to addressing their organisations 'top challenges'. When asked "What are the top issues you face at work?" leaders reported that 76% were people/relational and only 24% were financial/technical issues.[11] A Future of Jobs survey ranked EI as one of the top skills that would be required by 2020.[12] However, despite the high interest in EI, a survey by JCA Global across 50 UK organisations found that only 30% were actively using EI within their development or selection processes, despite over 90% recognising EI as 'important' or 'crucial' to areas such as working relationships, stress management, and leadership.[13]

A key application of EI has been in leadership development. A global study by Johnson & Johnson[14] on 358 of their managers found that high performers were significantly more 'emotionally competent' than other managers. Research by UCLA[15] indicated that only 7% of leadership success is attributed to intellect, the rest is attributed to trust, integrity, authenticity, honesty, creativity, presence, and resilience. A pool of senior managers from Siemens Global[16] who were trained in four EI domains (drive, initiative, team-working, and leadership) delivered an additional $1.5 million profit, double that of the comparison group that had no such training. In a large-scale study across industry sectors, EI explained nearly 60% of job performance across all managerial and executive levels. As part of the same study at AT&T, 91% of top performers were high in EI, while only 26% of low performers were high in EI. Egon Zehnder's[17] analysis of 515 senior executives found EI to be a better indicator of future success than either previous experience or IQ.

As suggested by the Zehnder study, organisations are not just interested in how EI relates to leadership performance, but what this can deliver by way of actual output and productivity. A number of studies that demonstrate the link between EI and business performance are summarised below:

— In one multinational consulting firm, partners scoring higher on 20 EI competencies earned 139% more than low EI partners.[18]

— L'Oréal sales agents selected on EI outsold sales people selected through the old recruitment procedures by $91,000 and had 63% less staff turnover.[19]

— Sales people at Met Life who scored higher on 'learned optimism' sold 37% more than the less optimistic individuals.[20]

— Insurance sales agents scoring higher in five key EI competencies had double the policy sales of lower scorers.[21]

— American Express introduced four days of EI training to all of its incoming financial advisers after finding that trained advisers increased business by 18%.[22]

— At Coca-Cola, division leaders who developed their EI competencies outperformed their targets by 15%. Division leaders who did not develop their EI were 15% below their targets.[23]

— At Sanofi-Aventis, a pharmaceutical company, salespeople with EI training outsold the control group by 12% (worth over $2 million per month).[24]

— When Motorola manufacturing implemented stress and EI programmes, 93% of employees increased their productivity.[25]

— A study on over 75,000 people in 15 workplace sectors across 125 countries found strong positive correlations between EI and various success factors of effectiveness, relationships, and well-being.[26]

— A meta-analysis on 43 separate studies found significantly strong correlations ($r=0.24$ to 0.30) between EI and job performance.[27]

As well as improving performance and productivity, several other benefits of EI have been found, such as:

— **Increased retention:** Across a sample of 875 employees, intention to stay almost doubled in those with high EI.[28]

— **Reduced attrition:**[21,23] In the US Air force, recruiters reported a $3 million immediate saving after using EI to select their recruiters.[29]

— **Fewer work-related accidents and grievances:** Lost-time accidents reduced by 50% in one manufacturing company after EI skills training.[30]

— **Greater career advancement:** EI scores were found to increase with seniority[31–33] across different job sectors.[33]

— **Increased 'servant leadership' and ethical practice:**[34,35] EI and trust were found to correlate positively with a people-oriented approach to leading others.[36]

— **Higher staff engagement and job satisfaction:**[37] In healthcare leaders, higher EI was linked to increased staff engagement during transformational change.[38]

The positive results from EI studies have been replicated by the EIP, showing that EI development is sustainable.[39,40] A sample of 189 leaders who completed the EIP showed an 18% improvement in their EIP scores six months after completing a three-day EI development programme. If this improvement in EI transferred directly into productivity, then conservative estimates indicate that an 18% improvement in productivity for senior managers would lead to 150% increase in pre-tax profits.[41] A case study presented at the UK National EI Conference by Skandia Group found middle managers to have a 20-32% increase in leadership performance following EIP coaching and training over a three-month period.[42] Validity studies have shown the EIP to correlate positively with performance and competency rating in several jobs sectors such as in the sales and financial sectors.[33] Further studies on the validity of the EIP may be found in the Technical Manual.[43]

9.1.1 The business demand for EI

There has been considerable growth in the field of EI at work since the early 1990s. In no small part, this rising popularity has been due to the writings of Daniel Goleman who has produced several accessible books.[44-46] His work became prominent in the business field following two papers in the Harvard Business Review (HBR), 'What makes a leader?'[47] and 'Leadership that gets results',[48] which rank as the most requested HBR articles to date. His work helped popularise some of the work by academics and researchers in the field, including Reuven Bar-On, who produced the EQi measure of EI,[49] and Mayer, Salovey, and Caruso, who developed the MSCEIT™ EI measure.[50]

There are other key reasons for the continuing interest in EI within business, such as neurological evidence on the importance of emotions for clear thinking, decision making, and effective behaviour. There has also been an increased acceptance of feelings being significant to performance, engagement, and retention in the workplace, and greater recognition in society generally, such as emotional literacy being taught in schools, politicians referring to EI, and popular business books on EI. In addition, there is a large body of academic research and practitioner evidence giving continued support to the importance of EI in workplace performance. Despite its widespread popularity, the concept of Emotional Intelligence remains contentious, primarily because of competing definitions and models, and its overlap with aspects of personality (see Appendix Two; Section 4).

Perhaps the main reason for organisations buying into EI is because there is an increased need for emotionally intelligent employees to meet the demands of current day working.[51] Some of these demands upon employees and the relevant EIP scales to help address these demands are now described.

The rate of change: Change is often seen as exponential, led by advances in technology, access to information, big data analytics, data protection, and increased globalisation. This typically comes with a high human toll, as employees are expected to be more adaptable and responsive to changing circumstances. For the 21st year in succession, Roffey Park's annual survey of managers reported managing change as their biggest organisational challenge, with workplaces becoming more diverse, virtual, and dispersed.[52] What demands does this place upon the EI of managers today? It may require being aware of their automatic and habitual responses (Self Awareness) and then learning how to move outside of their comfort zones to adapt to a changing world (Flexibility).

A changing economic climate: The health of the economy cascades down to organisations and to individuals. When the economy is buoyant, organisations experience rapid growth and individuals are expected to adapt quickly, take on greater responsibility, manage more resources, and deliver to higher expectations. During an economic slowdown, organisations consolidate and individuals are expected to do more with less, remain competitive with reduced resources, and cope with job uncertainty. The organisations and individuals who cope well with such changes have greater Emotional Resilience, and are adaptable enough to move outside of their comfort zones (Flexibility), and learn from the experience (Reflective Learning).

Increased competition: With globalisation, and in times of economic crisis, comes increased competition. To come out on top requires several EI attributes such as Emotional Resilience (to cope with and persevere after setbacks), Self Awareness (to draw on creativity and intuition), Connecting with Others (to engage with clients), and Balanced Outlook (to have a positive rather than pessimistic outlook).

Less hierarchy: Organisational structures are constantly being revised and a common trend has been the de-layering of hierarchies. Consequently, employees are given greater autonomy, independence, and accountability, and are expected to be more self-managed. This demands greater Self Management in areas such as knowing one's own strengths and weaknesses (Self Awareness), self-motivation (Goal Directedness) and self-confidence (Personal Power).

Increased team working: In tandem with the demand for greater Self Management, the demand for Relationship Management has been equally dramatic as new ways of working come in to play, such as virtual teams, collaborative working practices, matrix structures, and networking sites. Some of the relevant EIP attributes here include: valuing and appreciating an individual's differences (Regard for Others); forming, building, and maintaining relationships (Connecting with Others); knowing who and how much trust to place in others (Trust); and being known and trusted by others (Authenticity).

A job is not for life: Unlike 50 years ago, very few CEOs or company directors have dedicated their working lives to the same organisation. Such dedication is often seen as a handicap rather than an asset. Today's high fliers will not only work in different organisations but different industry sectors. This requires them to adapt to new environments and people (Connecting with Others), to continually learn from their experience (Reflective Learning), and to adopt versatile styles of working (Flexibility).

Increased job demands: Despite improved efficiency and speed in operating technology, the demands on the typical employee, such as working hours, information load, and job variety have dramatically increased. In a survey by PWC[53] of over 1000 CEOs from 54 countries, 97% said that their employees had to do more work than they would have done previously, but in the same amount of time. The main concern with this has been the rise in stress-related problems, such as absenteeism, low morale, illness, increased turnover, and under-performance.

EI in the workplace is about how people manage their emotional state under challenging conditions to perform effectively, which requires attributes such as: Emotional Resilience, Emotional Expression and Control, and Conflict Handling. EI is also about creating working cultures that engage people and help them to work to their strengths. This may include EI attributes such as Self Regard, Regard for Others, Self Awareness, Awareness of Others, and Reflective Learning. Just as the increased demand on leaders and employees requires greater EI, so too does the increased demand placed upon organisations to attract and retain the best people.

The war for talent: Attracting and retaining the best staff continues to be a challenge,[54] as the opportunity for travel, job change, transferability of skills, career growth, and personal development becomes more important to these aspiring leaders. The need for employers to motivate and satisfy employees is ever present. Understanding people's emotional needs (Awareness of Others), building loyalty (Connecting with Others), and creating trusting relationships (Trust) are significant factors in attracting and retaining skilled workers with high potential. In a 2015 study on the 'Best Companies to Work for' in 14 countries, EI was highlighted as an important factor influencing job satisfaction.[55]

An ageing population: People are living longer, retirement age is rising, and the characteristics of employees are changing with every generation (often referred to as 'baby boomers' and generations X, Y, and Z). Results from research based on the EIP have shown EI to increase with age and that different generations have different strengths and preferences.[33] Employers may wish to embrace these differences, such as drawing upon the experience and wisdom of older employees (Reflective Learning) and supporting the dynamic enthusiasm of younger employees (Flexibility).

Human capital: The UK economy has shifted from being predominantly product based (manufacturing and construction) to becoming more people led (services and knowledge). The net effect is that people are the primary resource for most organisations. Knowing how to maximise human potential (Relationship Management) and sustain performance (Goal Directedness) for ever greater productivity (Personal Power) can be leveraged through a greater understanding of EI in the workplace.

9.2   The relevance of EIP scales to leadership

Emotionally intelligent leadership is about developing the whole person, or in the words of Warren Bennis, "There is no difference between becoming an effective leader and becoming a fully integrated human being."[56] From the perspective of the EIP, a number of scales are of particular importance to emotionally intelligent leadership:

Self Regard: This is the cornerstone to all aspects of EI. It is evident that not all leaders are happy and do not necessarily hold themselves in high self-esteem. In fact, the opposite is often the case, where leaders are driven by a conditional sense of being OK, meaning they have unconscious drivers such as, "I am only OK ... if I have control, if I am perfect, if I am strong, if I please others, if I work hard etc." These may typically fit with the 'striving for achievement' characteristic of many leaders, but at what cost? One cost may be to relationships and the climate the leader creates, another may be a lack of Flexibility.

Flexibility: If a leader is driven to 'Be Perfect', 'Work Hard', or 'Be Strong' to support their Self Regard, then they run the risk of being rigid and dogmatic rather than responsive and adaptable to the demands of the present situation. Given the changing nature of organisations discussed in the previous section, any inflexibility in a leader lessens their effectiveness.

Authenticity: If a leader is driven to feel OK by 'Pleasing Others', they may respond by over committing themselves and therefore not being able to keep all of their promises, rather than being guided by their own inner principles. Being led by someone who is inconsistent and unpredictable creates considerable anxiety, as it becomes difficult to anticipate how they will respond or what they want. This is particularly problematic when the leader's mood affects how positive or negative they are towards others. Some of the greatest leaders may not be the most charismatic but are greatly trusted by their followers because of their consistency and principles (Gandhi, Nelson Mandela, the Dalai Lama, Steve Jobs, and Queen Elizabeth II).

Balanced Outlook: Research on the EIP[39] has shown senior leaders to have less extreme and more balanced EI scores than lower level managers. For example, senior managers are more likely to be realistic and considered, rather than emotionally impulsive or Over Optimistic. They tend to score in the middle on the multi-scales, rather than rebound from one extreme to the other, therefore being seen as calm, steady, and consistent. It may be that leaders with more extreme EI scores (possibly charismatic) are the ones who are noticed, yet this is neither a typical or necessary aspect of effective leadership.

Goal Directedness and Personal Power: Goal Directedness is knowing what we want, and Personal Power is believing we are able to make this happen. From EIP research,[33] high achievers and strong leaders often score highly on these two scales. The successful application of these is also dependent on having reasonably high Self Awareness.

Self Awareness: This is necessary in order for the leader to accurately calibrate and not to over-estimate their capacity to deliver. They should also have high Awareness of Others and humility so as to select the right advisers to balance and support them in areas where they are less strong.

Reflective Learning: Self Awareness also supports Reflective Learning, which is necessary in order to learn from experience and grow. Actively reflecting helps a leader to continuously improve themselves, so they can lead, influence, and get the best out of others.

Interpersonal Intelligence: All of the above scales relate to Personal Intelligence. Equally important to leadership is Interpersonal Intelligence; the leader is only one half of each and every interaction. Many leadership models emphasise the importance of relationships, for example Transformational Leadership[57] and Leader-Member Exchange Theory.[58] Sustainable leadership requires both personal and interpersonal intelligence, as a leader who lacks Self Management is unlikely to be skilled at, or able to sustain, effective Relationship Management.

Regard for Others: Having Regard for Others is the starting point and basis for effective Relationship Management. Holding a positive intent and attitude towards others leaks out in micro-behaviours that can be detected by others. Equally, a leader who has slick interpersonal skills but low Regard for Others may leave others feeling uneasy, despite having said and done all the 'right' things.

An exercise first used on an EI leadership programme at Stanford University[15] asked individuals to identify one person who had particularly influenced them. They were then asked to identify what it was about this person and what they did that made the difference. The usual response was that "This person believed in me", often more than the individual believed in themselves. Effective leaders have high belief in others (Trust and Regard for Others) and do so in a supportive way. They also have high Awareness of Others, the next relationship scale.

Awareness of Others: It is important that the leader accurately gauges the correct level of expectation to have of others. Too high expectations can leave people feeling anxious and disheartened, too low expectations and people may feel demotivated and not trusted. Awareness of Others is a vital tool for the leader; to know what others need and to give them the correct level of encouragement, advice, autonomy, or direction. Most other skills, habits, and behaviours to do with Relationship Management tend to occur as a natural consequence of having Regard for Others and Awareness of Others. One of these is Connecting with Others.

Connecting with Others: A survey by Gallup[3] identified the twelve questions which best predicted employee engagement. High on the list was that employees felt their boss cared about them. Forming trusting, honest, and caring relationships is a significant attribute of top leaders. Leaders who get the best out of others often form close bonds and go beyond transactional, business-like communication by sharing themselves (Authenticity), expressing vulnerabilities, and creating a closer level of trust.

9.2.1 Emotional Intelligence and leadership styles

Although many aspects of EI are relevant to effective leadership, it depends on the context as to which style of leadership and therefore which aspects of EI are most appropriate. One model to have identified six leadership styles is based on the original work of David McClelland at Harvard University in the 1970s that was linked to EI by Daniel Goleman.[28,47-48] These leadership styles have clear conceptual links with EI and are mapped against the EIP scales in Table 9.1.

EIP scales relevant to leadership styles

LEADERSHIP STYLE	ENCAPSULATING STATEMENT	LINKS TO EIP SCALES	WORKS WELL WHEN...
Coercive	"I expect others to do what I say without question"	Personal Power Goal Directedness Emotional Resilience Conflict Handling	There is a crisis Dealing with poor performers
Authoritarian	"I have a clear vision and lead people towards it"	Self Regard Goal Directedness Personal Power Authenticity	Change is needed Clear vision and objectives are required
Pace-setting	"I have clear standards and expect my team to meet them"	Emotional Resilience Goal Directedness Balanced Outlook Interdependence	Results are needed quickly
Affiliative	"I work closely with people to build effective working relations"	Regard for Others Connecting with Others Trust	Teams or individuals are facing stressful situations
Democratic	"I like to work as part of a team rather than taking the lead"	Regard for Others Awareness of Others Trust Interdependence	The team needs to own a project To get the most out of skilled and valued staff
Coaching	"I like coaching others, enabling them to perform effectively"	Regard for Others Awareness of Others Connecting with Others	Employees' skills need developing

Table 9.1

Key to emotionally intelligent leadership is being able to move between these leadership styles as and when appropriate (Flexibility), knowing when to use each leadership style (Awareness of Others), and knowing how to apply them (Reflective Learning). As with all aspects of EI, this is more likely if the person has the attitudes of high Self Regard and high Regard for Others (Ideal). A leader with high Self Regard and low Regard for Others (Critical) may overuse and misuse the Coercive, Authoritarian, and Pace-setting styles. A leader with low Self Regard and high Regard for Others (Submissive) is more likely to overuse and misuse the Affiliative, Democratic, and Coaching styles of leadership.

9.2.2 Emotional Intelligence and competencies

Most organisations define effective leadership behaviour through competencies. The relationship between EI and competencies is explained in Chapter One; 1.3.3; EI is the mechanism by which people develop and maintain their behavioural competence. Not surprisingly, therefore, many competencies are closely related to EI and are the backbone to several competency based EI measures.

In a study of 121 worldwide organisations, Goleman[17] found that 67% of competencies deemed to be essential for effective job performance were emotional competencies. He further supported his findings with a study by the Hay Group[45] of 40 companies, showing that 'star performers' were only 27% more likely to have greater strengths in cognitive competencies but were 53% more likely to have greater than average strengths in emotional competencies. In further work by Goleman and colleagues,[59] a study of 2000 supervisors and middle managers showed that 16 competencies distinguished the star performers from the average performers and that all but two of these were emotional competencies. This research led to the development of the Hay/McBer Emotional Competency Inventory (ECI 360)[60] recently revised to the Korn Ferry Emotional and Social Competency Inventory (ESCI 360)[28] which measures 12 behavioural competencies.

The JCA Global competency library[61] comprises four competency clusters which are split into eight supra-competencies, that further divide into 32 competencies, each consisting of 12 behavioural descriptors. The 32 competencies have been mapped against the EIP scales based on an importance and consensus rating by ten EI experts. The highest of these ratings are shown in Table 9.2, (empirical correlations are presented in the EIP technical manual).[43] Several of these competencies also form part of the Interview Guide (Table 7.4 on page 157).

The JCA Global competency framework

Table 9.2

ADAPT	
PROVIDING SUPPORT	**RELATED EIP SCALE***
Valuing people	2, 4, 9, 11
Behaving with integrity and authenticity	10
Upholding organisational values	10
Team working	2, 4, 9, 11, 15
ADAPTING TO CHALLENGES	**RELATED EIP SCALE***
Managing conflict	2, 4, 14
Showing resilience	1, 3, 5, 6, 10, 12
Responding to change	1, 5, 8, 12
Displaying flexibility	8

DELIVER	
MANAGING TASKS	**RELATED EIP SCALE***
Organising and prioritising	7
Following procedures and working with details	
Ensuring customer satisfaction	2, 4, 9
Delivering results	6, 7
PURSUING GOALS	**RELATED EIP SCALE***
Driving for success	6, 7
Displaying commercial awareness	
Acting with initiative	6, 8
Showing career ambition	1, 6, 7

THINK	
ANALYSING INFORMATION	**RELATED EIP SCALE***
Researching and investigating	
Analysing situations and making judgments	12, 16
Writing with impact	
Solving problems	12, 16

THINK	
LEARNING AND CREATIVITY	**RELATED EIP SCALE***
Learning agility	8, 16
Creativity and innovation	
Inspiring others	9, 13
Strategic and conceptual thinking	

INSPIRE	
SHAPING RELATIONSHIPS	**RELATED EIP SCALE***
Communicating and presenting	13
Influencing people	4, 10, 13
Building professional networks	4, 9, 15
Connecting with people	2, 4, 9, 15
PROVIDING LEADERSHIP	**RELATED EIP SCALE***
Directing and guiding	7
Coaching and developing others	2, 4, 9
Managing talent	2, 4, 11, 15
Making decisions	6, 7, 12, 16

*See Table 3.2 on page 56 for EIP scale labels.

There are clear benefits in relating EIP scales to competencies. Competencies are the result of practising EI, and EI is the practice of managing one's personality. In other words, there is a natural relationship between personality, EI, and competencies; EI is what turns human potential (personality) into effective behaviour and performance (competencies). Competencies are effective to the extent that they are supported by complimentary EI attitudes. In other words, by developing the related EIP scales (attitudes and habits) the individual will find it easier to develop the corresponding behavioural competencies. For example, a team leader is far more effective at coaching and developing others (competency) if they have high Regard for Others (an EI attitude).

9.3   The emotionally intelligent team

So far, this chapter has discussed EI in the context of individual leadership. EI is also applied widely in the context of teamwork and for improving relationships. There is clear evidence that EI not only improves performance of the individual, but also of teams.[62,63] JCA Global has developed a parallel team measure of EI, the Team EIP, to compliment the individual EIP instrument. Constructed by myself and Tim Sparrow (and updated in 2013),[64] both products share the same EI attitudes, principles, and theoretical framework. The table below shows the framework for the Team EIP.

The Team EIP framework

	Team Relationships	Team Intelligence
Behaviour	Collaboration	Effectiveness
Feeling	Openness	Motivation
Attitude	Climate	Morale

© 2013 JCA Global Ltd.

Table 9.3

As with the individual EIP, the arrows of influence move from the bottom upwards. The Attitude of the team (Climate and Morale) underpins the Feeling within the team (Openness and Motivation), which influences team Behaviour (Collaboration and Effectiveness).

Team EIP, as with the individual EIP framework is made up of two parts: Team Relationships (as opposed to Interpersonal Intelligence for the EIP) and Team Intelligence (as opposed to Personal Intelligence).

Team Relationships: Team members who positively value and respect each other (Climate) are more likely to be open and attentive towards one another (Openness), which leads to strong and effective relationships (Collaboration).

Team Intelligence: A team that is united by shared beliefs and confidence (Morale) is more motivated and engaged in whatever it is doing (Motivation), helping the team to perform well and achieve what it sets out to do (Effectiveness).

In contrast to the individual EIP framework, Team Relationships (Interpersonal Intelligence) is on the left and Team Intelligence (Personal Intelligence) is on the right. This is because it is necessary to have strong relationships between team members first (Team

Relationships) if the team as a whole is to perform effectively as a unit (Team Intelligence). The influence between each pair of scales is described below.

Attitude: Team members who respect and value one another (Climate) are likely to have greater shared belief in the team and what they can achieve (Morale).

Feeling: Team members who are open in their communication and aware of each other's feelings (Openness) are likely to have a collective energy and enthusiasm for what they set out to achieve (Motivation).

Behaviour: Team members who have strong relationships and work well together (Collaboration) are likely to behave and perform effectively as a team in achieving what they set out to do (Effectiveness).

9.3.1 The Team EIP scales

The six team scales are directly linked to the six parts of the individual EIP framework as shown below:

Team EIP scale links to the individual EIP framework

EIP FRAMEWORK	TEAM EIP SCALE	SCALE DEFINITION	RELATED EIP SCALE
Attitude	1 Climate	The degree to which team members have positive regard for one another and create an atmosphere of safety within the team	Regard for Others
	2 Morale	The shared belief and confidence this team has in itself, its members, and in what they set out to achieve	Self Regard
Feeling	3 Openness	How openly team members engage with one another and how aware they are of each other's feelings	Awareness of Others
	4 Motivation	The collective energy and enthusiasm this team has to succeed in what they set out to achieve	Self Awareness

Table 9.4

EIP FRAMEWORK	TEAM EIP SCALE	SCALE DEFINITION	RELATED EIP SCALE
Behaviour	5 Collaboration	The degree to which team members create strong interpersonal relations and work well together	Relationship Management
	6 Effectiveness	How effectively the team behaves and performs in order to achieve what they set out to do	Self Management

9.3.2 Applying the Team EIP

Unsurprisingly, the EI of a team is largely dependent on the EI of the individuals within it;[65] it is difficult to get effective collaboration and positive outcomes if individual team members are defensive and uncooperative. In particular, the EI of the team leader has a strong impact on the whole team by raising or lowering the emotional atmosphere.[66] However, team EI is more than the sum of its parts; it is quite possible to have high performing individuals who do not work well when placed together. Many elements of team EI come from the patterns of behaviour and attitudes that team members develop with one another rather than the EI of individuals.[67] It is therefore valuable to measure team EI separately from individual EI and provide team interventions alongside individual coaching. It is important not to confuse Team EIP with group facilitation of the EIP (described in Chapter Six; 6.5). With the Team EIP, team members are rating the team, not themselves, which reflects the team dynamics and relationships between team members. It is generally recommended that team members complete and explore their individual EIP first before doing the Team EIP. This way they can understand how they may be contributing personally to the team's strengths and development areas, so they may be more committed to both their own and the team's development. The relationship between individual and team EIP is shown in Table 9.5. The connecting arrows show that individuals with high Regard for Others support a positive team Climate; individuals with high Awareness of Others encourage Openness in teams; and individuals who are strong at Relationship Management build stronger team Collaboration.

The individual and Team EIP frameworks combined

	Personal Intelligence	Interpersonal Intelligence	Team Relationships	Team Intelligence
Behaviour	Self Management	Relationship Management	Collaboration	Effectiveness
Feeling	Self Awareness	Awareness of Others	Openness	Motivation
Attitude	Self Regard	Regard for Others	Climate	Morale

Table 9.5

© 2013 JCA Global Ltd.

The explanation of how to apply the Team EIP is not within the scope of this book and requires separate training, available through JCA Global. As with all psychometrics, it is important that the user is competent to use the Team EIP instrument, as well as having the appropriate skills for team facilitation. In terms of developing the EI of teams, many of the suggestions given in Chapter Eight are entirely relevant. Two of these suggestions in particular, providing opportunity for interaction and making change experiential, lend themselves well to team events.

9.4   The emotionally intelligent organisation

Today, Emotional Intelligence is well established as a model and process for coaching individuals and developing teams. However, there is far less research and practice on creating Emotional Intelligence within the organisation. This section briefly examines the application of EI in the organisation as measured by the Leadership Climate Indicator (LCI) and how this cascades down to teams and the individual.

Whatever activities it engages in, an organisation is more effective at what it does if it harnesses the full potential of all of its employees. It has been estimated that approximately 80% of activities in an organisation involve some collaboration.[68] The impact of improved engagement can be seen at an organisational level in terms of customer loyalty, productivity, profitability, reduced turnover, and improved well-being.[69] JCA Global sees the emotionally intelligent climate of an organisation as an integrated and interdependent whole, comprising of individuals, teams (relationships), and the organisation. This can be seen in Table 9.6, demonstrating the close relationship between scales of the EIP (individual), Team EIP (team) and LCI (organisation).

The emotionally intelligent organisation

Individuals display	Teams display	Organisations are
Self Regard	Morale	Encouraging
Regard for Others	Positive Climate	Innovative
Self Awareness	Motivation	Visioning
Awareness of Others	Openness	Trusting
Self Management	Effectiveness	Stretching
Relationship Management	Collaboration	Collaborative
EIP	Team EIP	LCI

© 2014 JCA Global Ltd.

Table 9.6

Evidence suggests that the organisational climate can significantly promote or inhibit emotionally intelligent behaviour.[70,71] As indicated by the top row of Table 9.6, creating an Encouraging organisational environment will foster teams that have higher Morale, which will support an individual's Self Regard. Equally, coaching and supporting individuals will ripple into their relationships,[72] which in turn will cascade across the organisation.[73,74] In other words, development can work through the individual, in teams, and across the organisation. Having any one of these elements does not automatically mean the others coexist. It is possible to have emotionally intelligent individuals and teams despite a negative organisational climate, such as when employees believe in the value of their work despite poor leadership from above and a poor economic climate. However, by far the greatest and most sustainable impact is achieved by applying all three elements in a combined intervention.

9.4.1 Measuring the Emotional Intelligence of an organisation

To measure the EI of an organisation, JCA Global developed the Leadership Climate Indicator (LCI).[75] The LCI is designed to focus on the behaviour of leaders as a key factor in determining the emotional climate or tone they set within the organisation. The LCI helps leaders build trust in the organisation and cultivate a leadership climate which supports a sustainable culture for high performance. The EI of leaders has been found to have a powerful impact on the climate and effectiveness of groups.[28,76–78] For instance, leaders who score higher in the EIP are rated more positively by 360 raters on all of the LCI scales.[79]

The LCI is completed by employees within the organisation who rate the behaviours of the leadership group, with the option of also rating their individual leaders. The questionnaire measures the extent to which leaders exhibit positive leadership behaviours (Inspiring and Including) that create a climate of trust in leaders, and in which people feel inspired to perform to their potential. It also measures negative leadership behaviours (Controlling and Withdrawing) which erode trust and engagement if used habitually. There are 12 scales grouped into four clusters. The 12 scales are all aspects of EI and are closely related to the EIP scales as shown in Table 9.7.

Leadership Climate Indicator (LCI) scales

Table 9.7

CLUSTER	DESCRIPTION	LCI SCALE	RELATED EIP SCALE
Inspiring	When leaders act in this way they generate a positive climate where people feel inspired, motivated, and challenged to move out of their comfort zones and perform at their best	Visioning	Goal Directedness
			Balanced Outlook
		Stretching	Personal Power
			Goal Directedness
		Encouraging	Regard for Others
			Awareness of Others
			Goal Directedness
			Connecting with Others
Including	By acting in this way, leaders generate trust, loyalty, and commitment and build emotional capital which can be drawn on to sustain performance and maintain trusted resilience in the face of pressure	Collaborative	Flexibility
			Trust
			Interdependence
		Trusted	Connecting with Others
			Authenticity
			Trust
		Appreciative	Regard for Others
			Awareness of Others
			Emotional Expression and Control

CLUSTER	DESCRIPTION	LCI SCALE	RELATED EIP SCALE
Controlling	Controlling behaviours can be effective and appropriate for mobilising energy in a short-term crisis, but if used habitually they erode trust and instil fear and defensiveness in others. Over time, a Controlling style can impede collaboration and innovation and can be toxic, leading to burnout and disengagement	Competitive	Mistrusting Aggressive
		Aggressive	Regard for Others (low) Emotionally Under Controlled Aggressive
		Demanding	Flexibility (low) Mistrusting Over Optimistic
Withdrawing	When leaders are operating in this cluster they tend to either detach themselves from people and issues, or become over reliant on others. Energy is low and there is a lack of innovation, healthy conflict, and connection with others. Leaders retreat into their comfort zones	Avoidant	Awareness of Others (low) Connecting with Others (low) Over Independent
		Dependent	Self Regard (low) Over Trusting Passive Dependent
		Rigid	Flexibility (low) Emotionally Over Controlled Pessimistic

The LCI data provides a rich resource for implementing appropriate organisational development interventions. For example, if the leadership behaviour is Aggressive and Competitive this may create the climate where employees feel anxious and intimidated. This leadership behaviour could be replaced by one that is more Appreciative and Encouraging so as to create a climate where people feel more engaged and motivated.

Associated with each of the LCI clusters is the emotional climate that leaders create through their behaviour, that is, "How does it feel to be in this organisation and to be led by this person?" The four clusters map onto the four quadrants of an established model of emotions.[80] This model separates emotions into either positive (pleasant) or negative (unpleasant) and high or low intensity. The close relationship between leadership behaviour and the emotional climate this creates in others is shown in Table 9.8.

The Emotions Matrix

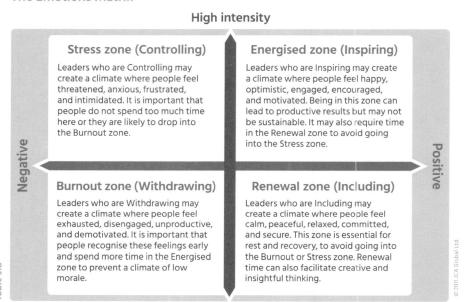

High intensity

Stress zone (Controlling)

Leaders who are Controlling may create a climate where people feel threatened, anxious, frustrated, and intimidated. It is important that people do not spend too much time here or they are likely to drop into the Burnout zone.

Energised zone (Inspiring)

Leaders who are Inspiring may create a climate where people feel happy, optimistic, engaged, encouraged, and motivated. Being in this zone can lead to productive results but may not be sustainable. It may also require time in the Renewal zone to avoid going into the Stress zone.

Burnout zone (Withdrawing)

Leaders who are Withdrawing may create a climate where people feel exhausted, disengaged, unproductive, and demotivated. It is important that people recognise these feelings early and spend more time in the Energised zone to prevent a climate of low morale.

Renewal zone (Including)

Leaders who are Including may create a climate where people feel calm, peaceful, relaxed, committed, and secure. This zone is essential for rest and recovery, to avoid going into the Burnout or Stress zone. Renewal time can also facilitate creative and insightful thinking.

Negative — Positive

Low intensity

Table 9.8

© 2011 JCA Global Ltd

Ideally, an organisation and its leaders will create an environment where individuals feel engaged and motivated to be in the Energised zone, where they have the opportunity for relaxation and recovery in the Renewal zone, where they spend only short periods in the Stress zone, and where they are supported when they fall into the Burnout zone.

9.5   An integrated approach to assessing Emotional Intelligence

In this chapter the case has been made for applying EI at an individual (leadership), team (relationships), and organisational (climate) level. Although discussed separately, they are all interdependent:[81] leaders who create a more emotionally intelligent climate foster better relationships which in turn, improve individual motivation. Additionally, EI should not be considered in isolation, as it forms part of a process for turning personality and potential into effective behaviour and performance. The relationship between these facets of performance is represented by the framework in Figure 9.1 (also see Chapter Six; 6.6). These different facets determine a large part of what constitutes effective organisational performance and can be measured by the range of JCA Global products.

The JCA Global products framework

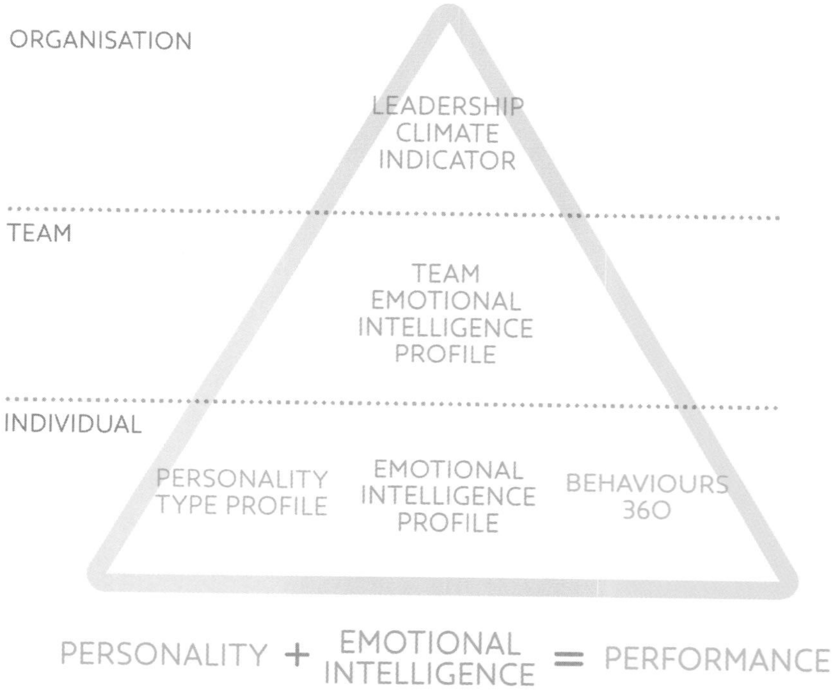

ORGANISATION

LEADERSHIP
CLIMATE
INDICATOR

TEAM

TEAM
EMOTIONAL
INTELLIGENCE
PROFILE

INDIVIDUAL

PERSONALITY   EMOTIONAL
TYPE PROFILE   INTELLIGENCE   BEHAVIOURS
                     PROFILE   360

PERSONALITY + EMOTIONAL = PERFORMANCE
              INTELLIGENCE

Figure 9.1

This final chapter has presented the business case for Emotional Intelligence, and described how EI may be applied to leadership, team and organisational assessment and development. The two appendices that follow provide further insight into the EIP scales and a historical overview of EI.

SUMMARY POINTS
FROM CHAPTER NINE

Emotional Intelligence has been shown to be measurable, developable, sustainable, and to predict performance. These are four criteria that are vital ingredients for leadership development.

Many of the demands on organisations such as increased competition, rapid change, an ageing workforce, and globalisation provide a compelling case for the need to develop EI attributes in the workplace.

There is now a substantial body of evidence demonstrating the benefit of EI for improving organisational productivity, performance, well-being,[32] and financial return.

EI is now firmly established as a central part of leadership performance, having been popularised by Daniel Goleman in the Harvard Business Review,[47] academically researched in leadership journals, recognised by many authoritative writers on leadership, and become a core part of many established leadership competency frameworks.

Emotional Intelligence may be measured at the individual (EIP), team (Team EIP), and organisational (Leadership Climate Indicator) levels. The greatest sustainable improvement in performance, engagement, and well-being[83] is achieved through interventions at all three levels.

The Team EIP scales map onto the six parts of the EIP framework, with the same dynamic relationship between them.

The Leadership Climate Indicator measures the key leadership behaviours (Inspiring, Including, Controlling, Withdrawing) which determine the emotional climate (Energised, Renewal, Stress, Burnout) of an organisation.

APPENDIX ONE
FURTHER INTERPRETATION OF THE 16 EIP SCALES

The EIP scale descriptions and scale combinations are interpreted in Chapter Five. For the EIP user who wishes to explore the EIP scales in greater detail, this appendix provides a more comprehensive description and analysis for each of the 16 scales.

SCALE 1: SELF REGARD

"No one can make you feel inferior without your permission"
Eleanor Roosevelt

1   Definition

Self Regard is scale 1 of the EIP questionnaire and is defined as the degree to which an individual values and accepts themselves.

2   Description

Low Self Regard: This may manifest as feelings of self-doubt and insecurity, worrying about shortcomings, and putting oneself down. Having low Self Regard may also distort a person's Self Awareness (scale 3), causing them to interpret experiences negatively, such as exaggerating problems or ignoring positives. Low Self Regard may be driven by certain unconscious negative attitudes such as: "I am only OK ... if everybody likes me, ... if I am perfect, ... if I am strong, or ... if I don't show my feelings." Negative attitudes may lead to rigid behaviours, such as insisting on being the centre of attention, avoiding people altogether, always wanting to be in charge, or avoiding any responsibility. Someone who has high Self Regard, however, accepts themselves unconditionally, 'warts and all', rather than feeling compelled to behave in a certain way in order to feel OK about themselves. A low score on Self Regard may also lower a person's Emotional Resilience (scale 5), Personal Power (scale 6), and Goal Directedness (scale 7).

High Self Regard: Self Regard is the basis for developing all aspects of Emotional Intelligence, in particular the Self Management scales. A high score on Self Regard helps an individual to build their Emotional Resilience, have a sense of Personal Power, and be goal directed. Having high Self Regard suggests that, for the most part, a person feels happy with themselves and who they have become, and they have a strong inner self-belief, even though there are aspects of themselves they may wish to develop. The exception to this would be if they are masking a low Self Regard through a low Regard for Others (scale 2). This is known as the 'Critical position' described in Chapter Four; 4.3.3. It may manifest as the individual finding fault in other people (so as to avoid looking at their own shortcomings), being arrogant, and seeing themselves as superior or more valuable than others.

3   Interpretation

Scale 1 forms the cornerstone to JCA Global's theory of Emotional Intelligence and the EIP framework. It greatly influences all of the EIP scales, forms one half of the Attitude Matrix, and is one of the eight Attitudes of Emotional Intelligence: 'However you are and others are, is OK'.

Unconditional Self Regard: Self Regard is experienced as the feelings an individual has about their self-concept (their identity or being), which may be conscious or unconscious and can be considered in three parts:

— Their sense of self-significance (or belonging)

— Their sense of self-competence (or self-efficacy)

— Their sense of self-liking (or self-acceptance and unique value)

Many people tend to believe (often unconsciously) that, "I am only OK if I do 'x', and if I do not do 'x' then I am Not OK." In other words, they have 'conditions' as to their self-worth and feeling OK. These conditions vary from person to person depending often on how adults treated them when they were children.[1]

Conditions of self-worth: Conditions of worth were originally defined by Carl Rogers[2] and are also referred to as 'drivers' as they drive a person's behaviour, although not in a healthy way. Drivers tend to endlessly push people, leading to exhaustion and burnout. The most common conditions of self-worth are Be Perfect, Be Strong, Please Others, Hurry Up, and Try Hard (but don't succeed). Conditions of self-worth are also forms of defensive behaviour, and are described in Chapter Four; Tables 4.5, 4.6 and 4.7.

The basis of self-acceptance: The ultimate purpose of Emotional Intelligence is to help individuals to be self-accepting and unconditionally OK (at least most of the time). This is achieved through dismantling the attitudes and beliefs, often acquired in childhood, that cause a person to feel they are not OK. These attitudes interfere with an individual achieving their innate potential and is neatly illustrated by Timothy Gallwey's 'Inner Game' book series[3] that introduces the formula: 'Performance = Potential − Interference'. That is, people naturally Perform to their Potential once their Interference factors (drivers and defences) are removed.

Links with other scales: Within the EIP framework, Self Regard is the cornerstone to Self Awareness and all other EIP scales. Self Regard and Self Awareness are fundamentally inseparable. Starting from the assumption, 'However you are and others are, is OK' (EI Attitude 1), to be truly self-aware is to be aware of this attitude, that 'I am OK' and therefore, 'I have high Self Regard'. Self Awareness is also feedback for developing Self Regard as it enables a person to be aware of which emotional needs are not being met (Chapter Eight; Table 8.2) such as the need for intimacy, attention, or recognition.

The Self Management scales are ordered by how closely they statistically correlate with Self Regard. Hence, Emotional Resilience is the first of the Self Management scales. All the EIP scales require the inner strength of Self Regard for them to be maintained. Further explanation of how Self Regard relates to the EIP scales is given within each of the scale descriptions that follow, and more information can be found in Chapter Five.

SCALE 2: REGARD FOR OTHERS

"If you want others to be happy, practise compassion. If you want to be happy, practise compassion" The Dalai Lama

1   Definition

Scale 2, Regard for Others, measures the degree to which an individual accepts and values others as people, as distinct from liking or approving of what they might do. Regard for Others is integrally related to Self Regard and should therefore be considered in relation to the previous scale and the Attitude Matrix described in Chapter Four; 4.3.

2   Description

Low Regard for Others: This scale underpins all of the Relationship Management scales for Emotional Intelligence. Having a low score on Regard for Others may hinder a person from Connecting with Others (scale 9), building Trust (scale 11), handling conflict (scale 14) and acting interdependently (scale 15). Low Regard for Others suggests someone may be judgmental of others, which is likely to impair their ability to be truly aware of people's differences (Awareness of Others) and therefore, they are likely to respond inappropriately to them. Judging others negatively may mean they are less inclined to listen to people, or adapt and respond to people's needs (Flexibility, scale 8), and that they may be critical, unsympathetic, and intolerant of others, rather than seeking to understand them.

High Regard for Others: Having a high Regard for Others helps an individual to connect with others, build trust, handle conflict, and act interdependently. High Regard for Others also suggests that they tend to be less judgmental of others, which enhances their ability to be truly aware of people's differences and therefore respond appropriately to them. By accepting and valuing people as they are, they may be more inclined to listen to people, seek to understand, adapt, respond to their needs, be supportive, sympathetic, and tolerant. Those with a very high Regard for Others continue to value and respect others, even if they dislike, disagree with, or disapprove of their behaviour.

3   Interpretation

Awareness of Others: Regard for Others is important because it underpins the right-hand pillar of the EIP framework (Interpersonal Intelligence). Directly above Regard for Others is Awareness of Others. If a person has low Regard for Others they perceive others through this lens, seeing them from a critical perspective. If they have less concern for others, they are also less likely to pay attention to other people's feelings and needs. Those with low Regard for Others tend to be more judgmental, critical, blaming, rejecting, mistrustful, and disregarding of others. As a result, they find it difficult to be accurately aware of others and their feelings. However, it is also possible that a person scores highly on Awareness of Others because they are hyper-vigilant and suspicious of others (due to a low Regard for Others and being Mistrusting), not because they have an accurate and balanced perception of them.

Appreciation: Showing regard for, belief in, and appreciation towards other people is one of the easiest and most powerful ways to raise EI in them. Evidence suggests that organisations that foster a culture of valuing others have happier and more productive employees. For example, the Gallup Q12 survey found that people with a best friend at work are seven times more likely to enjoy their jobs, have fewer accidents, and be more creative. The research also found that close friendships at work boost job satisfaction by 50%.[4] A key attribute of effective leadership is believing in the potential of others (Regard for Others) as by doing so, people are helped to believe in themselves. Believing in others is consistent with holding the EI Attitudes: 'However you are and others are, is OK', and 'People have a natural tendency towards growth and health.'

Appreciation may be considered at different levels in terms of how we communicate (see the Communication Grid, Chapter Eight; 8.8). The lowest level of appreciation is to ignore people as if they do not exist (a Put-down). An improvement on this is to acknowledge people and offer constructive Feedback although, all too often, Feedback is used as a way to disguise criticism and blame. More enlightened companies provide training courses in how to offer Praise, which is a conditional form of appreciation; people get recognition on condition that they perform well, are productive, and add value. The deepest level of appreciation is to show Value towards others, which is an unconditional form of appreciation, so even if a person makes a mistake they still feel valued. It is this level of appreciation that demonstrates Regard for Others, motivates individuals, creates loyalty, and builds long-term trusting relationships.

SCALE 3: SELF AWARENESS

"Few are those who see with their own eyes and feel with their own hearts" Albert Einstein

1   Definition

Self Awareness is the degree to which an individual is in touch with their physiology, feelings, and intuitions and is the basis for developing Emotional Intelligence.

The EIP framework of Emotional Intelligence shows that the causal arrows for Awareness of Others, Self Management, and Relationship Management derive from, and are dependent upon, developing Self Awareness. Consequently, it is fundamentally important to understand what Self Awareness is and what can be done to enhance it. Links between Self Awareness and other EIP scales are given in Chapter Five; 5.2.

2   Description

Low Self Awareness: This suggests that someone is less in touch with their feelings, wants, needs, and intuitions, which is likely to have a knock-on effect on most other aspects of their EI. For example, if an individual tends not to notice their feelings of frustration, these feelings are more likely to grow into feelings of anger or despair. If they do not notice how they feel under stress then they are less likely to learn what causes them stress and how to manage it effectively. If they don't notice feelings of joy, they may not learn to appreciate and enjoy the moment. One reason people stop paying attention to how they feel is because they do not like how they feel about themselves. If this is the case, then they may have also scored low on Self Regard (scale 1).

Scoring lowly on Self Awareness provides an ideal opportunity to improve someone's EI more generally, as increasing this single scale helps them to develop many other parts of their EI. For example, it is difficult to be aware of others' feelings (scale 4) if we do not notice our own feelings, and it is difficult to be goal directed (scale 7) if we are not in touch with what we want and like.

High Self Awareness: This suggests that the individual is likely to be closely in touch with their feelings, wants, needs, and intuitions which has a positive knock-on effect on other aspects of their EI. For example, if they tend to notice when they feel frustrated then they are more able to intervene and prevent the feeling escalating. If they notice their feelings under stress, they are more likely to learn what causes them stress and how to manage this effectively. Or, if they recognise feelings of joy, they are better able to know what they enjoy doing and what gives them satisfaction in life. It may be worth checking that their Self Regard score is also relatively high. Sometimes people with low

Self Regard are acutely self-aware of personal imperfections, resulting in a negatively biased self-perception.

3   Interpretation

Bodily awareness: Feelings are experienced in the body rather than the brain and are mediated largely through hormones rather than neurons (Chapter Two; 2.8). Different sources of feelings include: physiological (such as hunger, thirst, and nausea), emotional (such as anger, fear, and joy), and intuitive (such as gut feeling or inner knowing). An important element of Self Awareness is paying attention to the body's physical needs, such as the need for rest, recuperation, nutrition, and exercise. In this sense, the body may be likened to the workforce of an organisation. If the workforce are not looked after then they become demotivated, underperform, and eventually go on strike (through illness and depression), much like the human body.

Intuition: Intuition is an aspect of Self Awareness that people perceive through feedback from their body such as their 'gut feelings' rather than through cognitive thinking. Some people may be considered as naturally more intuitive than others, although intuition is something that everyone can develop with practice. Intuition is based on bodily awareness, so it is of the moment, transitory, and ever changing. Being intuitive involves self-monitoring to detect any changes that occur in the body which then inform our thinking and decision making. This monitoring process does not require constant conscious effort, although, for those low in Self Awareness, it may be needed initially. People are more likely to detect the quieter neurological and physical signals of intuition when they are relaxed and their brain is less active and noisy. Regularly checking-in with ourselves and our feelings will result in our intuition becoming more automatic and habitual with practice.

Self Knowledge: Self Knowledge is what a person knows about themselves (cognitively) based on their Self Awareness. For example, over time a person may start to notice that whenever they feel hungry their thinking deteriorates and they become irritable more easily. This is their Self Knowledge which has been acquired through reflecting upon (Reflective Learning, scale 16) their past experiences (Self Awareness). Having formed this piece of Self Knowledge, they know to eat something when they feel hungry, before their thinking deteriorates.

Self Regard: Self Awareness is highly dependent on Self Regard. If an individual is secure in their 'OKness', they can afford to be aware of whatever they are feeling without their value being threatened. However, if their 'OKness' is dependent on them being and feeling a certain way (a conditional self-worth) then they will judge the acceptability of what they feel which will impair their level of Self Awareness.

SCALE 4: AWARENESS OF OTHERS

"The greatest gift you can give another is the purity of your attention" Richard Moss

1   Definition

Awareness of Others is the degree to which a person is in touch with the feelings of others. This scale is fundamental to developing the relational aspects of Emotional Intelligence.

2   Description

Low Awareness of Others: If a person is less inclined to understand, empathise with, and intuit others' feelings, or to notice what people need and want, then they are less able to adapt or respond appropriately to them. For example, Conflict Handling (scale 14) depends on being aware of others' feelings and reactions, and Interdependence (scale 15) involves recognising others' needs and preferences. There are several possible reasons for a person being less aware of others: they may be inwardly focused and less interested in people; they may find it difficult to empathise; they may not be very observant of people; they may have low Regard for Others (scale 2) and not value others' feelings greatly; or they may believe that people are all the same or at least the same as them, so wrongly assume that they know how others are feeling. Underlying many of these reasons is often an unconscious attitude of, "I already know about people" or "I don't need or want to know about others", rather than being open to finding out.

High Awareness of Others: A person with a high Awareness of Others is likely to notice, understand, empathise with, and intuit what people feel, want, and need. This helps them to adapt and respond appropriately to others. This may also support them in developing their Conflict Handling, which depends on being aware of others' feelings and reactions, and Interdependence, which involves recognising the needs and preferences of others. Underlying their Awareness of Others may be EI Attitude 4, 'People are different', as well as an appreciation of individual differences. This may be reflected by a high score in Regard for Others (scale 2). If on the other hand their Regard for Others is low, their Awareness of Others may be negatively distorted and they may be hyper-vigilant of others because they assume people cannot be trusted.

3   Interpretation

There are a number of different ways of becoming aware of the feelings of others:

A   It may be a conscious cognitive process: "I notice that this person is tense and tapping their fingers on the table, and I therefore think that this person is feeling irritable or angry."

B   It may be an unconscious cognitive or intuitive process: "I don't know why, but I sense this person is annoyed about something."

C   It may be the cognitive consequence of the feeling process of empathy: "I notice that I feel irritable, but this is really somebody else's irritation, so I am aware of what the other person is feeling." This is also known as 'emotional contagion'.

Developing Awareness of Others is likely to require developing Self Awareness too. Lane and Schwartz[5] found these two functions of the brain to be closely related anatomically and to be almost indistinguishable early in a child's development.

Empathy: A person's ability to empathise with others in order to feel what others are feeling is hardwired within the limbic system of the brain. The evolutionary purpose of this is to help people predict how others are likely to behave and if they are a potential threat. There is a growing body of research into what is sometimes termed 'the social brain',[6] showing how people are emotionally connected. People have the capacity to pick up what others may be thinking and feeling from minute variations in their behaviour, such as their tone of voice and facial movements, much of which is only detected at an unconscious intuitive level. Psychologist Paul Ekman[7] has catalogued over 10,000 different facial expressions revealing that from birth, babies have an instinctive tendency to read their mother's face and to detect meaning in voices. It has also been established that empathy fires off the same neuronal patterns as the person being empathised with, such as wincing at someone else's pain. These so-called 'mirror neurons'[8] that reproduce emotions might also explain why emotions are contagious, such as laughing when others laugh and sharing emotions at a music concert. A similar set of neurons known as 'oscillator neurons' help people to coordinate themselves with others, such as when getting into rapport, connecting with others, and being in physical harmony (for example, an orchestra or dance group).

Alexithymia: People vary in the degree to which they naturally experience empathy. One group at the low end of the empathy spectrum are individuals with Alexithymia (from the Greek meaning 'lack of words for emotions'). Although they may not easily develop empathy, they can learn techniques or cognitive rules for developing their Relationship Management skills, such as, "When other people laugh, then laugh along" or "When someone looks at their watch, it may be time to end the conversation." But these learned rules are often poor substitutes for reading how people are feeling. For the majority of people, being more attentive and aware of people's feelings is something that can be improved with practice.

Relationship Management: Awareness of Others sits on the Interpersonal Intelligence side of the EIP framework and has a strong link with Relationship Management. An individual who lacks understanding and an Awareness of Others' feelings is less able to adapt or respond appropriately to them. For example, when making a presentation it is necessary to notice the energy of the audience. If the energy is low (people yawning, looking downwards, or slumping in their chairs) the presenter can take appropriate action by either taking a break or doing an activity.

The Relationship Management scales of the EIP are heavily dependent on developing Awareness of Others. For example, Trust (scale 11) requires accurately reading others to know whether to trust them; Conflict Handling (scale 14) depends on being aware of the feeling states and reactions of others; and Interdependence (scale 15) requires responsiveness to the feelings and needs of others.

Knowledge of Others: The link between Awareness of Others and Relationship Management is Reflective Learning (scale 16), as shown on the extended EIP framework. Through reflecting on past experiences with other people (Awareness of Others), a person forms their Knowledge of Others which informs how they choose to behave with others in the future (Relationship Management). For example, a line manager may notice that one of their reports has become unusually quiet; they look more serious, they don't have so much eye contact, and their communication towards them is more abrupt (Awareness of Others). From past experience they recognise this behaviour often happens when the individual is feeling unhappy or stressed (Knowledge of Others). The line manager may decide to check out their assumptions and have an informal chat with them.

Defensive behaviours: Low Awareness of Others can often be tracked back to low Regard for Others. If a person does not value others or see them as significant then they are unlikely to pay much attention to them and may choose to ignore them. Low Awareness of Others combined with low Regard for Others can result in a variety of defensive behaviours (described in Chapter Four; 4.3.2). The Blamer who is critical of others tends to have a negative perception of people, assuming others to be at fault. The Victim also makes negative assumptions about others, believing that people unfairly judge and pick on them. The Helper assumes that others are incapable of helping themselves and the Demander assumes that people do not like them unless they are receiving constant reassurance. The common thread in all of these defences is a negative assumption about other people, based on their own low Regard for Others. Making assumptions about others is a judgment; when people judge others this can reduce their capacity to accurately perceive and be aware of others.

Suspending judgment: A fundamental skill for improving Awareness of Others is to listen to others. Listening at a deeper level involves suspending judgment and keeping an open mind. Conversation is often predicated on the pattern, "You tell me your story, then I will tell you mine", which is an exchange of information rather than paying close attention to the other person. Deeper listening involves using all of our senses to detect the other person's feelings and the meaning behind their words. This also requires being aware of others in the moment, not being distracted by inner thoughts, or planning what to say next. Sometimes people get hampered by their own stories of other people, such as, "I think you feel this about me." These inner stories create an automatic block to being openly aware of others. The first step therefore to developing Awareness of Others is for the individual to develop their Self Awareness (scale 3) and to notice how their own feelings towards people may be interfering with their Awareness of Others.

People are different: Appreciating that 'people are different' is the fourth of the EI Attitudes. This principle is clearly tied in with Awareness of Others; if a person's attitude is that 'all people are the same' then there would be no need for them to think about other people. They would automatically assume that others feel the same way as they do in the same situation (a phenomenon known in psychology as 'projection'). For Awareness of Others, as with all EIP scales, it is useful to explore what underlying attitudes may be influencing a person's feelings, thoughts, and behaviours.

SCALE 5: EMOTIONAL RESILIENCE

"It is not whether you get knocked down; it is whether you get back up" Vince Lombardi

1   Definition

Emotional Resilience is the degree to which a person is able to pick themselves up and bounce back when things go badly for them.

2   Description

Low Emotional Resilience: Inevitably in life, people experience disappointment and setbacks. A low score suggests they may find this particularly difficult to cope with, becoming despondent and stressed. This does not mean that they have more problems than most people, but that they cope less well with life's challenges. They may tend to become overly anxious, catastrophise problems, assume problems are unsolvable, be unforgiving and critical towards themselves, feel that they have little control over events in their life (check this with their Personal Power score; scale 6), and tend to anticipate the worst (check this with their Pessimistic score; scale 12). If prolonged, low Emotional Resilience may affect their physical health and vice versa. If someone is living an unhealthy lifestyle they tend to have fewer inner resources to cope with adversity and setbacks.

High Emotional Resilience: A high score suggests that someone is particularly effective at applying their inner resources to cope with life's demands. They are more likely to: learn from a setback than let it get them down; anticipate success rather than failure (check this with their Balanced Outlook score; scale 12); remain calm in a crisis; think through problems rationally; look for and find solutions to challenges; be more forgiving towards themselves; and keep problems in perspective rather than ruminate over things they have little control over. They may also take care of themselves physically through exercise and nutrition which will support their recovery, particularly in times of stress and adversity. Check that their high score is genuine and not a Be Strong driver masking low Self regard (scale 1).

3   Interpretation

Self Regard: Emotional Resilience is clearly related to Self Regard. To hold on to self-worth and confidence in the face of disappointment or rejection, a person needs to believe "I am OK" (high Self Regard; scale 1). And to remain hopeful in a world filled with other people they need to believe "You are OK" too (high Regard for Others; scale 2). The Self Management scales are ordered according to their correlation with Self Regard – therefore, Emotional Resilience is at the top of the list. How easily a person picks themselves up when things go wrong is determined by how positive they feel about themselves. But if their Self Regard is low or highly conditional, then they take knocks hard and find it difficult to recover.

Stress: An area closely related to Emotional Resilience is stress. This is sometimes experienced as a rather confusing concept because the external and the internal sources of stress are often not adequately distinguished. What is perceived as stressful by one person may be perceived as exciting or fun by another. One piece of research has shown that librarians suffer more stress than fire fighters.[9] Much depends on the demands placed upon a person, how well these are met by an individual's resources for coping, and how much support they have. The greatest demands are often those that the individual places upon themselves. For example, the conditions of worth, described under scale 1 ("I am only OK if ... I please others, am strong, etc.") put significant self-imposed demands upon us. If we feel that we 'must' meet certain conditions in order to feel OK about ourselves then this is inherently stressful. Combined conditions of worth can be particularly stressful, such as to Be Perfect and Hurry Up. This combination compels someone to do everything just right and very quickly, which inevitably puts them under considerable pressure. This would be compounded by a Be Strong driver, meaning they ignore their feelings of stress, and further still by a Try Hard driver so they resist the need to rest, potentially driving their body to exhaustion and ill-health.

The most obvious antidote to this happening is to develop Self Awareness (scale 3) in order to pay greater attention to the body's feedback and to learn how to manage feelings of stress. Another important scale that supports Emotional Resilience is Connecting with Others (scale 9). Human beings are social animals and gain considerable benefit from sharing problems and receiving emotional support from others.

SCALE 6: PERSONAL POWER

"Between stimulus and response there is a space. In that space is our power to choose our response" Stephen Covey

1   Definition

Personal Power is the degree to which a person believes that they are in charge of and take sole responsibility for their outcomes, rather than viewing themselves as the victim of circumstances and/or of other people.

2   Description

Low Personal Power: This suggests that the individual may currently not believe that they have much influence or control over their circumstances. There are a number of possible reasons for this. They may have low Self Regard (scale 1) and feel despondent about themselves and their general self-worth, which may affect the confidence they have in their skills, abilities, and effectiveness to make things happen. Alternatively, they may have much higher Regard for Others (scale 2) than they do for themselves, which may cause them to feel they have little control over their circumstance and that they are dependent on other people (scale 15). It could be that they have low Self Regard and low Regard for Others and feel generally helpless and that nothing or nobody can make a difference. Or, they may hold the belief that their life and future is determined by factors other than themselves, such as fate, God, luck, other people, or chance. In all these cases, beliefs tend to be self-fulfilling – so if they believe they can or they believe they can't then this will probably be true for them. The consequences of having low Personal Power tend to mean that they externalise events by blaming others for failures, or, they may be self-critical and blame themselves, not acknowledging their own successes, avoiding responsibility, using phrases like "I couldn't help it" or "They made me", and generally feeling disempowered.

High Personal Power: This suggests that the individual has a strong sense of self determination and responsibility for what happens in their life and for creating their future. It is therefore important that they have a clear view of what they want (Goal Directedness; scale 7), so as to channel their energy in the appropriate direction. As Personal Power is often associated with having confidence in one's skills and abilities to create effective outcomes, they may also have a high Self Regard, although the two scales are different. If their Self Regard is low, they may expect a lot from themselves and be overly self-critical and demanding at the same time (possibly holding a Be Perfect condition of self-worth – refer to scale 1). If their Regard for Others is low they should be cautious that their high Personal Power doesn't spill over into being Over Optimistic (scale 12) about what they can achieve or Over Independent (scale 15) believing that they should go it alone.

3   Interpretation

Locus of control: Personal Power is closely related to the concept of 'internal locus of control', meaning the individual (as opposed to others, the situation, or the environment) has the largest effect on their own outcomes. Even when being constrained by others or blocked by circumstances, it is important for someone to recognise what power they do still have. There is a self-fulfilling prophecy to Personal Power which is highly correlated with effective performance and more generally to life outcomes. In a moving book by the Holocaust survivor Victor Frankl, 'Man's Search for Meaning',[10] he describes how people retained some degree of Personal Power despite the conditions of being imprisoned in a concentration camp. Frankl also describes how he felt the need to survive in order to tell the rest of the world of these atrocities, displaying a strong demonstration of the next EIP scale, Goal Directedness (scale 7).

Choice: The concept of choice often arises when discussing Personal Power. The extent to which an individual believes they have choice and control over their behaviour greatly influences their EI development as it is one of the EI Attitudes: Everyone is in control of and responsible for their actions. People are fully entitled to disagree with this and any of the EI Attitudes, but by adopting this attitude and assuming it to be true, a person is more likely to feel in control of their life and become more responsible and emotionally intelligent in how they choose to live their life. Of course, a person may choose not to be responsible for themselves, which is in itself a choice. Choice and Personal Power are not all or nothing concepts and may be practised and developed at different levels:

Level 1   The lowest level of Personal Power is to explain everything as being down to chance or fate and to entirely absolve themselves from any responsibility.

Level 2   The next level up is to attribute their circumstances and behaviour to unchangeable factors such as their upbringing or genetic factors, which are often used as excuses.

Level 3   A level on from this is to attribute outcomes to other people, such as blaming others or alternatively not accepting praise or recognition.

Level 4   High Personal Power is attained when a person believes they can choose how they respond to events, such as coping well with adversity or standing up for themselves.

Level 5   The highest level of Personal Power, and therefore the highest level of EI, is when a person believes they can choose and create their circumstances as well as how they respond to them. For example, being positive and friendly towards others is likely to be reciprocated with a positive and friendly response (circumstance).

Self Regard and Personal Power: Personal Power relates closely to one of the key three strands of Self Regard: a person's sense of self-competence and self-efficacy. However, it is entirely possible to score high on one of these scales and not the other. An individual may see themselves as very capable at influencing people or at playing ball games (high Personal Power), yet still feel awful about themselves as a human being (low Self Regard). Alternatively, they may feel incompetent at a particular task (low Personal Power) without letting this undermine their Self Regard. Remember that true Self Regard is unconditional and therefore not dependent upon having high scores on any of the other EIP scales.

SCALE 7: GOAL DIRECTEDNESS

"If you are not sure where you are going, you'll probably end up somewhere else" Laurence Peter

1   Definition

Goal Directedness is the degree to which the individual relates their behaviour to long-term goals.

2   Description

Low Goal Directedness: There are a number of reasons for a person not being goal directed. They may be unaware of what they actually want; they would benefit from developing their Self Awareness (scale 3). They may be easily distracted from their goals, tending to be impulsive or constantly seeking something new and exciting to do. Their attention may be directed towards the present or on the past rather than thinking and planning ahead, or they may focus more on meeting the needs of others at the cost of meeting their own needs. This is especially so if their Regard for Others (scale 2) is higher than their Self Regard (scale 1). The risk in all of these cases is that they do not create the outcomes or future they want.

High Goal Directedness: A high score suggests that the individual knows what they want and stays focused on achieving it. Knowing what they want is one key ingredient to general happiness; another is being able to make this happen (Personal Power; scale 6). They may also want to check that their high Goal Directedness is balanced with high Flexibility (scale 8) so that they know when to change or modify their goals and when to cut their losses. At the extreme, Goal Directedness may appear as being 'driven', where a person feels compelled to achieve their goals at almost any cost (if their Regard for Others is low, the cost may be to those around them).

3   Interpretation

Self Regard: Goal Directedness is strongly correlated with Self Regard (scale 1). In order to set goals and to align behaviour towards them, whatever the temptations or distractions, the individual needs to believe that they, and what they want, matter. One of the tricky things about Goal Directedness is that while the scale measures a single variable, there are two key factors which affect the level of a person's Goal Directedness – knowing what they want and not being easily distracted from achieving these goals.

Knowing what they want: In order to remain focused on what they want, people need first to know what it is that they want. Most people see this as a non-issue; of course, people know what they want, almost by definition. But actually, there are some people who are much less clear than others about what it is that they want from life. Sometimes this is because they don't really have an interest in anything, so it is hard for them to know what they want and what they should aim for. Some people do not know what they want because they have been taught to ignore their own feelings about what they want, like, and need (Self Awareness; scale 3). This may be because of expectations placed upon them as children, such as to please others (the message being that your feelings, wants, and needs are not as important as other people's). Or, they may have experienced that when they do make an effort to get their wants and needs met, they are unsuccessful, for example, as a child being told, "I want doesn't get", not being given much attention, or never being rewarded for making an effort. Giving children choices and allowing them to make decisions for themselves, rather than being Dependent on others (scale 15) is likely to lead to higher Goal Directedness as an adult.

Not being distracted: Even if someone does know what they want, their Goal Directedness may still be low if they allow themselves to be easily distracted. Those who allow themselves to be distracted by other people tend to hold the Submissive attitude (low Self Regard, high Regard for Others); they see their needs as less important than other people's or perhaps other people are more powerful than them and therefore will elbow them aside. An example of this would be when someone drops whatever they are doing immediately when asked to do something by others, even if what they are engaged in is important to them.

People may also be distracted from achieving their life goals not by other people but by themselves. For example, they may find time to watch hours of television but never get around to completing their qualifications or doing exercise. To counter this, they need to become consciously aware of what they are doing, of the choices they are making, and the likely long-term consequences of their choices. This may be done by checking-in with themselves at regular intervals: "Will this help me towards where I want to go?"; "Will I be glad later that I have spent time and energy doing this now?"; and to then adapt their behaviour according to the answers.

Impulse control: One particular kind of self-destructive distraction which is quite difficult to deal with is impulse control, such as eating chocolate bars when aiming to lose weight, or losing one's temper when trying to remain calm. It may seem to those who have poor impulse control that they have no choice in the matter, that they "Can't help it", but they can. Remember the EI Attitude: Everyone is in control of and responsible for their actions. If a person is regularly subject to such impulsive 'emotional hijacks', then they need to reflect on the pattern of their feelings and behaviour and the consequences this has for them (Reflective Learning; scale 16) over the short and long-term. They may also want to develop their Personal Power (scale 6) to choose more carefully how they manage their feelings and behaviour. Impulse control is also more difficult when our internal resources are depleted, such as when we are tired, thirsty, and hungry. Addressing these needs early also helps build Emotional Resilience (scale 5).

In an interesting series of experiments by Walter Mischel,[11] he observed how children as young as four years of age could resist temptation, such as not eating a marshmallow in order to secure a further marshmallow later on. The children in these experiments were followed up into adulthood where they found a remarkably strong correlation between the children's resistance to temptation (or impulse control) and their success later in life (as measured by their SAT scores, earnings, and happiness questionnaires). A conclusion drawn from this research was that learning to defer gratification to achieve longer-term goals is a vital emotional skill to develop early in life. Much of education, learning and self-development is rewarded by hard work, long-term investment, and early 'sacrifice'. These attitudes and behaviours can be inherently difficult for children to develop; they tend to be naturally opportunistic and live in the present moment. However, attitudes can be acquired, and with emotional maturity comes a greater capacity for foresight and aligning one's behaviour to longer-term goals.

Goal driven: There is a balance to be struck between impulse control (in order to build for the future) and living for the present. Some people have Goal Directedness as a condition of their self-worth: "I am only OK if ... I try hard, ... am perfect, ... etc." These are often individuals who are high achievers but are constantly striving for more, unable to enjoy the present and relax. Deferring gratification to this extent may mean they have an 'until' script such as: "I can't enjoy myself until I pass my school exams"; "I can't stop worrying until I get a job"; "I can't be happy until I am promoted"; "I can't switch off until the kids leave home"; "I can't relax until I have saved enough money"; "I can't take it easy until I retire ...". Their goals may not even be their own but the expectations that others (their parents, their family, their employers) have of them. Goal Directedness is not about being driven in this way and should be balanced with the next scale of Flexibility.

SCALE 8: FLEXIBILITY

"A ship in harbour is safe, but that is not what ships are made for"
John A. Shedd

1   Definition

Flexibility is the degree to which the individual feels free to adapt their thinking and their behaviour to changing situations. It is closely related to EI Attitude 7; Change is possible.

2   Description

Low Flexibility: This suggests that someone may be unwilling to move outside of their comfort zones and try new ways of doing things. One reason for this could be if they have a fear of failure and therefore avoid the risk of change, or they may assume that if they try something new they are bound to fail (Pessimistic; scale 12), which may be driven by low Self Regard (scale 1). This can lead to fairly rigid ways of behaving, unwillingness to experiment, and a lack of adaptation to changing circumstances, which in turn may inhibit creative thinking and learning from new experiences (Reflective Learning; scale 16). Another possibility is that they do not believe they can change the way they are and they have deeply ingrained habits of behaviour they are unaware of (Self Awareness; scale 3). In addition, if their Regard for Others (scale 2) is low, they may be unwilling to adapt to what others want.

High Flexibility: This suggests that the individual is willing to move outside of their comfort zones and try new ways of doing things which may be driven by a high Self Regard and an optimistic attitude towards change (Balanced Outlook; scale 12). This is good news as it is likely to help them to think creatively, to experiment, learn from experience, adapt to others, respond to changing circumstances, and to change their behavioural habits. It may be worth checking that their Goal Directedness (scale 7) is also high, otherwise they may lack direction and not see things through; or because some people are 'rigidly flexible' (as described later), they find it difficult to stick with one course of action. Remember, Flexibility is about the capacity to change, not the frequency of change.

3   Interpretation

Flexibility and Goal Directedness: This scale follows on from and provides necessary balance to Goal Directedness. As with all linear scales, a person cannot have too much Flexibility, rather they may have insufficient Goal Directedness. An individual who has a high capacity to flex but lacks Goal Directedness is likely to change direction constantly and not see things through. Equally, a person who is highly goal directed but lacks Flexibility is unlikely to shift their approach or position regardless of how futile the chosen direction may prove to be.

Rigid Flexibility: Some people are surprised that Flexibility is a linear, 'more is better' scale, rather than a multi, 'you can have too much of a good thing' scale. The crucial point in this respect is the definition. Flexibility refers not to the degree to which a person adapts, but the degree to which they feel free to adapt; they can easily adapt when necessary and appropriate, but can also stick to their guns when that is what is needed. Having the capacity to flex is not the same as being flexible. Some people, for example, are rigidly flexible in that they insist on always doing things differently and avoid any repetition or routine. In effect this is actually being inflexible, as true Flexibility involves adapting appropriately to circumstances, rather than insisting on change when change is not required. In order to adapt appropriately, people need to be aware of themselves and of others. If, for example, an individual begins to realise through their increased Self Awareness (scale 3) that they constantly change the way they behave because they get easily bored or they don't want people to get to know the real them, then they will begin to understand that their behaviour is likely to be maladaptive and ineffective. This may be because it is determined by their own internal fears, rather than by their inner principles (Authenticity; scale 10) or by the external needs of the situation.

Rigidity: The opposite of Flexibility is rigidity. People who are rigid, who stick to the same patterns of behaviour, thinking, or feeling, usually do this out of fear. They tend to stick with what they know, because they fear the unknown. Adapting behaviour appropriately often requires moving outside of one's comfort zones. If a person has low Self Regard, they may resist trying out new behaviours as this may expose them to discomfort, failure, and humiliation. Someone with high Self Regard on the other hand tends to build fewer boundaries around their behaviour because they have a more stable inner core. This allows them to experience failure as useful learning and as conditional feedback (about their behaviour rather than about their whole being) rather than causing them to feel terrible about themselves. Consequently, they are far more willing to experiment, learn through trial and error, and try new things out, thereby helping them to learn and develop more quickly.

Attitude scales: It is not just Self Regard (scale 1) that has an influence on a person's Flexibility, so too does their Regard for Others (scale 2). Having low Regard for Others is likely to reduce a person's willingness to flex and adapt themselves to the needs of others. If they assume that they are right and that others are wrong then they may be less aware of the needs of others and less reasonable and flexible in compromising or cooperating with the desires of others.

Habits: One way to develop Flexibility is through changing habits of behaviour (as explained in Chapter Eight; 8.6). Habits are unconscious and automatic responses people apply to a given situation, implying a degree of inflexibility and a lack of conscious choice. Another barrier to people changing their habits is if they do not believe that they can change (EI Attitude 7; Change is possible), and so they see no point in attempting to do so.

SCALE 9: CONNECTING WITH OTHERS

"Honesty and transparency make you vulnerable. Be honest and transparent anyway" Mother Teresa of Calcutta

1   Definition

This scale measures the extent and the ease with which an individual makes significant connections with other people.

2   Description

Low Connecting with Others: One reason for scoring low may be that the individual needs to develop some basic interpersonal skills, such as making small talk, listening to people, asking open questions, or remembering people's names. More underlying reasons could stem from a low Self Regard (scale 1), such as they are shy and retiring, they lack confidence with people, or they avoid initiating contact due to a fear of being ignored or rejected. Building connections with people requires investing time and energy into relationships, listening without judgment, being prepared to express feelings and vulnerabilities, and having Regard for Others (scale 2). If a person is guarded and does not give much away in how they present themselves, others may see them as detached or superficial. This could prevent them from forming close connections and trusting relationships with people (Trust; scale 11).

High Connecting with Others: A high score suggests that someone invests time and energy into maintaining and developing their relationships; they are open in sharing their thoughts, values, and ideas; and they are prepared to express their feelings and vulnerabilities. It is this willingness to take down their guard, to be spontaneous, to listen, and show others appreciation that helps them build close and trusting relationships. This may have several benefits, such as building networks with people at work, giving and receiving help in times of trouble (supporting their Emotional Resilience; scale 5), and generally enhancing the quality and depth of their relationships.

3   Interpretation

Openness and connectedness: This scale measures two things: personal openness (the depth of relationships) and personal connectedness (the breadth of relationships). People connect with others not just by spending time together, but above all by sharing their feelings and their vulnerabilities. This scale is therefore related to Emotional Expression and Control (scale 13), but also includes sharing thoughts and demonstrating connection through behaviour.

Self Awareness and openness: Openness with others begins by being open with oneself, which involves peeling off layers of awareness to reveal deeper levels of self-insight. Being open with others about feelings is closely dependent on Self Awareness (scale 3). If a person is not self-aware, they may not have much to be open about or their openness may lack depth and feeling. Once a person becomes self-aware, they can choose whether to share their thoughts and feelings or withhold them. One reason people avoid being open is because they fear that what they say may upset someone or cause conflict. This is often because people's first level of awareness and openness is to blame or finger point: "What I honestly think is ... you are an idiot." Explaining why they think this: "Because you ignore me"; and how they feel: "Which upsets me", is a deeper and more constructive level of openness and awareness. They could be more open still by explaining their own 'inner story': "I don't think you like me." This may reflect their underlying attitude: "People don't like me"; and the feeling they have towards themselves: "I fear I am not likeable." This example represents different levels of Self Awareness and openness, moving from a knee-jerk response of criticising others to explaining their behaviour, then their thinking, then their attitude, and finally their feelings towards themselves.

Scale links: Connecting with Others is a critical resource for developing EI in other areas such as Self Regard, Regard for Others, Awareness of Others, Emotional Resilience, Trust, Emotional Expression and Control, Conflict Handling, and Interdependence. The act of communicating with others and listening without judgment creates the opportunity to understand others, to be known by others, and for relationships to improve.

As with all EIP scales, Connecting with Others depends on the attitudes of Self Regard and Regard for Others. The 'Ideal' position on the Attitude Matrix (I am OK, you are OK) is required for making good connections with others. People respond to being valued and respected, so Regard for Others (You are OK) is obviously required. But there is also a risk involved in opening up to others. In order to take that risk, a person needs to be sure of their own value no matter what, so Self Regard (I am OK) is required too.

Risk being open: Building relationships takes time and involves the risk of being ignored and rejected, but the risk of not doing so or waiting for others to be open first, is far greater in the long run. An important element to openness is being spontaneous, natural, and uninhibited. Close relationships form when people let down their guard, are open, and have fun together ('child to child' in Transactional Analysis terms).[1] Some people find it difficult to develop their connection with others because they lack some basic interpersonal skills, such as how to introduce themselves, when to listen and talk, and how to show an interest in what a person is saying. Helping people learn these basic skills can make a profound difference to their relationships and hence their well-being.

A person's capacity for making connections with others impacts on the quality of their work performance. It enables them to network effectively, to build alliances, and to give and receive help. It also affects their whole life experience, since it largely determines the quality of their relationships. Also, as can be seen in the next scale, Authenticity (scale 10), being known (by being open) is a prerequisite for being trusted, which in turn is an essential element of effective leadership and team membership.

SCALE 10: AUTHENTICITY

"That you may retain your self-respect, it is better to displease the people by doing what you know is right, than to temporarily please them by doing what you know is wrong"
William J.H. Boetcker

1   Definition

Authenticity is the degree to which an individual invites the trust of others by being principled, reliable, consistent, and known.

2   Description

Low Authenticity: One reason others may not risk trusting a person is if they are difficult to get to know, difficult to read, or a 'closed book', in which case they may need to develop the previous scale of Connecting with Others (scale 9). Another reason people may not trust others is if, in the past, they have found them to be unreliable, unpredictable, and not keep their promises (low on Authenticity). One explanation for this would be if they are trying to please others by agreeing to do things that they are unable to deliver on. This may be because their Regard for Others (scale 2) is higher than their Self Regard (scale 1). A negative interpretation would be that they lack inner guiding principles and integrity which may manifest as inconsistent behaviour, such as betraying confidences, manipulating people, and saying things they do not believe.

High Authenticity: A high score suggests that the individual 'walks their talk', keeps their promises, behaves in the same ways when on their own as when observed by others, and is predictable in that they can be relied upon. They are likely to have largely resolved their inner conflicts and have integrity so that their behaviour is congruent with their beliefs and values. People therefore tend to see them as authentic which helps them to collaborate and build trusting relationships. Note that this scale reflects whether the individual is trusted by others and as such it is useful to get other people's feedback to validate their own self-perception.

3   Interpretation

Being trustworthy and knowable: Authenticity involves two steps, firstly being authentic and secondly being known to be so, which requires Connecting with Others (scale 9). If a person does not connect with others, then they will not be known to be trustworthy. Therefore, a person may not be trusted for two reasons: either because they are not known by others; or because they are known to be untrustworthy through experience.

Attitude scales: To be truly trustworthy and authentic requires both high Self Regard and high Regard for Others. People who do not value others are less inclined to keep their promises and so will let others down. People with low Self Regard tend to make promises they cannot keep, and are therefore seen as untrustworthy and inauthentic. Authentic people keep their promises, they have integrity and can be relied upon to behave consistently whether they are on their own or with others. The TA (Transactional Analysis) corollary of being emotionally intelligent is being an Integrated Adult ('Integrated' meaning integration between Parent, Adult, and Child 'ego states').[1]

Inconsistency: People who score high on all three parts of any multi-scale (a less common but possible result) may have low Authenticity. One reason for this profile is that the person wants to be liked, so they are constantly changing their behaviour to suit others, rather than checking if it is consistent with their own inner principles. Another possible explanation is if they are manipulative or inconsistent, such as being friendly one moment and aggressive the next. Inconsistency and unpredictability tends to make other people feel very uncomfortable; in a work setting people would rather work with a consistently firm or demanding boss than with one who is inconsistent and difficult to read. There is a clear neurological explanation for this: the limbic (emotional) brain is there to keep a person safe by anticipating what will happen next. If someone is difficult to read, the limbic brain panics and prepares for a possible threat.

A person can learn to detect whether their behaviour fits their inner principles by listening to their intuition. A part of the brain called the basal ganglia acts as an 'ethical rudder', providing intuitive feedback as to whether an action feels right and is in line with their guiding principles.

SCALE 11: TRUST

"You may be deceived if you trust too much, but you will live in torment if you don't trust enough" Frank H. Crane

1   Definition

Trust is the tendency for a person to place the right amount of trust in others. It measures the balance between being Mistrusting (too little trust), Carefully Trusting (the right amount of trust), and Over Trusting (too much trust). This is the first multi-scale on the EIP questionnaire. As with all multi-scales, a person can have too much Trust as well as too little of it.

2   Description

Mistrusting: Being Mistrusting is often the result of an avoidance of being Over Trusting, rather than choosing to be Mistrusting. For example, a security guard may be more inclined to be Mistrusting than risk being Over Trusting. There is also a self-fulfilling confirmatory bias in all aspects of Trust: if a person expects the best from others or expects to be let down by people then they tend to notice and look for evidence that supports their (usually unconscious) expectation. Mistrust in a person can also stem from not being able to anticipate how other people are going to behave towards them in terms of whether they are consistent and known (Authenticity; scale 10). When someone doesn't know about another person, they tend to create their own inner stories, which can lead to exaggeration, unfounded fear, and mistrust.

Carefully Trusting: The ideal Trust profile is to score highly on Carefully Trusting and lowly on both Mistrusting and Over Trusting. A person with this profile would be inclined towards trusting others, but at the same time would be wary of evidence and intuition that they should or should not trust a particular person about a particular matter.

Over Trusting: This profile indicates a tendency to be too trusting of people and an avoidance of being Mistrusting. It is often seen in counsellors and coaches who are keen to develop trust and rapport with their client, so may ignore indications of untrustworthiness. Consequently, they may 'tread on eggshells', agree unconditionally with a client's views, or fear challenging their clients for risk of being seen as Mistrusting.

People sometimes assume that more Trust is always better and many other measures of EI treat this scale (and most other multi-scales) as linear. Holding a more trusting view towards others in most circumstances is likely to be reciprocated but it is important to balance this with any potential consequences. For example, a person may be far more willing to risk trusting someone to look after their shopping bag than to look after their children, or more willing to lend them £5 than lend them their credit card.

Over Trusting to Mistrusting: It is possible for a person to score highly on both Over Trusting and Mistrusting but lowly on Carefully Trusting. This combination appears contradictory, being both over-trusting and under-trusting, but is not uncommon. A person who is Over Trusting is likely to be let down by others and then may swing to the other extreme of not trusting people, before gradually returning to their home position of Over Trusting people and so their pattern of behaviour continues. Another explanation for the apparent contradiction of scoring high on both Mistrusting and Over Trusting is that a person's level of trust is situationally determined. Some people can be Mistrusting of others in personal and relationship matters (perhaps because in the past they have been hurt by someone they loved), while at the same time tending to be Over Trusting in another part of their life such as in business and financial matters.

3   Interpretation

Patterns of trust: If a person has a pattern of being let down by people, it may be indicative of an underlying attitude such as, "People always let me down." They may reaffirm this attitude through their own behaviour by giving others too much responsibility, idealising people, or expecting too much from others (Over Trusting). Sooner or later the other person will not live up to their unrealistic expectations, so confirming their belief. Ironically, their mistrust of others is predicated by their Over Trusting behaviour. By recognising this and being more Carefully Trusting the individual will reduce both their Mistrusting and Over Trusting scores.

Attitude matrix: Trust is clearly linked with the Attitude Matrix (Chapter Four; 4.3). Coming from the Critical position (I am OK, you are not OK) an individual is more likely to be Mistrusting. From the Submissive position (I am not OK, you are OK) they are more likely to be Over Trusting. From the Ideal position (I am OK, you are OK) they are most likely to be Carefully Trusting, and from the Blocked Potential position (I am not OK, you are not OK) they may rebound between Over Trusting and Mistrusting.

Using intuition: One way to develop better judgment on how much to Trust others is to improve Awareness of Others (scale 4). Awareness of Others allows someone to read people more accurately and to know when and to what degree they may be trusted and depended upon. It is important for line managers to get the right balance of Trust. A manager who is Over Trusting may have unrealistic expectations of their staff, causing them to potentially fail and become disheartened. A manager who is Mistrusting may undervalue their staff, causing them to disengage and impair their development. Intuition is hardwired into deeper parts of the brain because of the evolutionary necessity to instantly ascertain whether someone is safe or a threat, friend or foe, and trustworthy or not. This is partly why Trust is so important to human relationships: if broken, it activates the primitive survival threat response, to move against others (fight), to move away from others (flight), or no movement – to disengage from others (freeze).

Trust is also related to the next scale, Balanced Outlook (scale 12). People who are Over Optimistic and assume the best in others tend also to be Over Trusting, but when they are let down by others, they may rebound to feeling disappointed (Pessimistic) and Mistrusting.

SCALE 12: BALANCED OUTLOOK

"A pessimist sees the difficulty in every opportunity; an optimist sees the opportunity in every difficulty" Sir Winston Churchill

1   Definition

Balanced Outlook is how well someone manages to balance optimism with realism. It is concerned with a person's general outlook on the world and where they stand in terms of being Pessimistic, Realistically Optimistic, and Over Optimistic. All the multi-scales are Relationship Management scales, except for Balanced Outlook which is more closely related to Self Management. This scale has therefore been included in the Self Management calculation for the Behaviour Matrix described in Chapter Four; 4.5.

2   Description

Pessimistic: Balanced Outlook tends to be a self-fulfilling attitude: if a person expects the worst then this is more likely to happen as the individual is not alert to potential opportunities. Those who are Pessimistic anticipate failure and are unconsciously drawn to making this happen, which undermines their level of commitment, motivation, morale, and enthusiasm towards tasks and life in general. For suggestions on how to create positive and realistic outcomes refer to Chapter Eight; 8.7.

Realistically Optimistic: The middle position is Realistically Optimistic. It is important to have a generally hopeful outlook and expectation, but not to ignore reality in the face of clear evidence. Even if a person thinks everything will go well, they still need an alternative plan in case it doesn't. As Oliver Cromwell said before a battle, "Put your trust in God, but be sure to keep your powder dry."

Over Optimistic: Unlike other EI measures that claim that more optimism is always better, Balanced Outlook is a multi-scale where the ideal position is to be Realistically Optimistic: being neither Pessimistic nor Over Optimistic. Being Over Optimistic (seeing the world through rose tinted glasses) suggests that someone is too ready to believe what they want to believe, without checking whether this is justified. This may prevent them from dealing effectively with the world as it actually is. The risk here is that they ignore potential problems, repeat the same mistakes, make too many unrealistic assumptions, and have poor judgment and decision making. Those who are Over Optimistic may also lack Flexibility (scale 8), by not learning from their mistakes or being unwilling to accept and adapt to changing reality.

Over Optimistic to Pessimistic: One explanation for being both Over Optimistic and Pessimistic is that the individual may rebound from expecting everything to turn out well

(Over Optimistic) to feeling disappointed and Pessimistic when things don't work out as they had hoped. The answer is to be Realistically Optimistic and to find the right balance of checking their hopes against reality while also remaining positive.

3   Interpretation

Attitude scales: Balanced Outlook has an interesting link with the Attitude Matrix (Self Regard, scale 1; and Regard for Others, scale 2). People who hold a Critical attitude (I am OK, You are Not OK) may be Over Optimistic about themselves and Pessimistic towards others. Consequently, they may ignore cautionary advice from others. Correspondingly, someone who holds a Submissive attitude (I am Not OK, You are OK) may be more Pessimistic about themselves and Over Optimistic towards others, and so seek reassurance from others. In other words, it depends on who is responsible for the outcomes as to their level of optimism or pessimism. Someone who is in the Blocked Potential position (I am Not OK, You are Not OK) is likely to be Pessimistic about both themselves and others. People can also swing from being Over Optimistic to Pessimistic, as their unrealistic assumptions that things are going to work out well (Over Optimistic) are often followed by surprise and disappointment when they don't (Pessimistic).

Attributional style: How a person attributes success and failure is also indicative of their outlook. A useful summary of this is the three P's of attribution: Personal, Permanent, and Pervasive. The pessimist tends to attribute failure internally (Personal), generalise the problem (Pervasive), and assume it will remain the same (Permanent). They do the reverse for success: "I got lucky" (non-Personal); "It was a one-off" (non-Pervasive); and "It won't last" (non-Permanent). For the Over Optimistic person, the opposite applies, and their perception of failure is: "It's not my fault" (non-Personal); "It doesn't matter" (non-Pervasive); and "I will do it again" (non-Permanent). Their perception of success is: "I can do anything" (Personal); "Everything is perfect" (Pervasive); and "Nothing can go wrong" (Permanent). The skill is to be optimistic but at the same time to not ignore reality, which, as with all EI scales, requires accurate Self Awareness (scale 3).

SCALE 13: EMOTIONAL EXPRESSION AND CONTROL

"Out of control emotions can make smart people stupid"
Byron Nelson

1   Definition

Emotional Expression and Control is the degree to which an individual is emotionally controlled, i.e. whether they achieve appropriate balance in the expression and control of their emotions.

2   Description

Under Controlled: Those who are emotionally Under Controlled may need to learn how to express their feelings. In the words of Aristotle's Nicomachean Ethics: "Anyone can become angry – that is easy, but to be angry with the right person, to the right degree, at the right time, for the right purpose, and in the right way – this is not easy."[12] Underpinning this is EI Attitude 5: Feelings and behaviour are separate. A young child may automatically and without hindrance express all of their emotions, such as having a tantrum, sulking, laughter, and unbridled excitement. However, part of emotional maturity is learning how to manage the expression of feelings. EI Attitude 3 (No one else can control our feelings) is also particularly relevant to this scale. Others may greatly influence how a person feels, but this does not mean they have control over their emotions. For those people who do allow others to dictate how they feel, they are likely to be vulnerable, easily manipulated, Dependent on others (scale 15), have low Personal Power (scale 6), and find it more difficult to manage their own behaviour and relationships. For suggestions on how to manage emotions refer to Chapter Eight; 8.4.

Free and in Charge: 'Free and in charge' means that the individual feels free to express their emotions but is also in control of when and how they do this. A low score on emotionally Under Controlled indicates that they can separate their behaviour from their feelings so as to be emotionally mature and even-tempered. A low score on emotionally Over Controlled indicates they tend not to suppress their feelings, so they are able to show people warmth and be emotionally responsive when appropriate. Having this balance on Emotional Expression and Control helps bring emotional maturity to their behaviour and closeness in their relationships.

Over Controlled: Most people have certain emotions which they are less comfortable in expressing than other feelings. For example, children who are brought up with a Be Strong driver may inhibit any expression of perceived weakness like crying, fear, or love, and children who are brought up with a Please Others driver may hide their feelings of anger, frustration, and dislike. There may be certain feelings that are less socially acceptable within a culture or less demonstrated within a family which become the individual's normal way of showing or hiding emotions. Issues can occur when someone does not find constructive ways to release their emotions, so they are expressed inappropriately, such as through passive-aggressive behaviour, stress, or ill-health. Being emotionally Over Controlled can also impair a person's relationships as they may be less able to connect with others (scale 9) and be less known or trusted by others (Authenticity; scale 10).

The emotional rebound: This scale provides a classic example of how people can swing from one extreme to the other on a multi-scale (the 'tuning fork' profile). People who tend to bottle-up their feelings (emotionally Over Controlled) are sooner or later likely to explode emotionally (emotionally Under Controlled), rather like keeping the lid on top of a kettle that eventually explodes. Many people who have this characteristic recognise that they are Under Controlled, especially as the results can be greatly damaging to their relationships, but they are often less aware that the cause comes from Over Controlled emotions. Instead of trying harder to keep their emotions under wraps, which only delays the explosion and makes it worse later, they should learn to notice their feelings sooner and let them out appropriately before they become overwhelming. As with all aspects of EI, the key to managing this process is to develop Self Awareness (scale 3) and to recognise their feeling patterns so that they are able to detect the early signs of emotions within their body.

3 Interpretation

Attitude scales: Emotional Expression and Control, as with all EIP scales, is underpinned by the Core Attitudes of Self Regard (scale 1) and Regard for Others (scale 2). An individual who comes from the Submissive position (I am not OK, you are OK) may believe that their thoughts and feelings are less important than other people's or that other people do not want to hear what they have to say. They may therefore hold themselves back and be emotionally Over Controlled. On the other hand, someone coming from the Critical position (I am OK, you are not OK) is less concerned with other people's feelings and believes that how they feel and what they think is more important and so they are Under Controlled in how they express their emotions. Sometimes being emotionally Under Controlled may appear to come from the Submissive position but it actually comes from a Blocked Potential position (I am not OK, you are not OK). When people are highly sensitive and become easily upset and catastrophise about their problems (low Self Regard, I am not OK), they are often highly self-absorbed rather than attentive to the needs of others. They feel that "My problems matter more than yours", and they do not take responsibility for their problems, tending instead to blame others and their circumstances (low Regard for Others, you are not OK).

Cultural differences: A further point to remember about this scale is that people's behavioural response may not accurately reflect their underlying emotional experience – that is, behavioural expression should be considered in context of the person's background. The Italian culture is renowned for being emotionally expressive; children may display pain differently from adults; men may be less inclined to cry; and people differ in how they display certain emotions.

Emotional labour: A popular area of emotional research in the workplace focuses on emotional labour, which is when an employee must alter their emotional expression in order to meet the display rules of an organisation.[13] When the required behaviour is congruent with their emotions this is known as 'surface acting'. When the required behaviour is incongruent with their emotions this is known as 'deep acting', such as being polite to a customer when feeling annoyed with them. Having emotional control is a useful short-term solution but in the long-term may lead to burnout.[14] The emotionally intelligent individual is authentic (scale 10), finding a way of understanding, accepting, or reframing events so that their attitudes are congruent with the emotions and behaviour they express, to meet the display rules of the organisation.

SCALE 14: CONFLICT HANDLING

"Out beyond ideas of wrongdoing and rightdoing there is a field. I'll meet you there" Rumi

1   Definition

This scale measures how well conflict is handled or how Assertive a person is. It is not the existence of conflict that is problematic in itself. Conflict is an inevitable part of life, since 'People are different' and want different things (EI Attitude 4). Handling conflict well is essential to maintaining relationships, dealing with confrontation, collaborating effectively, working creatively, and being productive.

2   Description

Passive: A high score on Passive suggests that the individual may avoid conflict, be overly accommodating, and less inclined to assert themselves or stand up for what they want. If their Self Regard (scale 1) is lower than their Regard for Others (scale 2), they may tend to put their own needs second, not express their needs, put up with things that are not right for them, and agree to things that they do not want. It is also worth considering whether they suppress their feelings too much (Over Controlled; scale 13) and whether they know what they want (Goal Directedness; scale 7), as it is difficult to assert themselves if they don't know what they want.

Assertive: Being Assertive suggests that someone stands up for what they want without undermining others, balances the needs of others with their own, focuses on tasks without ignoring people and creates mutually beneficial outcomes from conflict or confrontation. When combined with low scores on Passive and Aggressive, they are unlikely to back down from or avoid conflict, or become Aggressive or hostile towards others.

Aggressive: A high score on Aggressive suggests that someone may be overly Assertive, competitive, hostile, demanding, and perhaps dismiss the needs of others. One explanation for this is if their Regard for Others is lower than their Self Regard, in which case they may also be seen as a bully. Aggressive behaviour often masks a fear of not feeling in control, of losing out, or of feeling threatened. If they also have a tendency to feel angry, frustrated, and to be impatient this may adversely affect their physical health.

Passive and Aggressive: One reason for being high on both scales could be a tendency to rebound from being Passive (bottling up frustration) to Aggressive (being unable to contain feelings of anger). Learning to be more Assertive than Passive helps prevent feelings of anger from building up. Another explanation for this score is if the individual is passively Aggressive as described below.

3   Interpretation

Attitude scales: The relationship between Conflict Handling and the Attitude scales is very clear. Passivity is the expression of low Self Regard and high Regard for Others: "You are more significant and powerful than me, so I will not challenge you." Aggression is the expression of high Self Regard and low Regard for Others: "I am more important than you, so my wishes take priority over yours." The emotionally intelligent position is Assertive, high Self Regard and high Regard for Others: "Both of us matter, as do our interests." These Conflict Handling attitudes also map onto the Harvard model of negotiation. Assertive, is 'I Win, You Win'; Passive is 'I Lose, You Win'; Aggressive is 'I Win, You Lose'; and passive-aggressive is 'I Lose, You Lose'.[15]

Passive-aggressive: People who fall into the Blocked Potential position on the Attitude Matrix (low Self Regard and low Regard for Others) are likely to be passive-aggressive. For example, agreeing to do something but then not completing it, being unavailable at crucial times, criticising people behind their backs, or undermining agreed decisions after a meeting. What makes passive-aggressive behaviour more difficult to identify is that it is rarely expressed overtly and is normally done in a way that can be denied or justified.

Assertiveness skills: Assertiveness training often fails because it is not backed up by a corresponding change in the person's attitude. If an individual has a low Self Regard, then sooner or later they are likely to return to their Passive behaviour. Another reason could be because the new Assertive behaviours have not been sufficiently rehearsed and embedded at the experiential and emotional levels. When someone is required to be Assertive, they are likely to feel a degree of anxiety (as potentially they are in a conflict situation). Anxiety makes it more difficult to think clearly and so people often fall back on their habitual response. Rehearsing and practising a very specific new response to a conflict situation is usually more effective than teaching people multiple complex strategies. For example, when someone asks, "Can you do X for me?", instead of instantly saying "Yes" and dropping everything they are doing, they could recite a rehearsed phrase such as, "Can you give me a moment to check my schedule?" This gives them time to compose themselves, to think through what they want to do, and to reply with the most appropriate Assertive response.

Anger: As with all emotions, anger is an adaptive survival response that serves an important purpose. Anger helps raise adrenalin to prepare to fight. It also creates the energy and desire to rectify an injustice and challenge unfairness, driving much political reform and change in society.

However, chronic or extreme feelings of anger can have significant deleterious effects on a person's health, well-being, and relationships. The negative physiological effects of anger are numerous: it is the only emotion that reduces the pumping efficiency of the heart; it increases Cortisol production depleting the immune system; and the high state of arousal it creates puts considerable strain on the body. Chronic anger causes hypertension, increased cholesterol, damaged arteries, increased illness, leads to heart disease, and slows recovery. Chronic anger and Aggressive behaviour can also become habitual, as it often gets people's immediate needs met, such as 'winning' an argument, putting someone down, or taking control. However, these immediate gains are usually heavily outweighed by the consequences, such as irrational thinking, inappropriate behaviour, and damaged relationships. Despite being as common as anxiety, anger management is less culturally recognised and given far less prominence than stress management. Anger that turns into uncontrolled rage is a clear example of poor Emotional Intelligence (described as an 'emotional hijack' in Chapter Two; 2.3) and is associated with low Self Awareness (scale 3), low Awareness of Others (scale 4) low Emotional Resilience (scale 5), being emotionally Under Controlled, and poor Conflict Handling. Developing each of these scales, starting with Self Awareness, is at the root of reducing chronic anger and Aggressive behaviour.

SCALE 15: INTERDEPENDENCE

"Don't walk behind me, I may not lead. Don't walk in front of me, I may not follow. Just walk beside me and be my friend"
Albert Camus

1   Definition

Interdependence is the last of the Relationship Management scales. It measures how well an individual manages to balance taking themselves and others into account.

2   Description

Dependent: Scoring high on Dependent suggests that the individual prefers to work with other people, to have others around them for support, and to avoid independent activities. This may be because they are very extraverted and dislike working alone, or that they have a low Self Regard (scale 1) so lack the confidence to act independently, while also having high Regard for Others (scale 2) so assume that others know better than they do. The effect of this could be that they: avoid making independent decisions; ask people for help before thinking of a solution; seek regular reassurance and guidance from others; avoid too much responsibility; and find it difficult to work on their own. They may typically score low on Personal Power (scale 6) and be more Passive (scale 14).

Interdependent: The ideal profile pattern is to score relatively high on the middle scale, Interdependent, than on the other two extremes. This suggests that someone is equally comfortable and flexible at including others or working independently when appropriate. By not being Dependent on others, they are more likely to take the lead and responsibility when necessary and be willing to make decisions for themselves. By not being Over Independent, they are more likely to listen and communicate with people and be prepared to follow others when required. Having the capacity to work interdependently is necessary for effective team working, collaboration, building partnerships, and effective relationships.

Over Independent: Being Over Independent suggests that someone prefers to work on their own, to do things in their own way, and have less collaboration or teamwork activity. This may be because they are a more introverted person preferring to work alone, that they have low Regard for Others and see less value in what other people can contribute, or that they are Mistrusting (scale 11) so choose not to rely on others. The potential effects of being Over Independent are that they do not form close collaborative partnerships (scale 9), are less aware of others (scale 4), do not benefit from other people's contributions, miss out on opportunities to learn from others and the benefits of team working, and people may feel excluded by them.

Dependent and Over Independent: The least desirable profile pattern is to be high on both Dependent and Over Independent, but low on Interdependent. This suggests that they may be quite changeable depending upon the context. When they feel less confident they may be very Dependent on others, and when they no longer need support from others they may detach or drop them, leaving people feeling confused by their inconsistent behaviour towards them. In the long run this could jeopardise their relationships, as people may be cautious about offering them their support or feel rejected by them, which could make friendships, collaboration, and teamwork difficult to sustain.

3   Interpretation

Attitude scales: Interdependence requires both Self Regard (to work well independently) and Regard for Others (to work well with others). People who are Dependent may be coming from an Attitude of low Self Regard and high Regard for Others. They may lack a degree of confidence to make their own decisions and to act independently. Over Independent is effectively the reverse of this, reflecting an Attitude of high Self Regard and low Regard for Others.

Friend or Foe? People more naturally collaborate and group with people they know (who are familiar and similar) and move away from people they don't know. This is because the brain automatically classifies people as 'friend' or 'foe', and may classify someone they don't know as a foe (a potential threat) until proven otherwise. Perceiving someone as a foe reduces empathy, raises the threat response, and makes it more difficult to trust people. It is therefore important to interact openly with others so as to activate their 'friend' response. Interaction also releases oxytocin, a neurochemical that draws people closer and creates a sense of trust and safety in the other person.[16] A study by Gallup[17] showed that companies which encourage collaboration through informal contact, such as at the water dispenser, had greater productivity and well-being. Interaction and openness can easily be encouraged by organisations through practices such as networking, mentoring, social events, and informal meetings.

Personality type: Interdependence may be influenced to some degree by a person's personality type preference, either for introversion (Over Independent) or for extraversion (Dependent). However, through Emotional Intelligence a person can learn to manage their behaviour to be appropriate to the situation (Interdependent). This is a central part to the definition of EI: 'The practice of managing one's personality to be both personally and interpersonally effective.' Interdependence serves as a useful example of the relationship between EI and personality type which exists for all of the EIP scales.[18]

SCALE 16: REFLECTIVE LEARNING

"Hindsight is good, foresight is better, but insight is the best of all" Tim Sparrow

1   Definition

Reflective Learning is the degree to which Emotional Intelligence is enhanced by the individual reflecting on what they and others feel, think, and do. They may then notice the outcomes of their feelings, thoughts, and behaviour and alter their patterns accordingly. Unlike the other scales, Reflective Learning is not an aspect of Emotional Intelligence itself but is a vital prerequisite for developing Emotional Intelligence.

2   Description

Low Reflective Learning: Being low on this scale suggests that the individual rarely reflects upon their experiences consciously and/or intuitively, and that they may not have any formal approach for raising their own self-knowledge or for their personal development. The risk here is that they may tend to make the same mistakes or repeat patterns without learning from past experiences and adjusting their behaviour accordingly. Some possible reasons for this are: their attention is focused very much on the future or the present rather than reflecting on the past; they have little interest in personal development; they have never learned how to go about developing themselves or their relationships. Reflective Learning is important because it provides a process for developing all of the other EIP scales.

High Reflective Learning: Having a high score on this scale suggests that someone has a regular habit of reflecting upon their experiences consciously and/or intuitively, and that they put their learning into action to improve their personal and interpersonal effectiveness. This may mean that they know themselves well, they understand what motivates them, how they can change their behaviour, what triggers specific feelings for them, and how they can manage their emotional state. In order to make best use of this practice they should check that their Self Awareness (scale 3) is also high, as their experiential awareness provides the feedback necessary for later reflection.

3 Interpretation

Reflective Learning: Reflective Learning is an important part of the EIP framework as it enables the Feeling level (Awareness) to convert to the Behaviour level (Management) as shown in the extended EIP framework (Table A1.1).

The extended EIP framework

	Personal Intelligence	Interpersonal Intelligence
Behaviour	Self Management	Relationship Management
Knowledge	Self Knowledge	Knowledge of Others
Thinking	Self Reflection	Reflecting on Others
Feeling	Self Awareness	Awareness of Others
Attitude	Self Regard	Regard for Others

Table A1.1

© 1998 JCA Global Ltd.

Self Awareness v Self Knowledge: Not only do people need awareness in the moment, but they also need to adopt the practice of reflecting on their experience to convert their Self Awareness over time (a succession of moments) into Self Knowledge, and their Awareness of Others (scale 4) into Knowledge of Others. The practice of Reflective Learning is part of a continuous process of learning and developing: an individual becomes aware of their experience, reflects upon it, and evaluates it in relation to their existing Self Knowledge. This then helps them to either reinforce or update their Self Knowledge. In essence, Reflective Learning is the 'How to' part of the EI definition, which involves 'thinking about feeling to guide one's behaviour'. Another set of everyday descriptors used in the English language relating to the levels of the extended EIP framework are shown in Table A1.2.

Other descriptors of the EIP framework levels

DESCRIPTOR	DEFINITION	LINK TO THE EIP FRAMEWORK
Foresight	Making use of previous experiential learning to anticipate and choose future behaviour and responses	Self and Relationship Management
Insight	Understanding why we feel, think, and behave as we do	Self Knowledge
Hindsight	Reflecting upon and understanding past experiences	Reflective Learning
Mid-sight	Being aware of experiences in the moment	Self Awareness

Table A1.2

APPENDIX TWO
A HISTORICAL OVERVIEW
OF EMOTIONAL INTELLIGENCE

1   The evolution of emotion

In 1872, Charles Darwin[1] published 'The expression of the emotions in man and animals' to support his theory of evolution and natural selection. He argued that emotions evolved and were adapted over time providing a consistent emotional language across many species. A key piece of his evidence was observing the consistency across humans in their facial expression of emotions. This was positively supported 100 years later by the work of Paul Ekman (1977)[2] who mapped the subjective and physiological emotional experiences of people to distinct facial expressions. Ekman also found that certain emotions are universally recognised (even in cultures with no media influence). He proposed that there are six basic emotions: anger, disgust, fear, happiness, sadness, and surprise. This view, however, has been challenged by some modern cognitive theories of emotions discussed later.

Along similar lines, Robert Plutchick (1980)[3] defined eight basic emotions that were based on survival adaptations from as far back as the Cambrian era 600 million years ago. For example, sadness and grief are the response to a loss of something pleasurable, and surprise is the brief freezing response to a new stimulus (a possible threat). Plutchick placed the basic emotions into positive and negative pairings: joy versus sadness; anger versus fear; trust versus distrust; and surprise versus anticipation. From this, he derived an 'emotions wheel' where the basic emotions could be combined and modified through cultural conditioning, to form complex emotions, such as anger and disgust combining to form contempt. In contrast to Plutchick's theory, Nesse (1990)[4] and others proposed that emotions were selected in early Hominids when the human lineage diverged from the great ape, 5-8 million years ago, as an adaptation response to survival problems. For example, the emotions of desire and love were required to find a mate, and compassion in order to protect offspring.

Douglas Watt (2004)[5] offers a useful framework of evolution for understanding emotion and cognition as natural by-products of evolution to support the stable biological functioning of the organism (homeostasis). He argues that "emotion is an evolutionary extension of homeostasis, and likewise that cognition is an extension of emotion". In other words, evolution keeps what works and builds upon it to make it even better, so that emotions are at the service of homeostasis, and cognition is at the service of emotion. This suggests there is a pecking order of priority: homeostasis, emotion, cognition (which has parallels with Paul MacLean's[6] triune brain theory of evolution), reptilian (homeostasis), mammalian (emotion), and primate (cognition), as mentioned in Chapter Two; 2.1.

Evolutionary theories of emotion are largely consistent with the EIP basis for Emotional Intelligence, inferring that emotions stem from primitive parts of the brain, based initially on a survival response, and that complex emotions are more culturally defined than the basic emotions. Evolutionary theory tends to describe emotions as being relatively fixed and automated, while EI (and the EIP) emphasise how individuals can alter their emotional state and choose how they respond to their emotions, as explained by the later neuroscientific research on emotions.

2   The neuroscience of emotion

Research into the neural circuitry and anatomical foundations of emotion has lent considerable weight to explaining EI. This has often centred on the debate over whether emotions originate in the body and/or the brain. One of the earliest of these theories was by the psychologist William James who published 'What is an Emotion?' (1884)[7] and physiologist Carl Lange who independently developed a somatic feedback theory on emotion (1885)[8] which later became known as the James-Lange theory. They proposed that people perceive events and have bodily feelings (such as a change in heart rate, blood pressure, tight stomach, and sweaty palms) which they then label as physical sensation/emotion. For instance, when witnessing an external stimulus such as a grizzly bear, a person experiences trembling in the body, which they interpret as fear. In other words, the person's emotional reaction depends on how they interpret their physical reaction. The James-Lange theory was directly challenged by Walter Cannon[9] and his doctoral student Philip Bard[10] in the 1920s. Cannon argued that physiological responses were too slow for the rapid and intense experience of emotions. To demonstrate this, he showed that cats with different severed nerves (body to brain) still displayed full emotional responses, such as fear, in response to a barking dog. He also showed that physiological stimulation of the hypothalamus in the brain caused physiological changes in the body. From this, Cannon proposed, in his influential book Wisdom of the Body, that the physiological and conscious cognitive experience of emotions must occur simultaneously.

Whether emotions originate in the brain or the body continues to be debated today, although current research suggests that they originate in both. Elmer Green (1977),[11] who pioneered biofeedback for treatment of disease, states that "every change in the physiological state is accompanied by an appropriate change in the mental emotional state, conscious or unconscious, and conversely, every change in the mental emotional state, conscious or unconscious, is accompanied by an appropriate change in the physiological state". In her book, 'Molecules of Emotion', Candace Pert (1997)[12] gives a coherent biochemical rationale for emotions originating in both the brain and the body in the form of peptides, neuropeptides, and their receptors. She explains how peptides and neuropeptides flow freely in the circulatory system, acting as "information messenger molecules" which reach all organs and tissues of the body and brain, leading to complex physiological and neurological reactions, eventually culminating in emotional responses that influence actions and decision making. She refutes the Newtonian and Cartesian models of the body being a mechanistic clock-like organism and describes the body as "the unconscious mind... with an intelligence in the form of information (peptides) running all the system (body-mind) and creating behaviour". Her view of the body and emotions being 'intelligent' is also supported by the neurological perspective discussed next, which provides strong foundations for the concept of Emotional Intelligence.

One of the most significant pieces of neurological research in recent times in support of Emotional Intelligence is the Somatic Marker Hypothesis by Antonio Damasio (1994).[13] In economic theory, there is an assumption that decision making is devoid of emotion and is based purely on cost-benefit analysis. However, social environments are complex and unpredictable, requiring very rapid judgments based on large amounts of information, or what may be termed hunches, intuition, and gut feeling. The Somatic Marker Hypothesis is that cognitive decision making is influenced and simplified by the individual's emotional/physiological state (somatic markers) that directs them towards making more advantageous decisions. Somatic markers may be conscious or unconscious and are reinforced by past outcomes. For example, someone may feel happy and motivated to pursue a behaviour, or anxious and uncertain to avoid a course of action, depending on their previous experiences in similar situations.

Damasio studied patients with lesions to the brain in a region called the ventromedial prefrontal cortex (vmPFC).* He observed that these patients made decisions against their own interests and were unable to learn to make wiser decisions based on previous mistakes. To test his observation, Damasio adapted a decision-making game called the Iowa Gambling Task,[14] where participants selected from one of four decks of cards and learned to anticipate high-risk card decks from low-risk decks. The high-risk decks would give greater rewards but also higher penalties, and overall gave lower profits than the other card decks. Participants with damage to their vmPFC continued to make disadvantageous decisions, even when made aware of the consequences of their actions. A different region of the brain also involved in emotional decision making is the amygdala, and this is responsible for the fight-flight-freeze survival mechanism. Patients with damage to the amygdala were found to pursue more harmful and risky behaviours, while those with vmPFC damage, despite making disadvantageous decisions, did not engage in activity that would be immediately harmful to themselves. These findings provide evidence that emotions and where they are processed in the brain play an important role in informing sound judgment and decision making.

*Historical evidence has shown that frontal lobe damage is associated with impaired emotional expression, decision making, and social functioning. A classic example is of Phineas Gage,[15] a dynamite worker who suffered an iron bar through his head, damaging his frontal lobes. He survived with normal intellect, but it affected aspects of his personality, leading to him becoming irresponsible, untrustworthy, and impatient.

Another important finding from Damasio's research was that normal participants showed greater physiological anxiety (as measured by galvanic skin conductance response) just prior to picking up their card, which was absent in the vmPFC patients. In other words, their emotional response preceded their cognitive response, suggesting that thinking and decision making is largely influenced by feeling, one of the key propositions from the EIP SAFE-TBO model of Emotional Intelligence (Chapter Two; 2.3).

Several other neurological studies have confirmed the importance of emotions in informing thinking and decision making.[16] An intriguing piece of research by Tuan Pham (2012)[17] found that individuals who trust their feelings make more accurate predictions of future events than individuals who have low trust in their feelings. This 'Emotional Oracle Effect' was found across a variety of prediction domains, including the 2008 US Democratic presidential nomination, movie box-office success, the winner of American Idol, the stock market, college football, and even the weather!

In another example, V.S. Ramachandran (1998)[18] describes patients with Capgras syndrome who are unable to connect to their emotional memories. This means they recognise a close friend but have no emotional memory of them, and consider them to be an imposter. This further illustrates the dependence on emotions for accurate perception and decision making.

Other research has supported the view that emotions precede conscious awareness. Benjamin Libet (1985)[19] showed that the emotional trigger to act (an action potential) takes place 0.3 seconds before a person becomes aware of the desire to act. Joseph LeDoux (1996)[20] found that information is fast-tracked to the amygdala (brain region central to emotions) up to half a second before it reaches the neocortex, suggesting that emotional memories, impressions, and evaluations are made prior to the individual being conscious of them.

Advances in social and affective neuroscience have identified a specific network of brain regions that are involved in social and emotional cognition, called the Default Mode Network (DMN) or 'social brain'. According to Boyatzis (2018)[21] and other researchers in the field, this suggests that there are two different capacities for reasoning: 'empathic reasoning' (DMN) that facilitates social and emotional understanding, and 'analytical reasoning' (or the Task Positive Network (TPN) of brain regions) that attend to non-social problem solving. Interestingly, it has been found that these are opposing domains, meaning that doing one of them switches off the other.[22] The skill of EI is being able to switch fluidly between the two domains.

Although research based on neuroscience should be treated with caution,[23] the main point to emerge from this evidence is that emotions are a form of intelligence and wisdom. They provide sophisticated and instant feedback on how to respond, behave, and make decisions based on the wealth of accumulated emotional experience. These findings are consistent with evolutionary theory and the idea that emotions may have evolved to help people make better decisions.

Cognitive theories of emotion: Another area of research that lends support for the brain-body integration of emotions, and in that respect for EI, are cognitive theories of emotional processing.

An interesting experiment by Stanley Schachter (1962)[24] demonstrated the importance of cognitive appraisal (thinking) for interpreting a physiological experience as an emotion. Subjects were injected with epinephrine to induce physiological arousal, but in the absence of an actual emotion-evoking stimulus were unable to interpret their arousal as an experienced emotion. However, when presented with a stimulus (in the form of another person displaying an emotion such as anger or amusement) the subjects were observed to express related emotions. They called this the 'two factor theory of emotion', arguing that the experience of emotions requires both physiological and cognitive input. This research galvanised several cognitive theories of emotion. Some of the most influential of these include: Affect theory of emotion;[25] Judgment theory of emotions;[26] Mind and Body: Psychology of Emotion and Stress;[27] Cognitive appraisal theories on emotions;[28] and Intentionality of emotions.[29]

More recently, Perceptual theory (by Peter Goldie, 2004)[30] has claimed that cognition is unnecessary for interpreting emotion. This theory suggests that emotions are themselves perception, in that they represent a response to a situation; they have meaning and are about something. Emotions, rather like other senses such as vision or touch, provide information about the relationship between the individual and their world. Goldie describes emotions as "perceptions that have meaning", supporting the view that emotions are a form of intelligence within the body.

In a recent publication, 'How Emotions are Made', Feldman-Barrett (2017)[31] presents a coherent argument for a constructionist theory of emotions.[32] She proposes that emotions are created as goal-based concepts. For example, the concept of 'love' may have relevance to several goals, such as 'desire for others', 'help from others', or 'connection with others'. The goal of 'desire for others' for instance may invoke behaviours such as flirtation, romance, and sex, and create associations with more granular emotion such as passion, longing, and lust. Barrett proposes that emotional concepts are formed around diverse past experiences that have supported specific goals. Once emotional concepts are formed, they allow for rapid automatic processing of incoming stimuli that help predict, explain, and give meaning to an individual's internal and external world. The theory of constructed emotions contrasts with evolutionary theories that view emotions as relatively fixed templates, but is consistent with the EIP pattern matching theory described in Chapter Two; 2.4.

As well as the evolutionary, biological, and cognitive theories of emotion there is also an important social perspective that has clear relevance to EI. Emotions have a strong social and interpersonal component. James Averill (1980)[33] proposes that an emotional response is governed by social norms and expectations, and Brian Parkinson (1996)[34] proposes that emotions typically occur in particular social settings and have specific interpersonal functions, such as to trust others or to withdraw from people. This social aspect of emotions is discussed in the next section on Social Intelligence.

3   Social Intelligence

Emotional Intelligence has its origins in the concept of Social Intelligence, although the two concepts are often used interchangeably or together. Howard Gardner (1983)[35] separates out Intrapersonal (emotional) from Interpersonal (social) intelligences; Carolyn Saarni (1990)[36] describes Emotional Competence as including both emotional and social skills; and Reuven Bar-On (2000)[37] refers to the construct of EI as Emotional-Social Intelligence. Social Intelligence originates from the work of Edward Thorndike, who published 'Social Intelligence' in 1920,[38] describing socially competent behaviour as "the ability to understand and manage men and women, boys and girls, and to act wisely in human relations". Hunt (1928)[39] defined Social Intelligence as "the ability to deal with other people", and Wedeck (1947)[40] characterises it as "the ability to judge correctly, the feelings, moods, and motivations of others". The first instrument designed to measure socially intelligent behaviour in young children was produced by Edgar Doll in 1935.[41] Social Intelligence also has historical roots in personality theory and social psychology, such as George Kelly's Personal Construct Theory (1955).[42] This theory proposes that individuals form cognitive expectations, called personal constructs, to interpret and understand the social world in which they live. Personal constructs are the anticipation of events that influence how the individual behaves and may be likened to attitudes and pattern matching described in Chapter Two; 2.4.

Social Intelligence also draws heavily on human need theories,[43-45] asserting that behind much social behaviour are emotional drivers/needs, such as for affiliation, status, achievement, autonomy, and intimacy. These emotional drivers/needs include the human emotional needs described in Chapter One; 1.1, that lie behind the EIP model.

One other important element to Social Intelligence are theories of interpersonal behaviour and group dynamics. Two pioneers in this field were Kurt Lewin (1947)[46] and Will Schutz (1958).[47] Lewin is considered to be the father of modern social psychology and he established the National Training Laboratory in America as a way to develop social and emotional learning. Both Lewin and Schutz recognised the importance of experiential group encounter for personal growth, and the application of Emotional and Social Intelligence is much influenced by the principles laid down by their work.

Social Competence: A similar concept to Social Intelligence is Social Competence, which has its origins in terms such as 'social skills'[48] and 'social learning'.[49] Keith Topping (2000)[50] defines Social Competence as "the ability to integrate thinking, feeling, and behaviour to achieve social tasks and outcomes". By this definition people may be good at different elements of Social Competence: some people may be good at thinking and knowing what they should do, but be less good at dealing with the emotions of a social situation. Others may have learned a set of effective social skills but be less able to adapt them to unfamiliar situations. This fits with the principle of the EIP six-part framework that EI is multifaceted. In addition, the definition of Social Competence is similar to Part Two of the EIP definition of EI: 'the habitual practice of thinking about feeling, and feeling about thinking to guide one's behaviour.'

Practical Intelligence: Social Intelligence falls into the camp of what are termed non-cognitive or non-intellective intelligences. Another non-cognitive intelligence is Sternberg's (1985)[51] theory of Successful Intelligence, which can be identified by three key abilities: analytic, creative, and practical intelligence. Hedlund and Sternberg (2000)[52] give the following explanation of practical intelligence in relation to EI: "The ability to acquire knowledge, whether it pertains to managing oneself, managing others, or managing tasks, can be characterised appropriately as an aspect of intelligence. The decision to call this aspect of intelligence social, emotional, or practical intelligence will depend on one's perspective and one's purpose."

Alexithymia: At around the same time as there being an interest in exploring Social Intelligence, researchers began to examine the pathological end to this spectrum: the inability of individuals to recognise, understand, and describe emotions. This was later given the label of Alexithymia by Peter Sifneos (1973)[53] from the Greek meaning 'lack of words for emotions' and is characterised by:

— Difficulty identifying and distinguishing between feelings

— Difficulty describing feelings to others

— Constricted imagination

— An externally oriented cognitive style

Alexithymia is an aspect of personality originally identified by Ruesch (1948)[54] and Maclean (1949)[55] who observed patients with an inability to verbalise feelings despite sometimes displaying extreme emotions. Alexithymia has been partly attributed to early environmental influences, especially variations in their care-givers capacity to form attachment.[56] A similar construct to Alexithymia is Affective Orientation, described as "the degree to which people are aware of their emotions, perceive them as important, and actively consider their affective responses in making judgments and interacting with others".[57] Affective Orientation may be seen as a spectrum, from the very low end being Alexithymia to the high end representing EI.

Psychological Mindedness: Two concepts that closely parallel Alexithymia (or the opposite end of it) are Psychological Mindedness[58] and Emotional Awareness.[59]

Appelbaum defined Psychological Mindedness as "a person's ability to see relationships among thoughts, feelings, and actions, with the goal of learning the meanings and causes of his experiences and behaviours". Conte (1996)[60] extended the concept beyond self-focus, to include "both self-understanding and an interest in the motivation and behaviour of others", and identified four broad abilities:

— Access to one's feelings

— Willingness to talk about one's feelings and interpersonal problems

— Capacity for behavioural change

— An interest in other people's behaviour

Emotional Awareness is defined by Lane & Schwartz (1987)[59] as "the ability to recognise and describe emotions in one's self and others". They describe five levels of Emotional Awareness (which share structural characteristics with Piaget's (1950)[61] stages of cognitive development):

— Physical sensation

— Action tendencies

— Single emotions

— Blends of emotion

— Blends of blends of emotional experiences

There is much overlap between EI, Psychological Mindedness, and Emotional Awareness in terms of awareness of one's thoughts, feelings, and behaviours and those of others. However, EI is invariably defined as a positive attribute, while Psychological Mindedness may also exacerbate negative responses such as anxiety, feelings of loneliness, disappointment in others, and low self-esteem.[62,63] That is, too much Emotional Awareness can make a person 'wiser but sadder'. This is one of the criticisms also levelled at insight-based therapy, which requires a reasonable level of self-awareness.[64] One reason for this may be that Psychological Mindedness focuses on awareness of feelings (the middle level of the EIP framework) and less so on putting this into action (the top level of the EIP framework), which is a primary recommendation for developing EI.

Emotional Creativity: One other concept that came out prior to Goleman's popularisation of EI was Emotional Creativity. James Averill and Elma Nunley, in their book 'Voyages of the Heart' (1992),[65] describe Emotional Creativity as a constructionist view of emotions. They contrast this with the rationalist view of emotion (emotions as primitive responses that must be controlled) and the romanticist view of emotion of 'letting it all hang out'. They describe emotions as a construction analogous to language. Language has biological roots (as do emotions), but specific languages are a product of evolution (as are emotions) and within a language there is considerable opportunity for creativity such as for poetry and literature (as there is for learning to facilitate emotions creatively). They describe three levels of emotional creativity using the acronym ART:

Acquisition: The emotional maturity to experience, name, and differentiate emotions.

Refinement: A more sophisticated mastery of emotions to achieve the end goal, such as charisma to influence people.

Transformation: The expression of emotions that goes beyond the ordinary, as may be done symbolically in poetry, art, and music.

Emotional Literacy: A closely related concept to Emotional Intelligence is Emotional Literacy. Claude Steiner, a Transactional Analysis therapist, published the first paper on Emotional Literacy in 1974.[66] In his book Achieving Emotional Literacy (1997),[67] Steiner describes Emotional Literacy as "the ability to understand your emotions, the ability to listen to others and empathise with their emotions, and the ability to express emotions productively". He goes on to explain: "To be emotionally literate is to be able to handle emotions in a way that improves your personal power and improves the quality of life around you. Emotional literacy improves relationships, creates loving possibilities between people, makes cooperative work possible, and facilitates the feeling of community." According to Steiner, Emotional Literacy is about learning to understand your feelings and those of others, so as to facilitate relationships and deal skillfully with emotionally challenging situations. This is done by the individual looking at themselves, rather than at the external social context. Emotional Literacy has its roots in counselling and has been applied widely in educational contexts with children, helping them to identify and articulate their feelings. There is perhaps little to distinguish EI from Emotional Literacy, other than EI being applied more widely in the workplace.

Appendix Two has reviewed the history of Emotional Intelligence starting with the earliest theories on emotion and their evolution, which tended to see emotions as a mechanistic and adaptive response to survival. Since then, psychologists have long been interested in how people learn to manage their emotions and their relationships which has given rise to several concepts that are similar to EI, as summarised in Table A2.1.

Key theories relating to EI

CONCEPT	KEY THEORISTS	DATE
Social Intelligence	Edward Thorndike	1920[38]
Non-Cognitive Intelligence	David Wechsler	1943[82]
Psychological Mindedness	Stephen Appelbaum	1973[58]
Alexithymia (Affective Orientation)	Peter Sifneos	1973[53]

Table A2.1

CONCEPT	KEY THEORISTS	DATE
Emotional Literacy	Claude Steiner	1974[66]
Social Competence/Social Learning/Social Skills	Albert Bandura	1977[49]
Practical Intelligence	Robert Sternberg	1985[51]
Emotional Awareness	Richard Lane and Barry Schwartz	1987[59]
Emotional Competence	Carolyn Saarni	1990[36]
Emotional Creativity	James Averill	1992[65]

4   EI in the workplace

Psychologists and managers have been examining the social and emotional aspects of work since the Hawthorne experiments conducted by Elton Mayo in the 1930s.[68] One of these studies, known as the 'Hawthorne effect', found that workers increased productivity when they perceived they were being watched. Such experiments led to greater emphasis being placed on the social and emotional needs of workers. Post WW2, Kurt Lewin began developing programmes for leaders to manage human relations better in the workplace. These included the National Training Laboratories and, in the 1960s, 't' groups which focused on raising individuals' self-awareness and interpersonal sensitivity. In the 1980s, there was an expansion of leadership and personal development programmes, in areas such as stress management, self-motivation, team building, conflict handling, and leadership styles. This was followed in the 1990s by the emergence of EI and the growing popularity of executive coaching.

One of the earliest references to the term Emotional Intelligence was in 1966 by Barbara Leuner,[69] exploring the social roles of women, and later by Wayne Payne in 1985[70] who put forward the first model of EI in his doctoral thesis. In 1990 Peter Salovey and John Mayer[71] described an abilities-based approach to EI in a little-known published journal. It was not until 1995 when Daniel Goleman published 'Emotional Intelligence – Why it can matter more than IQ',[72] that EI managed to capture the interest of the popular business world. Goleman's book was seen as an egalitarian rebuttal to the Herrnstein and Murray book, The Bell Curve (1994)[73] that argued the importance of IQ for understanding social class in society. IQ was seen by many as hard, elitist, and difficult to develop, while EI (or EQ) was seen to be 'kind', something that all people could develop, and as relevant to work performance. In the same year EI was on the cover of Time magazine (Gibbs, 1995)[74] and EQ was selected as one of the most useful new words or phrases of 1995 by the American Dialect Society. The growth of interest, research, and publications in EI since this time has not relented and has led to the production of several established EI theories and measurement instruments, discussed next.

In the Encyclopaedia of Applied Psychology (2004),[75] Spielberger suggests that there are three major conceptual models of EI: an abilities model,[71] a social and emotional competencies model,[76] and a competency skills model.[77] Two other models that may be added to these are the personality trait model of EI[78] and the attitude-based EIP model of EI.[79] An important distinction between all of these models is whether they are measured objectively (the abilities model) or subjectively (self-perception/self-report). Self-perception measures of EI typically cluster a broad array of EI-related attributes, known as the mixed model. Boyatzis (2016)[80] makes a further distinction of measuring EI through observable behaviours, such as 360 ratings by others.

The abilities model of EI: Intelligence tests date back to 1905, when Alfred Binet[81] developed the first IQ tests which included 'judgment' as an integral part to using intelligence. David Wechsler (1939)[82] produced the WAIS (Wechsler Adult Intelligence Scale), one of the most widely recognised measures of intelligence, which included the subscales of comprehension, and picture arrangement which appear to measure aspects of Social Intelligence. In subsequent years, Wechsler described the non-intellective factors of intelligent behaviour and argued that models of intelligence would not be complete until these factors were adequately described (1943).[83] Within Wechsler's definition of intelligence, he includes "the capacity of the individual to act purposefully",[84] further reinforcing that there was a social aspect to intelligence. This led psychologists to focus their attention on the purpose of interpersonal behaviour[85] and this is turn influenced the likes of Salovey and Mayer (1990)[71] in their original abilities-based approach to EI called the MEIS (Multi-factorial Emotional Intelligence Survey), which was later updated in 1997 to the MSCEIT™[86] (Mayer, Salovey, Carusso Emotional Intelligence Test). This test measures four EI abilities:

1 Perceiving emotions

2 Using emotions

3 Understanding emotions

4 Managing emotions

A discussion of the relationship between the EIP model of EI and intelligence is given in Chapter One; 1.3.2.

Mixed models of EI: The mixed models of EI consist largely of self-report competency-based measures of EI. One of the earliest proponents of emotional competence was Carolyn Saarni (1990),[36] who describes emotional competence as including eight inter-related emotional and social skills:

— Awareness of one's own emotional state

— Skill in discerning the emotions of others

— Skill in using the vocabulary of emotion

— Capacity for empathic and sympathetic involvement towards others

— Skill in understanding that inner emotional state need not correlate to outer expression

— Skill at adaptive coping to aversive or distressing emotions

— Awareness of the structure or nature of relationships

— Capacity for emotional self-efficacy

One of the most recognised EI competency models was developed by Reuven Bar-On (1985),[87] who refers to the construct of Emotional Intelligence as Emotional and Social Intelligence. He defines it as "a cross-section of inter-related emotional and social competencies, skills, and facilitators that determine how effectively we understand and express ourselves, understand others and relate with them, and cope with daily demands". Bar-On coined the term Emotional Quotient (EQ) and developed one of the first measures of EI, the Emotional Quotient Inventory (EQ-i) – originally designed as an experimental instrument to examine emotionally and socially competent behaviour.[87] The most recent version of EQ-i (2.0)[88] assesses five broad subtypes of EI:

1 Self-perception

2 Self-expression

3 Interpersonal

4 Decision making

5 Stress management

Another well-established model of EI is by Daniel Goleman, who proposed four EI clusters that correspond to the top four parts of the EIP framework:

1 Self-awareness

2 Self-management

3 Social awareness

4 Relationship management

Goleman's contention was that people are born with general EI which determines their potential for developing EI competencies, as measured by the Emotional Competency Inventory (ECI)[89] and the Emotional and Social Competency Inventory (ESCI).[90] The ESCI competencies have been linked to underpinning needs, personality factors, and physiological states. For example, need for power drives teamwork, need for affiliation drives empathy,[91] and need for collaboration drives influence.[92] However, this was a post hoc rationalisation and it is noticeable that other EI measures do not have a set of underpinning principles as the EIP does.

A model that has gained significant ground in the literature and demonstrated strong validity is trait EI.[93] Petrides describes trait EI as "A Constellation of emotional self-perceptions located at the lower levels of personality hierarchies", which can be measured through the Trait Emotional Intelligence Questionnaire (TEIQ).[94] Research includes biological underpinnings for trait EI constructs, the location of trait EI personality in personality factor space (the so-called 'Big Five' and 'Giant Three'),[95] close relationships with the General Factor of Personality (GFP),[96] and meta-analytic evidence of incremental validity.[97]

On balance, practitioners often prefer the greater breadth of scales and validity of the mixed models,[98–100] while academic researchers favour the greater conceptual precision of the ability EI model.[101] For an overview on some of the mixed and ability measures of EI refer to Ackley (2016)[102] and Siegling et al. (2015).[103] The EIP falls within the mixed model approach to EI, but has its roots in attitudes rather than competencies, personality, or abilities. These unique differences are fully explained in Chapter Three; 3.2.4.

Criticisms of EI measures: A number of criticisms have been levelled at the concept of EI and EI measures. Perhaps the most significant of these is that EI is not an aspect of intelligence. Hans Eysenck[104] criticises the lack of scientific basis for the assumptions made by Daniel Goleman that EI is a form of intelligence. Several other eminent psychologists have also raised concerns about the theoretical foundations of EI. Edwin Locke[105] said that it is not another form of intelligence but is intelligence. Frank Landy[106] claimed that the few predictive validity studies for EI have shown little incremental validity beyond abstract intelligence or personality measures. In critical reviews of EI it has been described as an "elusive construct"[107] and as an "intangible myth".[108] Despite these challenges to the concept, other psychologists have found it useful to differentiate EI from other forms of intelligence[38,71,83] and evidence has been presented in this appendix for emotions being a form of intelligence.[12,13,20,21] For instance, a Pan-American study found the MSCEIT ability measure of EI to produce a second-order factor of intelligence that was incremental to other facets of general intelligence.[109]

A second key criticism, mainly of mixed EI, is that it is simply an aspect of personality. Mayer[110] suggests that terms used in EI such as motivation, emotion, cognition, and consciousness may be seen as the biological functions of personality. Hedlund[52] questions Goleman's model of EI as an attempt to capture almost everything that isn't IQ. Many EI attributes may be found in personality measures, such as the California Psychological Inventory[111] which includes scales of interpersonal effectiveness, self-acceptance, self-control, flexibility, and empathy. And, the NEO-PI-R includes items on empathy and awareness of feelings.[112] EI may also be seen to overlap with other personality models, such as the Hardy Personality,[113] the Constructive Thinker,[114] Ego Strength,[115] and

Self-actualisation.[116] Many EI attributes are also correlated with the Big Five personality characteristics, in particular, openness to experience,[117] awareness of feelings,[112] emotional attention,[118] and aspects of emotional vulnerability.[112] Given the varying definitions of EI, there is a danger of EI expanding into all areas of personality and it not being adequately differentiated.

The criticism of EI being an aspect of personality is legitimate in that personality may include a person's cognition, affect, behaviour, and attitude, which are all aspects of EI. However, the EIP draws specific distinctions between EI and personality temperament (see Chapter One; 1.3.1) and even defines EI as 'the practice of managing one's personality'. It is therefore expected that the EIP correlates to an extent with personality, but correlation does not mean they are the same thing. The EIP shows incremental validity beyond the Big Five dimensions[79] consistent with other established mixed measures of EI.[96,119] Petrides[97] argues that "trait EI organises under a single framework the main individual differences in affective personality, which up to now have been scattered across the basic Big Five personality dimensions and other models".

Another criticism of mixed EI measures is that they are mostly self-report, and that people who are low on EI may be less self-aware and therefore less able to accurately assess their own EI. Davis[120] found no correlation between individuals' estimates of their empathy and their scores on objective tests of empathy. Paulhus[121] found that self-report measures of intellect correlate quite modestly (0.2 to 0.3) with psychometric tests of mental ability. A person's self-perception is also influenced by their mood: happy people are more likely to say they understand their feelings, and unhappy people report being confused by them.[122]

These observations about self-report measures do raise some concerns, but despite this, self-report personality questionnaires have demonstrated reasonable validity in predicting performance and have stood the test of time.[123] EI self-report measures have also been found to be strong predictors of workplace performance[100,124] and to add unique variance as part of a multi-method approach to assessment.[124] Furthermore, good questionnaire design and validation mitigates against subjective bias and error. Also of importance is how the questionnaire is being applied; issues of faking and social desirability are far less likely when used for self-development than for selection and assessment. Another way to minimise error is to check the accuracy of an individual's self-perception (through discussing their item responses and scale scores) which is a key part of the self-development process when using the EIP (as explained in Chapter Six; 6.4). It should also be remembered, as with all self-report measures, that the EIP is only one source of feedback and should be considered alongside all other available findings such as 360 reporting, personal experience, and observations during the coaching process.

REFERENCES

Chapter One

1   Griffin, J. & Tyrrell, I. (2004). *The Human Givens. A new approach to emotional health and clear thinking.* (2nd edn.) East Sussex: Human Givens Publishing.

2   HSE Statistics. (2011). http://www.hse.gov.uk/statistics/causdis/stress/index.htm.

3   Seligman, M.E.P. In J. Buie (1988). 'Me' decades generate depression: individualism erodes commitment to others. *American Psychological Association Monitor.* Oct. 18.

4   Van Ghent, D. (1961). *The English Novel: Form and Function.* New York: Harper and Row.

5   Goleman, D. (1996). *Emotional intelligence: why it can matter more than IQ.* New York: Bantam Books.

6   Goleman, D. (1998). *Working with emotional intelligence.* New York: Bantam Books.

7   Goleman, D. (2006). *Social Intelligence: The new science of human relationships.* New York: Random House.

8   Descartes, R. (1637). transl. Veitch, J. (1924). *Discours de la méthode* (Discourse on the Method). An introduction to the *Essais,* which include the *Dioptrique,* the *Météores* and the *Géométrie.*

9   Darwin, C. (1872/1965). *The expression of the emotions in man and animals.* Chicago: University of Chicago Press.

10   Wechsler, D. (1943). Nonintellective factors in general intelligence. *Journal of Abnormal Social Psychology, 38,* 100-104.

11   Gardner, H. (1983). *Frames of mind.* New York: Basic Books.

12   Salovey, P. & Mayer, J.D. (1990). Emotional intelligence. *Imagination, Cognition, and Personality, 9,* 185-211.

13   Damasio, A.R. (1994). *Descartes' error: Emotion, reason and the human brain.* New York: Grosset/Putnam.

14   LeDoux, J. (1996). *The emotional brain: The mysterious underpinnings of emotional life.* New York: Simon and Schuster.

15   Lane, R.D. & McRae, K. (2004). Neural substrates of conscious emotional experience: A cognitive-neuroscientific perspective. In M. Beauregard (Ed.). *Consciousness, emotional self-regulation and the brain,* 87-122. Amsterdam: Benjamins.

16   Wolff, S. (1997/2005). *ECI Technical Manual.* Hay Group. Centre for Research and Innovation.

17   Bar-On, R. (1997). *The Emotional Quotient Inventory.* Toronto, Canada: Multi-Health Systems.

18   Maddocks, J. & Sparrow, T. (1998). *The Individual Effectiveness Questionnaire.* JCA Global Ltd.

19   Petrides, K.V., & Furnham, A. (2001). Trait emotional intelligence: Psychomteric investigation with reference to established trait taxonomies. *European Journal of Personality, 15,* 425-448.

20   Maddocks, J. (2007). Sustaining change through Emotional Intelligence. *The Coaching Psychologist, Vol 3.* (1).

21   Mattingly, V. & Kraiger, K. (In Press). Can emotional intelligence be trained? A meta-analytical investigation. *Human Resource Management Review.*

22   Murphy, K. & Dzieweczynski, J. (2005). Why don't measures of broad dimensions of personality perform better as predictors of job performance, *Human Performance, 18,* 343-357.

23   Costa, P.C. & McCrae, R.R. (1997). Longitudinal study of adult personality. In R. Hogan, J. Johnson & S. Briggs (Eds.), *Handbook of personality psychology,* 269-290. San Diego: Academic Press.

24   Sherman, S. & Freas, A. (2004). The Wild West of Executive Coaching. *Harvard Business Review, Nov, 82 (11),* 82-89.

25   Mikolajczak, M. (2009). Going Beyond the Ability-Trait Debate: The Three-Level Model of Emotional Intelligence. *Electronic Journal of Applied Psychology. 5(2):* 25-31.

26   O'Boyle, E., Humphrey, R., Pollack, J., Hawyer, T. & Story, P. (2011). The relations between emotional intelligence and job performance: A meta-analysis. *Journal of Organisation Behaviour, 32,* 788-818.

27   Joseph, D.L. & Newman, D.A. (2010). Emotional intelligence: An integrative meta-analysis and cascading model. *Journal of Applied Psychology, 95,* 54-78.

28   Andrei, F., Siegling, A. B., Aloe, A. M., Baldaro, B., Petrides, K. V. (2016). The incremental validity of the Trait Emotional Intelligence Questionnaire (TEIQue): A systematic review and mata-analysis. *Journal of Personality Assessment, 98,* 261-276.

29   Miao. C., Humphrey, R.H. & Qian. S. (2017). A meta-analysis of emotional intelligence and work attitudes. *Journal of Occupational and Organizational Psychology, 90,* 177-202.

30   Anderson, N., Bertua, C. & Salgado, J. (2005). The predictive validity of cognitive ability test: A UK meta-analysis. *Journal of Occupational and Organizational Psychology, 78 (3),* 387-409.

31   Thompson, H. (2010). *The stress effect. Why smart leaders make dumb decisions.* San Francisco: Jossey-Bass.

32   Feist, G.J. & Barron, F. (1996). *Emotional intelligence and academic intelligence in career and life success.* Paper presented at the Annual Convention of the American Psychological Society. San Francisco.

33   Duckworth, A.L. & Seligman, M.E.P. (2005). Self–discipline out does IQ in predicting academic performance of adolescents. *Psychological Science, 16 (12),* 939-44.

34   Jenkins, D. & Maddocks, J. (2005). Prison officers, emotional labour and the intelligent management of emotions. SDR, BPS conference. In J. Maddocks, *The EIP Technical Manual.* (2013).

35   Bar-On, R. (2000). Emotional and social intelligence: Insights from the Emotional Quotient Inventory (EQ-i). In R. Bar-On and J.D.A. Parker (Eds.), *Handbook of emotional intelligence.* San Francisco: Jossey-Bass.

36   Steiner, C. (1974). Scripts People Live. New York: Grove Press. Also see (2003) *Emotional Literacy; Intelligence With a Heart.* Fawnskin, California: Personhood Press.

37   Saarni, C. (1990). Emotional competence: How emotions and relationships become integrated. In R.A. Thompson (Ed.), *Socioemotional development.* Nebraska symposium on motivation, 36, 115-182. Lincoln: University of Nebraska Press.

38   Averill, J.R. & Thomas-Knowles, C. (1991). Emotional creativity. In K.T. Strongman (Ed.), *International review of studies on emotion, 1,* 269-299). London: Wiley.

39   Thorndike, E.L. (1920). *Intelligence and its use.* Harper's Magazine, 140, 227-235.

40   Bargh, J. A., Chaiken, S., Govender, R., & Pratto, F. (1992). The generality of the automatic attitude activation effect. *Journal of Personality and Social Psychology, 62,* 893-912.

41   Fazio, R. H., Sanbonmatsu, D. M., Powell, M. C., & Kardes, F. R. (1986). On the automatic activation of attitudes. *Journal of Personality and Social Psychology, 50,* 229-238.

42   Ajzen, I. (2007). *Attitudes, Personality and Behavior.* Maidenhead, England: McGraw-Hill Education.

43   Bem, D. J. (1970). Beliefs, *Attitudes, and Human Affairs.* Oxford: Brooks/Cole.

44 Eagly, A. H., & Chaiken, S. (1993). *The psychology of attitudes.* Fort Worth: Harcourt Brace.

45 Osgood, C. E., Suci, G. J., and Tannenbaum, P. H. (1957). *The Measurement of Meaning.* Urbana: University of Illinois Press.

46 Ernst, F.H., Jr. (1971). The OK corral: The grid for get-on-with. *Transactional Analysis Journal, 1 (4),* 33-42.

47 Bandura, A. (1977). *Social Learning Theory.* New York: General Learning Press.

48 Gallwey, W.T. (1986). *The inner game of tennis.* London: Pan.

49 Maddocks, J. & Hughes (2017). *The Emotional Intelligence Profile (EIP) 3.0 Technical Manual.* JCA Global Ltd.

Chapter Two

1 MacLean, P.D. (1973). *A triune concept of brain and behaviour.* Toronto: University of Toronto Press.

2 Eccles, J.C. (1991). *Evolution of the brain.* Routledge.

3 Chanes, L. & Feldman Barrett, L. (2016). Redefining the Role of Limbic Areas in Cortical Processing, *Trends in Cognitive Sciences. 20, 2,* 484-495.

4 Boyatzis, R. & Jack. A. (2018). The neuroscience of coaching. *Consulting Psychology Journal: Practice and Research. Vol. 70, No. 1,* 11-27.

5 Rose, K.D. (2006). *The Beginning of the Age of Mammals.* Baltimore: Johns Hopkins University Press.

6 Karasov, W.H. & Diamond, J. (1985). Digestive adaptations for fuelling the cost of endothermy. *Science, 228,* 202-204.

7 Griffin, J. & Tyrrell, I. (2014). *Why We Dream.* East Sussex: HG Publishing.

8 Dunbar, R. (1998). The social brain hypothesis. *Evolutionary Anthropology, 6,* 178-190.

9 Amaral, D.G., Price, J. L., Pitkanen, A. & Carmichael, S.T. (1992). Anatomical organisation of the primate amygdaloid complex. In J.P. Aggleton, (Ed.) *The amygdala: Neurobiological aspects of emotion, memory, and mental dysfunction.* New York: Wiley-Liss.

10 Forgas, J. (1995). Mood and judgment: The affect infusion model (AIM). *Psychological Bulletin,* Jan., 117 (1), 39-66.

11 LeDoux, J. (1996). *The emotional brain: The mysterious underpinnings of emotional life.* New York: Simon and Schuster.

12 Libet, B. (1985). Unconscious cerebral initiative and the role of conscious will in voluntary action. *Behavioural and Brain Sciences, 8,* 529-566.

13 Damasio, A.R. (1994). *Descartes' error: Emotion, reason and the human brain.* New York: Grosset/Putnam.

14 Goleman, D. (1996). *Emotional intelligence: why it can matter more than IQ.* New York: Bantam Books.

15 Cunningham, W.A. & Brosch, T. (2012). Motivational salience: Amygdala tuning from traits, values and goals. *Current Directions in Psychological Science, 21 (1),* 54-59.

16 Caruso, D.R. & Salovey, P. (2004). *The emotionally intelligent manager.* San Francisco: Jossey-Bass.

17 Makino, S., Gold, P.W. & Schulkin, J. (1994). Corticosterone effects on corticotropin-releasing hormone mRNA in the central nucleus of the amygdala and the parvocellular region of the paraventricular nucleus of the hypothalamus. *Brain Research, 640,* 105-12.

18   McEwen, B.S. (1992). Paradoxical effects of adrenal steroids on the brain: Protection verses degeneration. *Biological Psychiatry, 31,* 177-99.

19   O'Keefe, J. & Nadel, L. (1978). *The hippocampus as a cognitive map.* Oxford: Clarendon Press.

20   Yeo, B. T. et al. (2011) The Organization of the Human Cerebral Cortex Estimated by Intrinsic Functional Connectivity. *Journal of Neurophysiology, 106, 3,* 1125-1165.

21   Ekman, P. (1992). Facial expressions of emotion: New findings, new questions. *Psychological Science, 3,* 34-38.

22   Ybarra, O., Kross, E., Sanchez-Burks. (2014). The "big idea" that is yet to be: Toward a more motivated, contextual, and dynamic model of emotional intelligence. *Academy of Management Perspectives, 28(2),* 93-107.

23   Kraus, S.J. (1995). Attitudes and the prediction of behaviour: A meta-analysis of the empirical literature. *Personality and Social Psychology Bulletin, 21,* 58-75.

24   Griffin, J. & Tyrrell, I. (2004). *The Human Givens. A new approach to emotional health and clear thinking.* (2nd edn.) East Sussex: Human Givens Publishing.

25   Barrett, L.F. (2017). *How emotions are made, the secret life of the brain.* New York: Houghton Mifflin Harcourt.

26   Jouvet, M. (1965). Paradoxical sleep – a study of its nature and mechanisms. *Prog Brain Research, 18,* 20-57.

27   Dement, W. et al. (1967). Studies on the effects of REM deprivation in humans and in animals. In Kety, S.S., Ewarts, E.V. & Williams, H.L. (Eds.), Sleep and Altered States of Consciousness, *Proceedings of the Association for Research in Nervous and Mental Disease,* 45, 456-468.

28   Roffwarg, H.P., Muzio, J. & Dement, W. (1966). The ontogenetic development of the human sleep-dream cycle. *Science, 152,* 604-618.

29   Van der Helm, E., Yao, J., Dutt, S., Rao, V., Saletin, J.M. & Walker, M.P. (2011). REM sleep depotentiates amygdala activity to previous emotional experience. *Current Biology, 21, 23,* 2029-2032.

30   Gujar, N., McDonald, S., Nishida, M. & Walker, M. (2010). A role for REM sleep in recalibrating the sensitivity of the human brain to specific emotions. *Cerebral Cortex, 21 (1),* 115-123.

31   Selterman, D.F., Apetroaia, A.I., Riela, S. & Aron, A. (2014). Dreaming of You: behavior and emotion in dreams of significant others predict subsequent relational behaviour. *Social Psychological and Personality Science, 5(1),* 111-118.

32   Morrison, A.R. (1983). A window on the sleeping brain. *Scientific American, 248,* 86-94.

33   Vogel, G.W. (1979). A motivational function of REM sleep. In Drucker-Colin, R., Shkurovich, M. & Sterman, M.B. (Eds.) The Function of Sleep. *Academic Press,* 233-250.

34   Jouvet, M. & Michel, F. (1959). Correlations electromyographiques du sommeil chez le chat decortique et mesencephalique, *Comptes Rendus de la Societe Biologie,* 154: 422-425. Referenced in Griffin (2014). Why We Dream. HG Publishing. East Sussex.

35   Booth-Kewley, S. & Friedman, H.S. (1987). Psychological predictors of heart disease: a quantitative review. *Psychol Bull.* May, 101 (3), 343-362.

36   McEwen, B. & Stellar, E. (1993). Stress and the individual: mechanisms leading to disease. *Arch Intern Med, 153,* 2093-101.

37   Barret, L.F. & Simmons, W.K. (2015). Interoceptive Predictions in the Brain, *Nature Reviews Neuroscience, 16 (7),* 419-429. In Barrett, L.F. (2017). How emotions are made, the secret life of the brain. New York: Houghton Mifflin Harcourt.

38   McCraty, R. (2015). Heart Brain Neurodynamics: The Making of Emotions. In *Issues of the Heart: The Neuropsychotherapist special issue,* M. Dahlitz, & Hall, G., (Eds). Brisbane: Dahlitz Media: 76-110.

39   Edwards, S.D. (2016). Influence of HeartMath Quick Coherence Technique on psycho-physiological coherence and feeling states. *African Journal for Physical Activity and Health Sciences, 22(4:1),* 1006-1018.

40   Plutchik, R. (1980). *Emotion, a psychoevolutionary synthesis.* New York: Harper & Row.

41   Crivelli, C., Jarillo, S., Russell, J.A. & Fernández-Dols, J. (2016). Reading Emotions from Faces in Two Indigenous Societies, *Journal of Experimental Psychology, 145 (7),* 830-843.

42   Toohey. P. (2011). *Boredom. A lively history.* New Haven and London: Yale University Press.

43   Lövheim, H.A. (2012). A new three-dimensional model for emotions and monoamine neurotransmitters. *Medical Hypotheses, 78 (2),* 341-348.

44   Tomkins, S. (1962). *Affect Imagery Consciousness: The Positive Affects.* New York: Springer.

45   Pert, C. (1997). *Molecules of emotion. The science behind mind-body medicine.* New York: Touchstone.

Chapter Three

1   Maddocks, J. & Hughes, D. (2017). *The Emotional Intelligence Profile 3.0 Technical Manual.* JCA Global Ltd.

2   Maddocks, J. (1997). *The Maps Indicator, Users Manual.* JCA Global Ltd.

3   Lapierre, R. (1934). Attitudes vs. actions. *Social Forces, 13,* 230-237.

4   Festinger, L. (1962). *A theory of cognitive dissonance.* London: Tavistock Publications.

5   Eagly, A. & Chaiken, S. (1993). *The psychology of attitudes.* Fort Worth: Harcourt Brace.

6   Huczynski, A. & Buchanan, D. (2001). *Organizational behaviour: An introductory text.* Harlow: Financial Times Prentice Hall.

7   Makin, P. & Cox, C. (2004). *Changing behaviour at work: A practical guide.* London: Routledge.

8   Damasio, A.R. (1994). *Descartes' error: Emotion, reason and the human brain.* New York: Grosset/Putnam.

9   LeDoux, J. (1996). *The emotional brain: The mysterious underpinnings of emotional life.* New York: Simon and Schuster.

10   Lane, R.D. & McRae, K. (2004). Neural substrates of conscious emotional experience: A cognitive-neuroscientific perspective. In M. Beauregard (Ed.). *Consciousness, emotional self-regulation and the brain,* 87-122. Amsterdam: Benjamins.

11   Schutz, W. (1958). *FIRO, a three-dimensional theory of interpersonal behaviour.* WSA, New York: Holt, Reinhart & Winston.

12   Berne, E. (1964). *Games people play.* New York: Grove Press.

13   Griffin, J. & Tyrrell, I. (2004). *The Human Givens. A new approach to emotional health and clear thinking.* (2nd edn.) East Sussex: Human Givens Publishing.

14   Maddocks, J. (2007). Sustaining change through Emotional Intelligence. *The Coaching Psychologist, Vol 3. (1).*

15   Boyatzis, R. E. (2016). Commentary on Ackley (2016): Updates on the ESCI as the behavioral level of emotional intelligence. *Consulting Psychology Journal: Practice and Research, 68(4),* 287-293.

16   Joseph, D. L., & Newman, D. A. (2010). Emotional intelligence: an integrative meta-analysis and cascading model. *Journal of Applied Psychology. Vol. 95 No. 1,* 54-78.

17   Segon, M. & Booth, C. (2015). Virtue: The Missing Ethics Element in Emotional Intelligence. *Journal Business Ethics.* 128, 789-802.

18   Mayer, J. D., Salovey, P., & Caruso, D. (2008). Emotional intelligence: New ability or eclectic traits? *American Psychologist.*

19   Austin, E. J., Farrelly, D., Black, C. & Moore, H. (2007). Emotional intelligence, Machiavellianism and emotional manipulation: does EI have a dark side? *Personality and Individual Differences.* Vol. 43, No. 1, 179-189.

20   Judge, T. A., Piccolo, R. F., & Kosalka, T. (2009). The bright and dark sides of leader traits: a review and theoretical extension of the leader trait paradigm. *The Leadership Quarterly,* 20(6), 855-875.

21   Schlegelmilch, B. B., & Thomas, H. (2011). The MBA in 2020: Will there be one? *Journal of Management Development, 30(5),* 474-482.

22   Kraus, S. J. (1995). Attitudes and the prediction of behavior: A meta-analysis of the empirical literature. *Personality and Social Psychology Bulletin, 21,* 58-75.

23   Ybarra, O., Kross, E., & Sanchez-Burks, J. (2014). The "big idea" that is yet to be: Toward a more motivated, contextual, and dynamic model of emotional intelligence. *Academy of Management Perspectives, 28(2),* 93-107.

24   Fiori, M. (2009). A new look at emotional intelligence: a dual-process framework, *Personality and Social Psychology Review, Vol. 13,* 21-44.

25   Baumeister, R. F., Vohs, K. D., DeWall, C. N., & Zhang, L. (2007). How emotion shapes behavior: Feedback, anticipation, and reflection, rather than direct causation. *Personality and Social Psychology Review, 11,* 167-203.

26   Mikolajczak, M. (2009). Going Beyond the Ability-Trait Debate: The Three-Level Model of Emotional Intelligence. Electronic *Journal of Applied Psychology. 5(2):* 25-31.

27   Cherniss, C. (2010), Emotional intelligence: toward clarification of a concept. *Industrial and Organizational Psychology, Vol. 3 No. 2,* 110-126.

28   Joseph, D. L., Jin, J., Newman, D. A., & O'Boyle, E. H. (2015). Why Does Self-Reported Emotional Intelligence Predict Job Performance? A Meta-Analytic Investigation of Mixed EI. *Journal of Applied Psychology, 100(2),* 298-342.

29   Perls, F. (1969). *Gestalt therapy verbatim.* Moab: Real People Press.

30.   Grinder, J. & Bandler, R. (1979). *Frogs into princes: Neuro linguistic programming.* Moab: Real People Press.

31   Cattell, R.B. (1946). *The description and measurement of personality.* New York: World Book.

32   Kline, P. (2000). *Handbook of psychological Testing* (2nd ed.). London: Routledge.

33   Jung, C.G. (1921). *Psychological Types.* Princeton, New Jersey: Princeton University Press.

34   Maddocks, J. (2013). *The Emotional Intelligence Profile (EIP) Technical Manual.* JCA Global Ltd.

35   O'Boyle, E. H., Humphrey, R. H., Pollack, J. M., Hawver, T.H., & Story, P. A. (2011). The relation between emotional intelligence and job performance: a meta-analysis. *Journal of Organizational Behavior, 32,* 788-818

36   McCleskey, J. (2014). Emotional intelligence and leadership A review of the progress, controversy, and criticism. *International Journal of Organizational Analysis, 22(1),* 76-93.

37   Miao, C., Humphrey R.H. & Qian, S. (2017). A meta-analysis of emotional intelligence and work attitudes. *Journal of Occupational and Organizational Psychology, 90,* 177-2012.

Chapter Four

1   Ernst, F.H., Jr. (1971). The OK corral: The grid for get-on-with. *Transactional Analysis Journal,* 1 (4), 33-42.

Chapter Five

1   Maddocks, J. & Hughes, D. (2017). *The Emotional Intelligence Profile (EIP) 3.0* Technical Manual. JCA Global Ltd.

Chapter Six

1   Maltz, M. (1960). Psycho-Cybernetics: *A New Way to Get More Living out of Life.* Englewood Cliffs: Prentice-Hall.

2   Lally, P., Jaarsveld, C., Potts, H. & Wardle, J. (2010). How are habits formed: Modelling habit formation in the real world. *European Journal of Social Psychology.* October, 40 (6) 998-1009.

3   Festinger, L. (1962). *A theory of cognitive dissonance.* London: Tavistock Publications.

4   Burch, N. (1970). Learning a New Skill is Easier Said than Done. *Gordon Training International,* 198.

5   Maddocks, J. (2008). *Personality Type Profile user manual.* JCA Global Ltd.

6   Jung, C.G. (1921). *Psychological Types.* Princeton, New Jersey: Princeton University Press.

7   Maddocks, J. (2006). Linking Emotional Intelligence with Jungian Typology. *APT Bulletin of Psychological Type, Vol. 29, No. 3.*

8   Maddocks, J. & Hughes, D. (2017). *The Emotional Intelligence Profile 3.0 Technical Manual.* JCA Global Ltd.

9   Csikszentihalyi, M. (1990). *Flow: The psychology of optimal experience.* New York: Harper & Row.

10   Prochaska, J.O. & DiClemente, C.C. (1983). Stages and processes of self-change of smoking: Toward an integrative model of change. *J Consult Clin Psychol. Jun, 51 (3),* 390-5.

11   O'Leary, V. E., & Ickovics, J. R. (1995). Resilience and thriving in response to challenge: An opportunity for a paradigm shift in women's health. *Women's Health: Research on Gender: Behavior; and Policy, I,* 121-142.

Chapter Seven

1   Boothroyd, P., Gravell, R., Hughes, D., Maddocks, J. & Noble, S. (in press). *Emotional Intelligence in the STEM sector.* JCA Global Ltd.

2   Boyatzis, R. E., Rochford, K., & Cavanagh, K. (2017). Emotional intelligence competencies in engineer's effectiveness and engagement. *Career Development International, 22(1),* 70-86.

3   Pittenger, L. M. (2015). Emotional and social competencies and perceptions of the interpersonal environment of an organization as related to the engagement of IT professionals. *Frontiers in Psychology, 6,* 623.

4   Hochschild, A. R. (1983). *The Managed Heart: Commercialisation of Human Feeling.* Berkeley: University of California Press.

5   Ballantyne and Povah (2016). *Assessment and Development centres.* 2nd ed. Abingdon: Routledge.

6   The BPS qualification in Test Use. The British Psychological Society Psychological Testing Centre. www.psychtesting.org.uk

7   Maddocks, J. & Hughes, D. (2017). *The Emotional Intelligence Profile 3.0 technical manual.* JCA Global Ltd.

8   Lawrence, A. (2011). "The Big AI". *Select International,* Inc.

9   Kaiser, R.B., LeBreton, J.M., & Hogan, J. (2015). The Dark Side of Personality and Extreme Leader Behavior. *International Association of Applied Psychology. 64 (1),* 55-92.

10   Hogan, R. & Hogan, J. (2001) Assessing Leadership: A view from the dark side. *International Journal of Selection and Assessment. 9,* 40-51.

11   Horney, K. (1945). *Our inner conflicts.* New York: Norton.

12   Ones, D.S. & Viswesvaran, C. (1998). The effects of social desirability and faking on personality and integrity assessment for personnel selection. *Human Performance, 11(2/3),* 245-269.

13   Smith, D.B. & Ellingson, J.E. (2002). Substance versus style: A new look at social desirability in motivating contexts. *Journal of Applied Psychology, 87,* 2, 211-219.

14   Lench, H.C., Flores, S. A., & Bench, S.W. (2011). Discrete Emotions Predict Changes in Cognition, Judgment, Experience, Behavior, and Physiology: A Meta-Analysis of Experimental Emotion Elicitations. *Psychological Bulletin. Vol. 137, No. 5,* 834-855.

Chapter Eight

1   Rintzler, A. & Brown, D. (2002). *Fast Start Learning.* Resource Associates Corporation. PA: Reading.

2   Maddocks, J. (2007). Sustaining change through Emotional Intelligence. *The Coaching Psychologist, Vol 3.* (1).

3   Murphy, M. (2012). *Hiring for attitude.* McGraw-Hill.

4   Pavlov, I.P, transl., ed. Anrep., G.V. (1927). *Conditioned reflexes: An investigation of the physiological activity of the cerebral cortex.* London: Oxford University Press.

5   Grinder, J. & Bandler, R. (1979). *Frogs into princes: Neurolinguistic programming.* Moab: Real People Press.

6   Libet, B. (1985). Unconscious cerebral initiative and the role of conscious will in voluntary action. Behavioural and Brain Sciences, *8,* 529-566.

7   Baumeister, R., Bratslavsky, E. & Finkenauer, C. (2001). Bad is stronger than good. *Review of General Psychology, 5, (4).*

8   Eisenberger, N. & Lieberman, M. (2009). The pains and pleasures of social life. *Science,* 323, (5916), 890-891.

9   Maslow, A.H. (1943). A theory of human motivation. *Psychological Review,* 50 (4), 370-396.

10   Rock, D. (2008). SCARF: A brain-based model for collaborating with and influencing others. *NeuroLeadership Journal, Dec., 1 (1).*

11   Langer, E. & Rodin, J. (1977). The effects of choice and enhanced personal responsibility for the aged: A field experiment in an institutional setting. *Journal of Personality and Social Psychology,* 191-198.

12   Festinger, L. (1962). *A theory of cognitive dissonance.* London: Tavistock Publications.

13   Greenberger, D. & Pandensky, C. (1995). *Mind over mood: Change how you feel by changing the way you think.* New York: Guildford Press.

14   Kahneman, D. & Tversky, A. (1979). Prospect theory: An analysis of decisions under risk. *Econometrica. 47 (2),* 263-29.

15   Cabello, R., & Fernández-Berrocal, P. (2015). Implicit theories and ability emotional intelligence. *Frontiers in Psychology. Vol. 6. Article 700.*

16   Dweck,C.S.(1999). *Self-theories: Their Role in Motivation, Personality and Development.* Philadelphia: Taylor &Francis/Psychology Press.

17   Cousins, N. (1976). Anatomy of an illness as perceived by the patient. *N Engl J Med, 295 (26),* 1458-63.

18   Bandler, R. & Grinder, J. (1975). *The Structure of Magic I: A Book about Language and Therapy.* Science and Behavior Books Inc. pp. 5-6.

19   Griffin, J. (2005). 'PTSD: Why some techniques for treating it work so fast'. *The Human Givens Journal. 12 (3).*

20   Bandler, R. (1993). *Time for a Change.* Meta Pubns. p. vii. ISBN 978-0-916990-28-2.

21   Callahan, R. (2001). *Tapping the healer within.* Chicago: III Contemporary Books.

22   Shapiro, F. (2001). *EMDR: Eye Movement Desensitization of Reprocessing: Basic principles, protocols and procedures* (2nd edn.) New York: Guildford Press.

23   Ruden, R.A. (2011). *When the Past Is Always Present: Emotional Traumatization, Causes, and Cures.* New York: Routledge, Psychosocial Stress Series.

24   Lench, H.C., Flores, S. A., & Bench, S.W. (2011). Discrete Emotions Predict Changes in Cognition, Judgment, Experience, Behavior, and Physiology: A Meta-Analysis of Experimental Emotion Elicitations. *Psychological Bulletin. Vol. 137, No. 5,* 834-855.

25   Bishop, S.R., Lau, M., Shapiro, S., Carlson, L., Anderson, N.D., Carmody, J., et al. (2004). Mindfulness: A proposed operational definition. Clinical Psychology: *Science and Practice, 11(3),* 230-241.

26   Gotink, R.A., Meijboomb, R., Vernooij, M., Smits, M., & Huninka, M.G. (2016). 8-week Mindfulness Based Stress Reduction induces brain changes similar to traditional long-term meditation practice – A systematic review. *Brain and Cognition, 108,* 32-41.

27   Thompson, H. (2010). *The stress effect. Why smart leaders make dumb decisions.* San Francisco: Jossey-Bass.

28   Griffin, J. & Tyrrell, I. (2014). *Why We Dream.* HG Publishing: East Sussex.

29   Feinstein, J., Duff, M. & Tranel, D. (2010). Sustained experience of emotion after loss of memory in patients with amnesia. *Proceedings of the National Academy of Sciences of the United States of America. April 27, 107 (17),* 7674-7679.

30   Berlin, H.A. (2011). The Neural Basis of the Dynamic Unconscious. *Neuropsychoanalysis, 13 (1).*

31   Griffin, J. & Tyrrell, I. (2004). The Human Givens. A new approach to emotional health and clear thinking. (2nd Edn.) East Sussex: Human Givens Publishing.

32   Edelman, G. (1987). *Neural Darwinism: The theory of neuronal group selection.* New York: Basic Books.

33   Beehr, T. & Newman, J. (1978). Job stress, employee health and organisational effectiveness: A facet analysis, model and literature review. *Personnel Psychology, 31 (4),* 665-699.

34   Sparrow, T. & Knight, A. (2006). *Applied emotional intelligence: The importance of attitudes in developing emotional intelligence.* Chichester: Wiley.

35   Buckingham, M. (2003). *Building the strength-based organisation.* The Gallup Organisation (Online: www.gallup.com).

Chapter Nine

1   Mattingly, V. & Kraiger, K. (In Press). Can emotional intelligence be trained? A meta-analytical investigation. *Human Resource Management Review.*

2   Hodzic, S., Scharfen, J., Ripoll, P., Holling, H., & Zenasni, F. (2017). How Efficient Are Emotional Intelligence Trainings: A Meta-Analysis. *Emotion Review Vol. 10 No. 2,* 138-148.

3   Gallup Inc. (2010). *Employee engagement. What's your engagement ratio?* Gallup Inc. Performance Optimisation.

4   Zenger, J. & Folkman, J. (2009). *The extraordinary leader: turning good managers into great leaders.* New York: McGraw-Hill.

5   Freedman, J. (2008). *Workplace issues report.* Six seconds.

6   Goleman, D. (1996). *Emotional intelligence: why it can matter more than IQ.* New York: Bantam Books.

7   Research by Forum Corporation on Manufacturing and Service Companies, (1989-1995), cited in Orioli, E. (2000). *Leader know thyself: Measuring and developing leadership using the EQ Map.* Workshop presentation at Linkage Emotional Intelligence Conference, Chicago, IL.

8   Murphy, M. (2012). *Hiring for attitude.* McGraw-Hill.

9   Denning, S. (2004). *The seven highest values of organisation storytelling.* Braintrust Presentation.

10 Dulewicz, V., Dulewicz, C. & Young, M. (2005). The relevance of emotional intelligence for leadership performance. *Journal of General Management.* Braybrooke Press Ltd.

11 Freedman, J. & Stillman, P. (2016). *The Business Case for Emotional Intelligence.* Six seconds.

12 Schwab, K. & Samans, R. (2016). *The Future of Jobs Employment, Skills and Workforce Strategy for the Fourth Industrial Revolution 2016.* World Economic Forum.

13 Maddocks, J. (2015). *The Emotional Intelligence of the human resources sector 2007-2015.* JCA Global Ltd.

14 Cavallo, K. (2006). *Emotional competence and leadership excellence at Johnson & Johnson: Europe's Journal of Psychology, Vol 2, No 1.*

15 Cooper, R. & Sawaf, A. (1996). *Executive E.Q. Emotional Intelligence in Leadership and Organisations.* New York: The Berkley Publishing Group.

16 Bradberry, T. (2002). *Emotional intelligence and leader job performance.* Unpublished manuscript.

17 Egon Zehnder study on failed executives. Cited in D. Goleman (1998). *Working with emotional intelligence.* New York: Bantam Books.

18 Boyatzis, R. (1999). Self Directed Change and Learning as a Necessary Meta-Competency for Success and Effectiveness in the twenty-first century. In Sims, R. and Veres, J. (Eds.). *Keys to Employee Success in Coming Decades.* London: Quorum books.

19 Spencer, L., McClelland, D. & Kelner, S. (1997). *Competency assessment methods: History and state of the art.* Boston: Hay/McBer.

20 Seligman, M. (1990). *Learned optimism: how to change your mind and change your life.* New York: Knopf.

21 Hay/McBer Research and Innovation Group (1997). Cited in D. Goleman (1998). *Working with emotional intelligence.* New York: Bantam Books.

22 Cannon, K. (1999). *Conference Proceedings,* NexusEQ 2000.

23 McClelland, D. (1999). Identifying competencies with behavioral-event interviews. *Psychological Science, 9 (5),* 331-339.

24 Rozell,E.J., Pettijohn, C.E. & Parker, R.S. (2006). Emotional Intelligence and Dispositional Affectivity as Predictors of Performance in Sales People. Cited in Freedman, (2016). *The Business Case for Emotional Intelligence.* Six Seconds.

25 McCraty, R., Atkinson, M. & Tomasino, D. (2003). Impact of a Workplace Stress Reduction Program on Blood Pressure and Emotional Health in Hypertensive Employees. *Journal of Alternative and Complementary Medicine, 9 (3),* 355-369.

26 Freedman, J. & Fariselli, L. (2016). *Emotional Intelligence and Success.* Six Seconds.

27 O'Boyle, E., Humphrey, R., Pollack, J., Hawyer, T. & Story, P. (2011). The relations between emotional intelligence and job performance: A meta-analysis. *Journal of Organizational Behavior, 32,* 788-818.

28 Boyatzis, R., Guise, S., Hezlett, S., Kerr, P., & Lams, S. (2017). *Emotional and social competency inventory. Research guide and technical manual.* Korn Ferry.

29 Handley, R. (1999). *Conference Proceedings,* NexusEQ 2003.

30 Pesuric, A. & Byham, W. (1996). The new look in behavior modeling. *Training and Development,* 25-33.

31 Freedman, J., Procicchiani, T., & Lorenzo F. (2016). *The State of the Heart.* Six Seconds.

32 Momm, T., Blickle, G., Liu, Y., Wihler, A., Kholin, M., & Menges, J. (2015). It pays to have an eye for emotions: Emotion recognition ability indirectly predicts annual income. *Journal of Organizational Behavior. Vol. 36(1),* pp.147-163.

33 Maddocks, J. & Boothroyd, P. (2017). *The Emotional Intelligence of the sales sector.* JCA Global Ltd. Also see previous white papers on *EI in the HR sector* (2015), *EI in the Finance sector* (2014) and, *A decade of EI* (2011), available from JCA Global Ltd.

34 Barbuto, J.E., Gottfredson, K. & Searle, T.P. (2014). An Examination of Emotional Intelligence as an Antecedent of Servant Leadership. *Journal of Leadership & Organizational Studies. Vol. 21 No. 3.* 315-323.

35 Deshpande, S.P. (2009). A study of ethical decision making by physicians and nurses in hospitals. *Journal of Business Ethics. 90,* 387-397.

36 Du Plessis, M., Zani, W., & Petrus, N. (2015). The influence of emotional intelligence and trust on servant leadership. *SA Journal of Industrial Psychology, Vol. 41. No 1.*

37 Vyas, E. (2015). *The Relationship between Healthcare Leaders' Emotional Intelligence, Leader Performance Outcomes, and Employee Work Engagement during Transformational Change.* Six Seconds.

38 Meisler, G. (2014). Exploring emotional intelligence, political skill, and job satisfaction. *Employee Relations, Vol. 36 Iss: 3,* 280-293

39 Maddocks, J. (2011). *A Decade of Emotional Intelligence.* JCA Global Ltd.

40 Boothroyd, P., Gravell, R., Hughes, D., Maddocks, J., & Noble, S. (2018). *Emotional Intelligence in the STEM sector.* (In print). JCA Global Ltd.

41 Sibson, R.E. (1976). *Increasing employee productivity.* New York: AMACOM, 12.

42 Knight. A (2006). *Proceeding from the national EI conference.* Windsor. Centre for Applied EI.

43 Maddocks, J. & Hughes, D. (2017). *The Emotional Intelligence Profile 3.0 technical manual.* JCA Global Ltd.

44 Goleman, D. (1996). *Emotional intelligence: why it can matter more than IQ.* New York: Bantam Books.

45 Goleman, D. (1998). *Working with emotional intelligence.* New York: Bantam Books.

46 Goleman, D. (2006). *Social Intelligence: The new science of human relationships.* New York: Random House.

47 Goleman, D. (1998). What makes a leader? *Harvard Business review,* November–December, 95, 99.

48 Goleman, D. (2000). Leadership that gets results. *Harvard Business review, March-April, 81,* 79-90.

49 Bar-On, R. (1997). *The Emotional Quotient Inventory (EQ-i): A test of emotional intelligence.* Toronto, Canada: Multi-Health Systems, Inc.

50 Mayer, J.D., Salovey, P. & Caruso, D.R. (2002). *Mayer-Salovey-Caruso Emotional Intelligence Test (MSCEIT™).* Toronto, Canada: Multi-Health Systems, Inc.

51 Petrie, N. (2011). *Future Trends in Leadership Development, White Paper, Centre for Creative Leadership,* www.ccl.org/leadership/pdf/research/futuretrends.pdf.

52 Lucy, D., Wellbelove, J., Poorkavoos, M., & Hatcher, C. (2018). *The Management Agenda 2018.* Horsham: Roffey Park Institute.

53 PriceWaterhouseCoopers (2009). *Twelfth annual global CEO survey.*

54 McKinsey & Company (2001). The War for Talent. *The McKinsey Quarterly, 3 (37).*

55 Edmans, A., Li, L. & Zhang, C. (2015). Employee Satisfaction, Labor Market Flexibility, and Stock Returns Around the World. European Corporate Governance Institute (ECGI) – *Finance Working Paper No.* 433/2014.

56 Bennis, W. (1999). *On Becoming a Leader.* New York: Basic Books.

57 Joyce, E., Judge, T. A. (2004). Personality and Transformational and Transactional Leadership: A Meta-Analysis. *Journal of Applied Psychology. 89 (5):* 901-910.

58 Graen, G. B. & Canedo, J. (2016). The new workplace leadership development. Oxford Bibliography on Management. New York: Oxford University Press.

59 Goleman, D., Boyatzis, R. & McKee, A. (2002). *The New Leaders. Transforming the art of leadership into the science of results.* London: Time Warner.

60 Boyatzis, R. E., Goleman, D. & Hay/McBer. (1999). *Emotional competence inventory.* Boston: HayGroup.

61 JCA Global Ltd. (2016). *JCA Global Competency framework.* Available on request.

62 Elfenbein, H.A., Polzer, J.T. & Ambady, N. (2007). Can teams have emotional skills? The case of recognizing others' emotions. In C.E.J. Härtel, N.M. Ashkanasy & W.J. Zerbe (Eds.), *Research on emotion in organizations: Functionality, Intentionality and Morality.* Oxford: Elsevier/JAI Press.

63 Ilarda, E. & Findlay, B. (2006). Emotional intelligence and propensity to be a team player. *E-Journal of Applied Psychology: Emotional Intelligence, 2 (2),* 19-29.

64 Maddocks, J. (2013). *The Team Emotional Intelligence Profile (Team EIP) Technical Manual.* JCA Global Ltd.

65 Prati, L., Douglas, C., Ferris, G., Ammeter, A. & Buckley, M. (2003). Emotional intelligence, leadership effectiveness, and team outcomes. *International Journal of Organizational Analysis, 11 (1),* 21-40.

66 Lewis, K.M. (2000). When leaders display emotion: How followers respond to negative emotional expression of male and female leaders. *Journal of Organizational Behavior, 21,* 221-234.

67 Druskat, V.U. & Wolff, S.B. (2001). Group emotional competence and its influence on group effectiveness. In C. Cherniss & D. Goleman (Eds.), *Emotional competence in organisations:* San Francisco: Jossey-Bass.

68 Landy, C. (1983). *Understanding organisation.* London: Penguin.

69 Buckingham, M. (2003). *Building the Strength-Based Organisation.* The Gallup Organisation (Online: www.gallup.com).

70   Wong, C. & Law, K. (2002). The effect of a leader and follower emotional intelligence on performance and attitude: An exploratory study. *Leadership Quarterly, 13,* 243-274.

71   Cartwright, S. & Pappas, C. (2008). Emotional intelligence, its measurement and implications for the workplace. *International Journal of Management Reviews, 10,* 149-171.

72   Foo, M.D., Elfenbein, H., Tan, H. & Aik, V. (2004). Emotional intelligence and negotiation: The tension between creating and claiming value. *International Journal of Conflict Management, 15 (4),* 411-429.

73   Bachman, W. (1988). *Nice Guys finish first.* New York: Praeger.

74   George, J.M. & Bettenhausen, K. (1990). Understanding psychosocial behaviour. *Journal of Applied Psychology, 75,* 698-709.

75   Maddocks, J. & Seex, S. (2011). *The Leadership Climate Indicator. Users Manual.* JCA Global Ltd.

76   Kelner, S. Rivers, C. & O'Connell, K. (1994). *Managerial style as a behavioural predictor or organisational climate.* Boston: McBer.

77   Kozlowski, S.W. & Doherty, M.L. (1989). Integration of climate and leadership: Examination of a neglected issue. *Journal of Applied Psychology, 74,* 546-553.

78   Litwin, G. & Stringer, R.A.J. (1968). *Motivation and organisational climate.* Boston: Harvard University, Graduate School of Business Administration, Division of Research.

79   Maddocks. J. (2017). Does the Emotional Intelligence of leaders influence the emotional climate of the organisation? *Assessment & Development Matters. Autumn 2017 – Vol. 9.* No.3.

80   Russell. J. (1980). "A circumplex model of affect". *Journal of Personality and Social Psychology 39:* 1161-1178.

81   William, D. (1994). *Leadership for the 21st century.* Boston: Hay Group.

82   Sánchez-Álvareza, N., Extremerab, N. & Fernández-Berrocalc, P. (2015). The relation between emotional intelligence and subjective well-being: A meta-analytic investigation. *The Journal of Positive Psychology. August* 1-10.

83   Kaji, J. (2018). *The rise of the social enterprise. The 2018 Deloitte Global Human Capital Trends.* Deloitte Insights.

Appendix One

1   Stewart, I. & Joines, V. (1987). *TA today: A new introduction to transactional analysis.* Nottingham: Lifespace Publishing.

2   Rogers, C.R. (1959). A theory of therapy, personality and interpersonal relationships, as developed in the client-centered framework. In S. Koch (Ed.), *Psychology: A study of science,* New York: McGraw Hill.

3   Gallwey, W.T. (1986). *The inner game of tennis.* London: Pan.

4   Buckingham, M. (2003). *Building the Strength-Based Organisation.* The Gallup Organisation. (Online: www.gallup.com).

5   Lane, R.D. & Schwartz, G.E. (1987). Levels of emotional awareness: A cognitive developmental theory and its application to psychopathology. *American Journal of Psychiatry, 144,* 133-143.

6   Van Overwalle, F. (2009). Social cognition and the brain: A meta-analysis. *Human Brain Mapping, 30,* 829-858.

7   Ekman, P. (1973). *Darwin and facial expression: A century of research in review.* New York: Academic Press.

8   Iacoboni, M., Woods, R.P., Brass, M., Bekkering, H., Mazziotta, J.C. & Rizzolatti, G. (1990). Cortical mechanisms of human imitation. Science 286 (5449), 2526-2528.

9   Saddiq, S. (2006). *Librarians 'suffer most stress'*, http://news.bbc.co.uk/1/hi/4605476.stm.

10   Frankl, V. (1959). *Man's search for meaning:* the classic tribute to hope from the holocaust. London: Random House/Rider.

11   Mischel, W., Shoda, Y. & Rodriguez, M.L. (1992). Delay of gratification in children. In G. Lowenstein & J. Elster (Eds.), *Choice over time,* New York: Russell Sage Foundation.

12   Aristotle, transl. Chase, D.P. (2008). *Nicomachean Ethics.* Book 2, Chapter 6.

13   Hochschild, A.R. (1979). Emotion Work, Feeling Rules, and Social Structure. *American Journal of Sociology, 85,* 551-575.

14   Naisberg-Fennig, S., Fennig, S., Kienan, G. & Elizur, A. (1991). Personality characteristics and proneness to burnout: A study among psychiatrists. *Stress Medicine, 7 (4),* 201-205.

15   Fisher, R., Ury, W. & Patton, B. (1991). *Getting to Yes: negotiating Agreement Without Giving In.* Second Edition. New York: Penguin Books.

16   Kosfeld, M., Heinrichs, M., Zak, P.J., Fischbacher, U. & Fehr, E. (2005). Oxytocin increases trust in humans. *Nature, 453,* 673-76.

17   Gallup Inc. (2010). *Employee engagement. What's your engagement ratio?* Gallup Inc., Performance Optimisation.

18   Maddocks, J. (2006). Linking Emotional Intelligence with Jungian Typology. *APT Bulletin of Psychological Type, Vol. 29,* No. 3.

Appendix Two

1   Darwin, C. (1872/1965). *The expression of the emotions in man and animals.* Chicago: University of Chicago Press.

2   Ekman, P. (1977). Biological and cultural contributions to body and facial movement. In J. Blacking (Ed.). *The anthropology of the body.* London: Academic Press.

3   Plutchik, R. (1980). *Emotion, a psychoevolutionary synthesis.* New York: Harper & Row.

4   Nesse, R. (1990). Evolutionary explanations of emotions. *Human Nature,* 1, 261-289.

5   Watt, D.F. (2004). Consciousness, Emotional Self-Regulation and the Brain Review Article. *Journal of Consciousness Studies, 11 (9),* 77-82.

6   MacLean, P.D. (1973). *A triune concept of brain and behaviour.* Toronto: University of Toronto Press.

7   James, W. (1884). What is an emotion? *Mind, 9,* 188-205.

8   Schioldann, J. (2011). "On periodical depressions and their pathogenesis" by Carl Lange (1886). *History of psychiatry, 22,* 85, Pt.1, 108-130. Also in Amdisen, A. (1985). "Carl Lange på fransk visit i psykiatrien [C. Lange's flying visit to psychiatry]". Dansk *Medicinhistorisk Aarbog,* 14, 9-40.

9   Cannon, W.B. (1927). The James-Lange theory of emotion: A critical examination and an alternative theory. *American Journal of Psychology, 39,* 10-124.

10   Bard, P. (1928). A diencephalic mechanism for the expression of rage with special reference to the sympathetic nervous system. *American Journal of Physiology, 84,* 490-516.

11   Green, E. & Green, A. (1977). *Beyond biofeedback.* San Francisco: Delacorte Press.

12   Pert. C. (1997). *Molecules of emotion. The science behind mind-body medicine.* New York: Touchstone.

13   Damasio, A.R. (1994). *Descartes' error: Emotion, reason, and the human brain.* New York: Grosset/Putnam.

14   Bechara, A., Damasio, A.R., Damasio, H. & Anderson, S.W. (1994). Insensitivity to future consequences following damage to human prefrontal cortex. *Cognition,* 50, 7-12.

15 Harlow, J.M. (1868). Recovery from the Passage of an Iron Bar through the Head. *Massachusetts Med Society, 2*, 327-347.

16 Zeelenberg, M., Nelissen, R.M.A., Seger, M., Breugelmans, S. M. & Pieters, R. (2008). On emotion specificity in decision making: why feeling is for doing. *Judgment and Decision Making, 3 (1)*, 18-27.

17 Tuan Pham, M., Lee, L. & Stephen, A.T. (2012). Feeling the Future: The Emotional Oracle Effect. *Journal of Consumer Research, 39 (3)*, 461-477.

18 Ramachandran, V. S. & Blakeslee, S. (1998). *Phantoms in the Brain.* London: Fourth Estate.

19 Libet, B. (1985). Unconscious cerebral initiative and the role of conscious will in voluntary action. *Behavioural and Brain Sciences, 8*, 529-566.

20 LeDoux, J. (1996). *The emotional brain: The mysterious underpinnings of emotional life.* New York: Simon & Schuster.

21 Boyatzis, R. & Jack. A. (2018). The neuroscience of coaching. *Consulting Psychology Journal: Practice and Research. Vol. 70, No. 1*, 11-27.

22 Jack, A. I., Dawson, A. J., Begany, K. L., Leckie, R. L., Barry, K. P., Ciccia, A. H., & Snyder, A. Z. (2012). fMRI reveals reciprocal inhibition between social and physical cognitive domains. *NeuroImage, 66C*, 385-401.

23 Button, K. (2011). Power failure: why small sample size undermines the reliability of neuroscience. *Nature Reviews Neuroscience, 14*, 365-37.

24 Schachter, S. & Singer, J. (1962). Cognitive, Social, and Physiological Determinants of Emotional State. *Psychological Review, 69*, 379-399.

25 Tomkins, S. (1962). *Affect Imagery Consciousness: The Positive Affects.* New York: Springer.

26 Solomon, R.C. (1977). The logic of emotion. *Noûs, 11*, 41-49.

27 Mandler, G. (1984). *Mind and Body: Psychology of emotion and stress.* New York: Norton.

28 Roseman, I. J. (1984). Cognitive determinants of emotions: A structural theory. In P. Shaver (Ed.), *Review of Personality and Social Psychology: Vol. 5.* Emotions, relationships, and health, Beverly Hills: Sage.

29 Lazarus, R.S. (1991). *Emotion and adaptation.* New York: Oxford University Press.

30 Goldie, P. (2004). Emotion, feeling, and knowledge of the world. In R.C. Solomon (Ed.), *Thinking About Feeling: Contemporary Philosophers on Emotions.* Oxford: Oxford University Press.

31 Barrett, L.F. (2017). *How emotions are made, the secret life of the brain.* Houghton Mifflin Harcourt. New York.

32 Barrett L. F. & Simmons, W.K., (2015). Interoceptive Predictions in the Brain. *Nature Reviews Neuroscience 16 (7):* 419-429.

33 Averill, J.R. (1980). A constructivist view of emotion. In R. Plutchik & H. Kellerman (Eds.), *Emotion: Theory, research, and experience,* New York: Academic Press.

34 Parkinson, B. (1996). Emotions are social. *British Journal of Psychology, 87*, 663-683.

35 Gardner, H. (1983). *Frames of mind. The Theories of Multiple Intelligences.* New York: Basic Books.

36 Saarni, C. (1990). Emotional competence: How emotions and relationships become integrated. In R.A. Thompson (Ed.), *Socioemotional development.* Nebraska symposium on motivation, 36, 115-182. Lincoln: University of Nebraska Press.

37 Bar-On, R. (2000). Emotional and social intelligence: Insights from the Emotional Quotient Inventory (EQ-i). In R. Bar-On and J.D.A. Parker (Eds.), *Handbook of emotional intelligence.* San Francisco: Jossey-Bass.

38 Thorndike, E.L. (1920). Intelligence and its uses. *Harper's Magazine,* 140, 227-235.

39 Hunt, T. (1928). The measurement of social intelligence. *Journal of Applied Psychology, 12,* 317-334.

40 Wedeck, J. (1947). The relationship between personality and psychological ability. *British Journal of Psychology, 36,* 133-151.

41 Doll, E.A. (1935). A generic scale of social maturity. *American Journal of Orthopsychiatry, 5,* 180-188.

42 Kelly, G.A. (1955). *A theory of personality: The psychology of personal constructs.* New York: Norton.

43 Atkinson, J.W. (1981). Studying personality in the context of an advanced motivational psychology. *American Psychologist, 32,* 117-129.

44 McClelland, D.C. & Koestner, R. (1992). The achievement motive. In C.P. Smith, J.W. Atkinson, D.C. McClelland & J. Veroff (Eds.), *Motivation and personality: Handbook of thematic content analysis.* New York: Cambridge University Press.

45 Murray, H.A. (1938). *Explorations in personality.* New York: Oxford Press.

46 Lewin, K. (1951). *Field Theory in Social Science.* New York: Harper.

47 Schutz, W. (1958). *FIRO, a three-dimensional theory of interpersonal behaviour.* New York: Holt, Reinhart & Winston.

48 Combs, M.L. & Slaby, D.A. (1977). Social-skills training with children. In B.B. Lahey & A.E. Kazdin (Eds.), *Advances in Clinical Child Psychology, 1,* 161-201. New York: Plenum.

49 Bandura, A. (1977). *Social Learning Theory.* Englewood Cliffs: Prentice-Hall.

50 Topping, K. (2000). The Effectiveness of school based programs for the promotion of Social Competence. In R. Bar-On and J.D.A. Parker (Eds.), *The Handbook of Emotional Intelligence.* San Francisco: Jossey-Bass.

51 Sternberg, R.J. (1985). *Beyond IQ: A triarchic theory of human intelligence.* New York: Cambridge University Press.

52 Hedlund, J. & Sternberg, R.J. (2000). Too Many Intelligences. In R. Bar-On and J.D.A. Parker (Eds.), *Handbook of emotional intelligence.* San Francisco: Jossey-Bass.

53 Sifneos, P.E. (1973). The prevalence of alexithymic characteristics in psychosomatic patients. *Psychotherapy and Psychosomatics, 22,* 255-262.

54 Ruesch, J. (1948). *The infantile personality. Psychosomatic medicine, 10,* 134-144.

55 MacLean, P.D. (1949). Psychosomatic disease and the "visceral brain": Recent developments bearing on the Papez theory of emotion. *Psychosomatic Medicine, 11,* 338-353.

56 Schore, A.N. (1994). Affect regulation and the origin of the self: *The neurobiology of emotional development.* Hillsdale: Erlbaum.

57 Booth-Butterfield, M. & Booth-Butterfield, S. (1994). The affective orientation to communication: Conceptual and empirical distinctions. *Communications Quarterly, 42,* 331-344.

58 Appelbaum, S.A. (1973). Psychological mindedness: Word, concept, and essence. *International Journal of Psycho-Analysis, 54,* 35-46.

59 Lane, R.D. & Schwartz, G.E. (1987). Levels of emotional awareness: A cognitive-developmental theory and its application to psychopathology. *American Journal of Psychiatry, 144,* 133-143.

60 Conte, H.R. & Ratto, R. (1997). Self-report measures of psychological mindedness. In M. McCallum & W.E. Piper (Eds.), *Psychological mindedness: A contemporary understanding,* Mahwah: Erlbaum.

61 Piaget, J. (1950). *The psychology of intelligence.* London: Routledge & Kegan Paul.

62 Farber, B.A. (1989). Psychological-mindedness: Can there be too much of a good thing? *Psychotherapy, 26,* 210-217.

63 Fenigstein, A. (1984). Self-consciousness and the over perception of self as a target. *Journal of Personality and Social Psychology, 47,* 860-870.

64 Piper, W.E., Joyce, A.S., McCallum, M. & Azim, H.F.A. (1998). Interpretive and supportive forms of psychotherapy and patient personality variables. *Journal of Consulting and Clinical Psychology, 66,* 558-567.

65 Averill, J.R. & Nunley, E.P. (1992). *Voyages of the heart. Living an emotionally creative life.* New York: The Free Press.

66 Steiner. C. (1974). Scripts People Live. New York: Grove Press. Also in Steiner. C., (2003). *Emotional Literacy; intelligence with a heart.* Fawnskin: Personhood Press.

67 Steiner, C. & Perry, P. (1997). *Achieving Emotional Literacy.* London: Bloomsbury.

68 Mayo, E., (1949). *Hawthorne and the Western Electric Company. The Social Problems of an Industrial Civilisation.* Abingdon: Routledge.

69 Leuner, B. (1966). Emotional intelligence and emancipation: A psychodynamic study of women. *Prax Kinderpsychol Kinderpsychiatr. Aug-Sep, 15 (6),* 196-203.

70 Payne, W.L. (1983/1986). A study of emotion: developing emotional intelligence; self integration; relating to fear, pain and desire. *Dissertation Abstracts International, 47,* 203A, (University microfilms No. AAC 8605928).

71 Salovey, P. & Mayer, J.D. (1990). Emotional intelligence. *Imagination, Cognition, and Personality, 9,* 185-211.

72 Goleman, D. (1995). *Emotional intelligence; why it can matter more than IQ.* New York: Bantam Books.

73 Herrnstein, R.J. & Murray, C. (1994). *The bell curve: Intelligence and class in American life.* New York: The Free Press.

74 Gibbs, N. (1995). Cover story. New brain research suggests that emotions, not IQ, may be the true measure of human intelligence. *Time Magazine, 146 (14).*

75 Spielberger, C. (Ed.) (2004). *Encyclopedia of Applied Psychology.* Boston: Elsevier Academic Press.

76 Bar-On, R. (1997). *The Emotional Quotient Inventory (EQ-i): A test of emotional intelligence.* Toronto: Multi-Health Systems, Inc.

77 Goleman, D. (1998). *Working with emotional intelligence.* New York: Bantam Books.

78 Petrides, K.V., & Furnham, A. (2000). On the dimensional structure of emotional intelligence. *Personality and Individual Differences, 29,* 313-320.

79 Maddocks, J. & Hughes, D. (2017). *The Emotional Intelligence Profile 3.0 technical manual.* JCA Global Ltd.

80 Boyatzis, R. E. (2016). Commentary on Ackley (2016): Updates on the ESCI as the behavioral level of emotional intelligence. *Consulting Psychology Journal: Practice and Research, 68(4),* 287-293.

81 Binet, A. (1905), transl. Paul, K. (1907). L'Annee Psychologique, 12, 191-244. Trench, Trubner & Co Ltd., London.

82 Wechsler, D. (1939). *The Measurement of Adult Intelligence.* Baltimore: Williams & Witkins.

83 Wechsler, D. (1943). Nonintellective factors in general intelligence. *Journal of Abnormal Social Psychology, 38,* 100-104.

84 Wechsler, D. (1958). *The measurement and appraisal of adult intelligence (4th edn.)*. Baltimore: Williams & Wilkins.

85. Zirkel, S. (2000). Social intelligence: The development and maintenance of purposive behavior. In R.Bar-On and J.D.A. Parker (Eds.), *Handbook of emotional intelligence*. San Francisco: Jossey-Bass.

86 Mayer, J.D., Salovey, P. & Caruso, D.R. (1997, 2002). *Mayer-Salovey-Caruso Emotional Intelligence Test (MSCEIT™)*. Toronto, Canada: Multi-Health Systems, Inc.

87 Bar-On, R. (1985). The development of an operational concept of psychological well-being. *Unpublished doctoral dissertation* (first draft), South Africa: Rhodes University.

88 Stein, S. (2011). *The complete EQi 2.0. experience*. Toronto: Multi-Health Systems inc.

89 Boyatzis, R.E., Goleman, D. & Hay/McBer. (1999). *Emotional competence inventory*. Boston: HayGroup.

90 Boyatzis, R.E. (2007). *The Creation of the Emotional and Social Competency Inventory (ESCI)*. Boston: HayGroup.

91 Burruss, J.A. & Boyatzis, R.E. (1981). *Continued validation of a competency model of alcoholism counselors in the Navy* (Report to the US Navy on contract number N002-44-80-C0521). Boston: McBer and Company.

92 McClelland, D.C. (1985). *Human motivation*. Glenview: Scott, Foresman & Co.

93 Petrides, K. V., & Furnham, A. (2001). Trait emotional intelligence: Psychometric investigation with reference to established trait taxonomies. *European Journal of Personality, 15,* 425-448.

94 Petrides, K. V., Mikolajczak, M., Mavroveli, S., Maria-Jose, Sanchez-Ruiz., Furnham, A., Juan-Carlos., & Pérez-González (2016). Developments in Trait Emotional Intelligence Research, *Emotion Review. Vol. 8. No. 4*. 335-341.

95 Petrides, K. V., Pita, R. and Kokkinaki, F. (2007). The location of trait emotional intelligence in personality factor space, British Journal of Psychology, Vol. 98. No. 2, 273-289.

96 Van der Linden, D., Pekaar, K.A., Bakker, A.B., Schermer, J.A., Dunkel, C.S., Vernon, P.A. et al (2017). The general factor of personality and emotional intelligence: a meta-analysis. *Psychological Bulletin 143:* 36-52.

97 Andrei, F., Siegling, A. B., Aloe, A. M., Baldaro, B., & Petrides, K. V. (2016). The incremental validity of the Trait Emotional Intelligence Questionnaire (TEIQue): A systematic review and meta-analysis. *Journal of Personality Assessment, 98,* 261-276.

98 Cartwright, S., & Pappas, C. (2007). Emotional intelligence, its measurement and implications for the workplace. *International Journal of Management Reviews, 10,* 149-171.

99 Joseph, D. L., & Newman, D. A. (2010). Emotional intelligence: an integrative meta-analysis and cascading model. *Journal of Applied Psychology, Vol. 95. No. 1,* 54-78.

100 Joseph, D. L., Jin, J., Newman, D. A., & O'Boyle, E. H. (2015). Why Does Self-Reported Emotional Intelligence Predict Job Performance? A Meta-Analytic Investigation of Mixed EI. *Journal of Applied Psychology, Vol. 100, No. 2,* 298-342.

101 Jordan, P. J., Dasborough, M. T., Daus, C. S., & Ashkanasy, N. M. (2010). A call to context, *Industrial & Organizational Psychology, Vol. 3. No. 2,* 145-148.

102 Ackley, D. (2016). Emotional intelligence: A practical review of models, measures, and applications. *Consulting Psychology Journal: Practice and Research.*

103 Siegling, A., Saklofske, D., & Petrides, K.V. (2015). Measures of Ability and Trait Emotional Intelligence, Chapter 14, 381-414. In Boyle, J., Saklofske, D., Matthews, G. (2014) (Ed.) *Measures of personality and social psychological constructs.*

104 Eysenck, H. (2000). *Intelligence: A New Look.* New Brunswick: Transaction Publishers.

105 Locke, E.A. (2005). Why emotional intelligence is an invalid concept. *Journal of Organizational Behavior, 26 (4),* 425-431.

106 Landy, F.J. (2005). Some historical and scientific issues related to research on emotional intelligence. *Journal of Organizational Behavior, 26,* 411-424.

107 Zeidner, M., Matthews, G. & Roberts, R.D. (2001). Slow down, you move too fast: Emotional intelligence remains an 'elusive' intelligence. *Emotion, 1 (3),* 265-275.

108 Matthews, G., Roberts, R.D. & Zeidner, M. (2003). Development of emotional intelligence: A skeptical – but not dismissive – perspective. *Human Development, 46,* 109-114.

109 MacCann, C., Joseph, D. L., Newman, D. A., & Roberts, R. D. (2014). Emotional intelligence is a second-stratum factor of intelligence: Evidence from hierarchical and bifactor models. *Emotion, 14,* 358-374.

110 Mayer, J. & Salovey, P. (1995). Emotional intelligence and the construction and regulation of feelings. *Applied and Preventive Psychology, 4 (3)* 197-208.

111 Gough, H.D. (1986). *The California Psychological Inventory.* Palo Alto: Consulting Psychologists Press.

112 McCrae, R.R. & Costa, Jr., P.T. (1991). Adding Liebe und Arbeit: The full five-factor model and well-being. *Personality and Social Psychology Bulletin, 17,* 227-232.

113 Kobasa, S.C. (1979). Stressful life events, personality and health: An inquiry into hardiness. *Journal of Personality and Social Psychology, 37,* 1-11.

114 Epstein, S. (1998). *Constructive thinking: The key to emotional intelligence.* Westport: Praeger.

115 Block, J.H. & Block, J. (1980). The role of ego-control and ego-resiliency in the organization of behavior. In W. A. Collins (Ed.), *Development of cognition, affect, and social relations:* The Minnesota symposia on child psychology, 13. Hillsdale: Erlbaum.

116 Goldstein, K. (1934). *The organism: a holistic approach to biology derived from pathological data in man.* New York: Zone Books.

117 Schutte, N.W., Malouff, J.M., Hall, L.E., Haggerty, D.J., Cooper, J.T., Golden, C.J. & Dornheim, L. (1998). *Development and validation of a measure of emotional intelligence. Personality and Individual Differences, 25,* 167-177.

118 Salovey, P., Mayer, J.D., Goldman, S.L., Turvey, C. & Palfai, T.P. (1995). Emotional attention, clarity, and repair: Exploring emotional intelligence using the Trait Meta-Mood Scale. In J. W. Pennebaker (Ed.), *Emotion, disclosure, and health,* Washington DC: American Psychological Association.

119 Miao, C., Humphrey R.H. & Qian, S. (2017). A meta-analysis of emotional intelligence and work attitudes. *Journal of Occupational and Organizational Psychology, 90,* 177-2012.

120 Davis, M. & Kraus, L. (1997). Personality and accurate empathy. In W. Ickes (Ed.), *Empathic accuracy.* New York: Guilford Press.

121 Paulhus, D. (1998). Self-Report Measures of Intelligence: Are They Useful as Proxy IQ Tests? *Journal of Personality, 66 (4),* 525-554.

122 Mayer, J.D. & Gaschke, Y.N. (1988). The experience and meta-experience of mood. *Journal of Personality and Social Psychology, 55,* 102-111.

123 Morgeson, F.P. Campion, M. et al. (2007). Reconsidering the use of personality tests in personnel selection contexts. *Personnel Psychology, 60 (3),* 683-729.

124 Keefer, V.K. (2015). Self-Report Assessment of Emotional Competencies: A Critical Look at Method and Meaning. *Journal of Psychoeducational Assessment. Vol. 33 (1)* 3-23.

INDEX

ABOUT THE AUTHOR

Jolyon (Jo) Maddocks is a founder of JCA Global and a chartered occupational psychologist.

He is the author of several highly influential and widely used products and programmes on Emotional Intelligence which have helped thousands of people develop their self-esteem, enhance their relationships and improve their performance at work.

One of Jo's interests is competing in endurance sports, which has given him first-hand experience of the attitudes and behaviours necessary for sustaining high performance under pressure. These are attributes which Jo believes all people can develop through Emotional Intelligence.